Y0-DWE-139

Ethnic Diversity and Conflict
in Eastern Europe

LEARNED SOCIETIES ·

the Joint
Committee
on Eastern
Europe
Publication
Series
Number 8.
THE SOCIAL

THE AMERICAN COUNCIL OF

SCIENCE RESEARCH COUNCIL

The Index was prepared by

Peter F. Sugar

Ethnic Diversity and Conflict in Eastern Europe

PETER F. SUGAR
EDITOR

ABC-Clio
Santa Barbara, California/Oxford, England

Library of Congress Cataloging in Publication Data

Main entry under title:
Ethnic Diversity and Conflict in Eastern Europe.
    Based on a conference on ethnicity in Eastern Europe held June
11-13, 1976, in Seattle, Wash., sponsored by the Joint Committee on
Eastern Europe.
    Includes bibliographical references and index.
    1. Europe, Eastern—Ethnic relations—Congresses.
2. Nationalism—Europe, Eastern Congresses.
3. Ethnicity—Congresses. 4. Anthropological
linguistics—Congresses. I. Sugar, Peter F. II. Joint Committee on
Eastern Europe.
HN372.E74   305.8'00947   80-12032
ISBN 0-87436-297-0

ABC-Clio, Inc.
Riviera Campus
2040 Alameda Padre Serra, Box 4397
Santa Barbara, California 93103

Clio Press, Ltd.
Woodside House, Hinksey Hill
Oxford, OX1 5BE, England

Manufactured in the United States of America

TABLE OF CONTENTS

PREFACE

The Joint Committee on Eastern Europe of the
American Council of Learned Societies and
the Social Science Research Council identified several areas needing research during
its Fall, 1975 meeting. The subjects were
all of general interest within the scholarly
community and the Committee determined there
was need for "seminal volumes" to encourage
their detailed study. The Joint Committee
commissioned scholars in the several fields
to organize conferences dealing with each
topic and funded the subsequent meetings.
I was selected to organize a conference to
discuss Ethnicity in Eastern Europe and
this volume resulted from that conference.
      The conference was convened because
ethnicity has been a factor in determining
the developments and issues that have
emerged in Eastern Europe from the middle
of the eighteenth century until the present,
and there is need for a more general understanding of its impact. A study of recent
literature indicates that area specialists
are not always familiar with the theoretical
aspects of ethnicity, or with specialized
studies concerning other areas and regions.
Scholars who specialize in Asian Studies,
African Studies--the Middle East or Latin
America--may be unfamiliar with developments
in Eastern Europe or pay little attention to

them. Accordingly, the conference on Ethnicity in Eastern Europe was organized to bring together East European specialists, scholars interested in ethnic studies involving other areas, and theoreticians. The papers contributed by these scholars were distributed to the participants in advance of the conference where they were discussed, but not formally presented.

In planning the conference and selecting the topics for discussion it seemed to me that no three-day conference could possibly deal with all of the diverse aspects of ethnicity. Ethnicity plays a role in practically all internal relationships within a community--the establishment of authority and the development of institutions--and it affects inter-community relationships as well. Accordingly, I felt it necessary to limit the discussions to four key topics:

Language as the Basis for Ethnic Identity

The Influence of State Policy on Ethnic Persistence and Nationality Formation

Economic and Class Differentiation and Ethnicity

Religion and Ethnicity

Each topic was discussed first by a theoretician or by an area specialist working outside of East Europe (See Chapters II, IV, VI and VIII) and then by East European specialists (Chapters III, V, VII and IX). Chapter I, the "Problemstellung," was the keynote and the other essayists delayed drafting their contributions until they had read it.

Four expert commentators were invited to participate in the conference and although their comments and critiques are not reproduced in this volume were most helpful when the papers were rewritten following the conference. We acknowledge with appreciation the valuable contributions made by Professor John Gumpers (University of California, Berkeley) who commented on Chapters II and III; Professor Stanley Kimball (Southern Illinois University) who reviewed Chapters IV and V; Professor William Lockwood (University of Michigan) who critiqued Chapters VI and VII; and, finally, Dr. Donald L. Horowitz (Brookings Institution) who read Chapters VIII and IX. As the convener of the conference and editor of the papers which are published here I was responsible for selecting the topics for discussion and for determining the procedures and formats to be employed. I, therefore, accept full responsibility for any shortcomings that may have ensued.

The conference was convened on June 11 through June 13, 1976 in Seattle, Washington. The participants discussed the selected topics freely and openly and the conference closed with the feeling that we could have profitably spent more time listening to each other. We also agreed that the mix of specialists, theorists, and experts in other areas had been helpful. We learned a good deal from each other although we all had to become familiar with a diversity of languages in order to communicate effectively. In fact, the use of several languages made it clear that the papers discussed at the conference would have to be rewritten to record faithfully the proceedings. As a result of the rewriting the reader will note that each essayist references the chapters prepared by the others. Despite the differing qualifications and interests of the essayists the reader will also note that there is a certain communality--a common stress on certain key factors--in these essays. That quality was missing in the first drafts presented prior to the conference. Still, the papers differ in style and point of view. This collection is therefore more than a mere collection of scholarly papers. Indeed, we hope that it is a "seminal volume."

The participants gratefully acknowledge the support of the Joint Committee on Eastern Europe in convening the conference and the efforts of Mrs. Barbara O'Halloran of Seattle in organizing the meeting and preparing the manuscript. I must also thank the participants for preparing their original manuscripts in time to be distributed prior to the meeting--and for their diligence in meeting the deadline for rewriting their papers after the meeting was over.

Peter F. Sugar

Seattle, Washington
1979

xii

CHAPTER I

ETHNIC GROUPS AND NATIONALITIES

by

Paul R. Brass

There are three ways of defining ethnic groups--in terms of objective attributes, with reference to subjective feelings, and in relation to behavior. An objective definition assumes that, though no specific attribute is invariably associated with all ethnic categories, there must be some distinguishing cultural mark that clearly separates one group of people from another, whether that mark or marks be language, territory, religion, color, diet, dress, or any of them. The problem with objective definitions is that it is usually extremely difficult to determine the boundaries of ethnic categories in this way.[1] The difficulty with subjective definitions is that they make it impossible to answer the basic question of how a group of people arrives at subjective self-consciousness in the first place. Behavioral definitions are really a form of objective definition since they assume that there are specific, concrete ways in which ethnic groups behave or do not behave, particularly in relation to and in interaction with other groups.

1

2

Behavioral definitions merely suggest that
there are cultural differences between
ethnic groups, but that the critical distinctions reveal themselves only in
interaction with other groups.[2] But, the
existence of explicit codes of behavior and
interaction is rather more characteristic,
more all-pervasive, and more evident in
simple than in complex societies in which
people may establish their separateness
with reference to specific attributes without adopting an entirely distinct code of
behavior.

     Subjective definitions will not, there-
fore, serve the analytical purposes of this
study, whereas interactive definitions lack
the universality required. The most appropriate definition for the aims of this
essay is one that begins with objective
cultural markers but which recognizes that
they are susceptible to change and variation. Any group of people dissimilar from
other peoples in terms of objective cultural
criteria containing within its membership
either in principle or in practice the
elements for a complete division of labor
and for reproduction forms an ethnic
category. The objective cultural markers
may be a language or dialect, distinctive
dress or diet or customs, religion, or race.
The inclusion in the definition of the
phrase "contains within its membership
either in principle or in practice the elements for a complete division of labor and
for reproduction" is designed to emphasize
the cultural basis of ethnicity and to

distinguish ethnic categories from other
social categories based on class or gender
or age grades.

Ethnicity is a sense of ethnic identity, which has been defined by De Vos as
consisting of the "subjective, symbolic or
emblematic use" by "a group of people . . .
of any aspect of culture, in order to differentiate themselves from other groups."[3]
This definition can be used for the analyt-
ic purposes required here by altering the
last phrase to read "in order to create
internal cohesion and differentiate themselves from other groups." An ethnic group
that uses cultural symbols in this way is a
subjectively self-conscious community that
establishes criteria for inclusion into and
exclusion from the group. At this point,
matters of descent, birth, and a sense of
kinship may become important to ethnic
group members, for the methods of inclusion
and exclusion into the group often involve
the explicit or tacit adoption of rules of
endogamy and exogamy. Ethnicity or ethnic
identity also involves, in addition to
subjective self-consciousness, a claim to
status and recognition, either as a superior
group or as a group at least equal to other
groups. Ethnicity is to ethnic category as
class consciousness is to class.[4]

Ethnicity is an alternative form of
social organization and identification to
class, but it is a contingent and change-
able status that, like class, may or may
not be articulated in particular contexts
or at particular times.[5] Ethnic groups

that use ethnicity to make demands in the
political arena for alteration in their
status, in their economic well-being, in
their civil rights, or in their educational
opportunities are engaged in a form of interest group politics which has become
prominent in the United States during the
past decade or so and which seeks to improve
the well-being of group members as individuals.[6] However, some ethnic groups in other
contexts go further and demand that
corporate rights be conceded to the group
as a whole, that they be given not just
individual educational opportunities on the
same basis as others, but that they be given
control over the public system of education
in their areas of concentration so that they
can teach the history, language, and culture
of their group to their own children. They
demand a major say for the group in the
political system as a whole or control over
a piece of territory within the country,
or they demand a country of their own with
full sovereignty. In the latter case, the
ethnic group aspires to national status
and recognition. Insofar as it succeeds
by its own efforts in achieving any one of
these goals either within an existing state
or in a state of its own, it has become a
nationality or a nation.[7] A nation, therefore, may be seen as a particular type of
ethnic community,[8] or, rather, as an
ethnic community politicized, with recognized group rights in the political
system.[9]

Nations may be created by the transformation of an ethnic group in a multiethnic state into a self-conscious
political entity or by the amalgamation of
diverse groups and the formation of an
inter-ethnic, composite or homogeneous
national culture through the agency of
the modern state. Although the two
processes of nation-formation have different starting points and raise quite
different kinds of analytical and theoretical questions, the end result historically
has been sometimes the same, and the two
processes have much in common.[10] In both
cases, the effort is made to give subjective and symbolic meanings to merely
objective distinctions between peoples and
to increase the number of attributes and
symbolic referents that they have in common
with each other and that distinguish them
from other groups. Ethnic nationalism and
state-centered nationalism may be seen,
therefore, as sub-types of a more general
process of identity formation, defined as
the process of intensifying the subjective
meanings of a multiplicity of symbols and
of striving to achieve multi-symbol
congruence among a group of people defined
initially by one or more central symbols,
whether those symbols are ethnic attributes
or loyalty to a particular state.[11] More
often than not, ethnic demands center
initially around a single central symbol,
such as language, religion, territory, or
color. In the movement to create greater
internal cohesion and to press more

effectively ethnic demands against rival
groups, ethnic and nationalist elites
stress increasingly the variety of ways in
which the members of the group are similar
to each other and collectively different
from others. This effort, however, creates
its own problems because the selection of
additional symbols inevitably involves
either the loss of potential adherents or
the need to persuade or coerce group members
to change their language, religion, behavior, or dress. It also may lead nationalist
leaders into expansionist military adven-
tures and conflicts with other states when
the drive to achieve multi-symbol congruence
involves irredentist claims. It is important to recognize that this striving for
multi-symbol congruence is pursued by
ethnic group leaders as much as by state-
builders. If the process is more or less
successful, the nationality created out of
an ethnic group is sure to be quite a
different social formation from the initial
group.

The process of nationality-formation
may or may not be pursued to the point
where political structures are made
congruent with the nationality by creating
an autonomous or independent self-governing
unit. Similarly, the process of nation-
building by state authorities may or may not
succeed in creating relatively homogeneous
national groups congruent with the territorial boundaries of the state. More often
than not, ethnic groups that come into
conflict in multi-ethnic societies reach

accommodations with each other. State
authorities also usually find that it is
politically wiser to recognize and tolerate
some forms of cultural diversity rather than
impose a total uniformity by forcible means.
Tolerance of diversity may take the form of
recognition of the corporate rights of
ethnic groups within the state or the removal of specific symbols from the concept
of the nation and their relegation to the
private sphere as, for example, happened
with religion in the United States. However, both processes of nationality-formation and state-building may be pushed
beyond pluralist accommodations to extreme,
even pathological limits, to expulsions,
counter-expulsions, the exchanges of population groups and even to genocide.
    Although the processes of forming
nationalities out of ethnic groups and of
building national cultures to conform with
state boundaries are similar in many
respects, the principal interest centers on
outlining more precisely the process of
nationality-formation rather than the process of state-building, and on developing
a theory to account for the reasons why some
ethnic groups become communities or
nationalities and pursue successfully their
social, economic, and political goals while
others do not. The process of nationality-
formation is one in which objective differences between ethnic groups acquire
increasingly subjective and symbolic
significance, are translated into a
consciousness of and a desire for group

solidarity, and become the basis for successful political demands. There are two
stages in the development of a nationality.
The first is the movement from ethnic
category to community. Depending on the
context, this stage may involve such changes
as the creation of a self-conscious language
community out of a group of related speakers,[12] the formation of a caste association
from a caste category, or a community of
believers from the followers of a particular
religious leader. The subjective meanings
of symbols of identity are intensified and
become more relational (interpersonal) than
personal or instrumental. Language becomes
not merely a means of communication, but a
priceless heritage of group culture;
religion becomes not only a matter of
personal belief and of a relationship between a person and a deity, but a collective
experience that unites believers to each
other; familiar places and historical sites
become sacred shrines and "freedom
trails."[13] At this stage also the effort
to bring multiple symbols in congruence
begins. The leaders of the movement to
create a language community may, at the
same time, stake a claim to the dominance
of that language in a particular territory;
the supporters of the demands of a religious
community may also seek protection for the
language or script in which their religious
texts are written and may promote the
identification of the language with the
religion and encourage its increasing use
by all believers.

This process of development of communities from ethnic categories is particularly associated with the early stages of modernization in multi-ethnic societies where languages have not yet become standardized, where religious groups have not become highly structured and compartmentalized, and where social fragmentation is prevalent. However, the transition may occur even in post-industrial societies such as the United States, where Negroes have become Blacks, Mexican-Americans Chicanos, and many other ethnic groups have rediscovered their origins and identities.

The second stage in the transformation of ethnic groups involves the articulation and acquisition of social, economic, and political rights for the members of the group or for the group as a whole. Depending upon the perceived needs and demands of the group, its size and distribution, its relations with other groups, and the political context, demands may aim at relatively modest civil, educational, and political rights and opportunities for the individual members of the group or for recognition of the group's corporate existence as a political body or nationality. Insofar as an ethnic group succeeds by its own efforts in achieving and maintaining group rights through political action and political mobilization, it has gone beyond ethnicity to establish itself as a nationality.

The delineation of the process of nationality-formation in this manner

10

suggests several problems that require
explanation. First, what are the conditions under which ethnic groups become
communities and under which ethnic demands,
ethnic competition, and ethnic conflict
take place? Second, what are the conditions under which an ethnic community is
likely to make the major demand for status
as a nationality and what are the requirements for success? Third, how does one explain the transformations that take place
in the culture, in the behavior, and in the
boundaries of a people as it undergoes the
movement from ethnic group to nationality?
Fourth, since it is also evident that
ethnic and nationality movements frequently
ebb and flow over time within the same
group, how can one explain the resurgence
of ethnicity and nationalism among diverse
groups of people at different times and in
different places? The focus of the remainder of this chapter will be on the first
two questions, but the analysis will also
touch, at several places, on the last two.

Ethnic Differentiation: From Ethnic Groups
to Communities

The movement from ethnic group to community
is a transition that some groups never make,

that others make initially in modern times,
and that still others undergo repeatedly
at different points in time. In the first
category are the various "lost" peoples and
speakers of diverse dialects who have merged
into or are merging into other peoples--the
Cornish in the United Kingdom, the Frisians
in Holland, the Sorbs and Wends of Eastern
and Central Europe, the Maithili-speaking
people and numerous other dialect-speakers
in north India. In the second category are
the newly-formed ethnic groups and nationalities of the nineteenth and twentieth
centuries--the Welsh and the Irish, the
nationalities in Austria-Hungary, the Ibos
in Nigeria, the Naga tribes in northeastern
India and most of the language communities
of contemporary India, the Malays in Malaysia. In the last category are the ancient
peoples of the world, Jews, Han Chinese,
Egyptians, and the major nationalities of
Western Europe.
    What are the conditions that determine
whether or not one group will merge into
another group, or will establish or re-
establish and redefine its identity? The
richness of a group's cultural heritage,
the stage of development of its language,
and the distinctiveness of its religious
beliefs do not by themselves predetermine
that one group of people will be more
internally solidary than another and will
be more likely to perpetuate itself through
time. Absence of or loss of a distinctive
language has not prevented Blacks in the
United States or Celtic groups in the United

Kingdom, or non-Hebrew, non-Yiddish speaking Jews in the United States from acquiring or maintaining a sense of ethnic identity. By the same token, over the centuries in Europe, old, fully standardized, written languages--Latin, Anglo-Saxon, Provençal, Low German, Church Slavonic--some of them spoken by peoples occupying compact geographical areas, have been "submerged" while other languages have replaced or absorbed them.[14] Moreover, despite the fact that European culture, civilization, and science have for centuries been dominated increasingly by the three great languages, English, French, and German, this has not prevented "the growth of linguistic diversity in Europe from 16 [standard] languages in 1800 to 30 in 1900 and to 53 in 1937"[15] and the attendant development of language communities among many of them.

Distinctive minority religious groups in modern times have often developed into ethnically self-conscious communities, but it has also often happened, particularly in Eastern Europe, that religious differences have been used or even created to establish or emphasize barriers that have non-religious origins between peoples. The attempt to establish an Uniate Church in Bulgaria, which culminated in the development of a separate hierarchy of Eastern Orthodoxy, has over time served to reinforce the ethnic separateness of Bulgarians from Greeks, but it was not religious distinctiveness that initially inspired the rise

of Bulgarian ethnic consciousness. Islam
in non-Muslim states often has provided a
strong basis for Muslim separatism, but
again it is not the distinctiveness of Islam
as such in relation to other religions that
is decisive, for the degree of Muslim
communal self-consciousness varies in
different contexts. For example, in Eastern
Europe, Islam has served more effectively
as a basis for ethnic separatism in Yugoslavia than in Albania.[16] Nor, finally,
can Jewish religious distinctiveness explain Jewish ethnic separatism that
culminated in Zionism, for Jews chose often
enough to assimilate in Eastern Europe when
conditions were favorable.
     The process of creating communities
from ethnic groups involves the selection
of particular dialects or religious
practices or styles of dress or historical
symbols from a variety of available alternatives. It will be shown below that it
is always the case that particular social
groups, leaders, or elites stand to benefit
and others to lose from the choices that
are made.

ETHNICITY AND ELITE COMPETITION
Ethnic communities are created and transformed by particular elites in modernizing
and in post-industrial societies undergoing
dramatic social change. This process invariably involves competition and conflict
for political power, economic benefits, and
social status between competing elite,
class, and leadership groups both within and

among different ethnic categories. Several
scholars of ethnicity and nationality have
pointed out that modernization and industrialization in large, multi-ethnic societies
tend to proceed unevenly and often, if not
always, to benefit some ethnic groups or
some regions of a country more than others.[17] However, inequality between
different ethnic groups or culturally
distinct regions does not by itself spur
the development of communal or national
consciousness. Speakers of an unstandardized local dialect in a backward rural
region of a modernizing country may very
well go on speaking their language and
cultivating their fields without becoming
concerned that their language is being
neglected and without developing any sense
of solidarity.[18] They may do so either
because they are completely in the backwash
of modernization, remote from urban life-
styles and only marginally affected by new
educational opportunities and new means of
mass communication and transportation, or
because the locally powerful economic,
religious and political elites find it to
their advantage to cooperate with external
authorities and adopt the language and
culture of the dominant ethnic group in
order to maintain or enhance their own
power. Relevant examples here are the
Anglicized Welsh aristocracy in Wales in
the nineteenth century, the Polonized
Lithuanian nobility in Lithuania, and the
Magyarized Romanian nobility in Transylvania. This kind of cooperation between

internal elites and external authorities
usually leads to a situation of persistent
ethnic differences among the mass of the
people, but without the articulation of
ethnic demands.

Ethnic self-consciousness, ethnically-
based demands, and ethnic conflict can occur
only if there is some conflict either between indigenous and external elites and
authorities or between indigenous elites.
Four sources of elite conflict that may spur
the development of ethnic communalism or
separatism in pre-industrial or early
modernizing societies are those a) between
a local aristocracy attempting to maintain
its privileges against an alien conqueror;
b) between competing religious elites from
different ethnic groups; c) between religious elites and the native aristocracy
within an ethnic group; and d) between
native religious elites and an alien
aristocracy.

Most alien conquerors in pre-industrial
societies strive to gain control over the
land and landholders by either imposing a
new aristocracy or gaining the collabora-
tion of the old aristocracy or by establishing a direct relationship between the state
and the peasantry. Where such an effort is
successful, as with the imposition by the
Habsburgs of a predominantly non-Czech,
Catholic landlord class in the Czech lands
in the seventeenth century, the development
of ethnic consciousness among the conquered
people may be delayed until industrial
development leads to the formation of new

social classes.[19] Where the conqueror
lacks the degree of control necessary to
achieve one of these goals and the native
aristocracy lacks the military strength to
establish its independence, but retains its
control over the land, the nobility may
promote an indigenous ethnic separatism to
support its local dominance. A leading
example of this type of development in
Eastern Europe is what Barany has called
the "aristocratic nationalism" promoted by
the Magyar nobility in the nineteenth century.[20] The Romanian boyars in Moldavia
and Wallachia in the eighteenth and early
nineteenth centuries also used symbols of
Romanian nationalism as a basis for
preserving and extending their own privileges under Ottoman rule.[21] The success
of a native aristocracy in this regard
will depend on its relations with the
tenantry and on its ability to prevent
alliances forming between its tenants and
the state authorities to undermine its local
control. The Polish aristocracy was far
less successful than its Magyar counterpart
and found in both the 1830 and 1863 rebel-
lions that it could not carry with it most
of the Polish-speaking and, even less, the
non-Polish speaking peasantry of the former
eastern territories of the Polish commonwealth.[22]
    A second type of inter-ethnic elite
conflict may occur when the dominant external group attempts to impose its religion
or permits proselytizing activities among
an indigenous population. In that case, the

local religious elites will naturally move
quickly to defend their interests in promoting ethnic consciousness by attempting
to arouse their followers in defense of the
native religious system. Such competitive
proselytization has, of course, been endemic
for centuries in the East European countries.

The third type of elite competition is
intra-ethnic. When a native aristocracy
collaborates with an external or colonial
authority, it may or may not adopt the
religion of the external group, but it almost always adopts and promotes the alien
culture in a way that threatens the
authority of indigenous religious leaders.
This kind of division between traditional
religious elites and native landlords,
though a common early cleavage that has
spurred movements of ethnic communalism
in many modernizing societies, has not been
prominent in Eastern Europe.

In Eastern Europe, the fourth type of
conflict, between indigenous religious
elites and local, but alien aristocracies
was more common than intra-ethnic conflicts.
Thus, in non-Magyar areas of Austria-
Hungary under the control of the Magyar
nobility, such as Slovakia and Transylvania,
and in the Balkans under Ottoman rule where
the Turks controlled the land, as in Serbia
and Bulgaria, ethnic identities and the
early stages of nationalism were promoted
by parish priests and "the native lower
clergy."[23] Sometimes inter-ethnic and
intra-ethnic conflicts of this sort merge

in complex ways, as in Transylvania in the
eighteenth century where the Orthodox and
Uniate clergy sustained a sense of Romanian
ethnic identity among a peasantry dominated
by an oppressive Magyar and Magyarized
Romanian aristocracy. Many of the Orthodox
clergy themselves were hardly distinguishable from the peasants whom they served and
they resented the privileged position which
the Protestant and Catholic churches and
clergy were accorded in the area. Their
desire to enhance their own status and
their identification with the interests of
the peasantry suffering at the hands of the
Calvinist and Catholic Magyar nobility led
some of them into a union with the Roman
Catholic Church (the Uniate Church) and to
an effort to gain support from the Habsburg
Court for improvements in the status of the
Romanian peasantry.[24]
It is with such conflicts either
between competing landholders and alien
conquerors, between competing religious
elites, or between religious leaders and
local aristocracies that the first stages
of ethnic transformation often begin. In
the latter two cases, the conflicts spur
movements of religious revival which seek
two objectives that are critical for the
shaping of ethnic boundaries, namely, the
removal from indigenous religious practices
and beliefs of alien forms derived from
interaction with other religions and the
promotion of education in either the
vernacular language or the language of the
scriptures. If the dominant indigenous

elite is collaborationist and there is only
one external alien authority or group, the
local counterelite will be in a position
exclusively to manipulate ethnic particularist symbols to challenge the leadership
of its rivals and it will appeal to alternative social classes in doing so. Thus, the
religious counterelite will have the edge
in capturing the allegiance of the masses
as modernization proceeds and it will promote the education of new classes in the
vernacular language, whose support will
ultimately be brought to bear in overthrow-
ing the old elite.

     Where both religious and linguistic
symbols are potential bases for differentiating one ethnic group from another,
it is easy to understand how the process
of promoting multi-symbol congruence begins.
It is often a mistake, however, in early
modernizing societies to assume either that
such symbols are likely to be congruent to
begin with or that it is a pre-existing
congruence that predisposes ethnic groups
towards differentiation and conflict.
Rather, it is more often the case that the
choice of the leading symbol of differentiation depends upon the interests of the
elite group that takes up the ethnic cause.
Religious elites will usually select as
the leading symbol the group's religion,
and language will be used, insofar as
possible, as a secondary reinforcing symbol
of unity. Moreover, the religious elites
will attempt to promote the congruence of
language with religion by promoting

education and by publishing religious
pamphlets in the vernacular. Thus, in
Transylvania at the end of the seventeenth
century, Orthodox Romanians established the
Romanian Uniate Church. In the middle of
the eighteenth century, the monks at a
monastery in Blaj established a printing
press for the publication of books in
Romanian.[25] They also proceeded to emphasize the Latin origin of the Romanian
language, "two of the seminarians composed
a Romanian grammar" in 1780, and the Latin
alphabet was adopted to replace the Cyrillic
script. In this way, Romanian ethnic
consciousness came to be based upon the dual
symbols of religion and language.[26] However, where the clergy itself is ethnically
stratified, the lower clerics may adopt
language--the "language of the people"
versus the liturgical language--as its
central symbol and demand that a separate
church be established congruent with the
language of the ethnic community. Thus,
the Bulgarian monks in the eighteenth
century resisted the dominance of the
Greek Orthodox clerics and the Greek litur-
gy by promoting the development of the
Bulgarian popular language and a separate
Bulgarian church.[27] The religious difference between Croatian Catholics and
Orthodox Serbs has been reinforced linguistically by the use of the Latin alphabet
by Croats and the Cyrillic script by Serbs
to write the common Sergo-Croatian language.

   In some cases it is easier to promote
such a congruence of linguistic and religious symbols than in others. The strength
of modern Polish nationalim, based primarily on language,[28] has been reenforced
by the fact that nearly all Poles are also
Catholics and are to be distinguished,
therefore, on both linguistic and religious
grounds from other Slav peoples.[29] However,
such a congruence was never achieved in
Albania where ethnic consciousness has been
based upon language in the face of continued
religious diversities.[30] In Slovakia, the
existence of a significant Protestant
minority less receptive to Slovak ethnic
appeals than the majority Roman Catholic
population constituted a political obstacle
to the achievement of Slovak demands in the
interwar period when many Slovak Protestants
supported instead the idea of "Czechoslova-
kism."[31]
   Moreover, in the course of development
of a people from an ethnic category to a
community or to a nation, communal and
nationalist leaders may emphasize different
symbols and promote alternative conceptions
of the group's boundaries. For example,
in the development of the Greek nation from
the nineteenth century up to the present
time, competing ideas of the boundaries of
the nation have appeared, depending upon
how Greek leaders have chosen to combine
the three symbols of Greek Orthodoxy, the
Greek language, and Greek descent from the
Hellenic peoples of antiquity.[32] Some
Greek leaders confined their nationalist

aspirations to the creation of a political
unit congruent with that group of people who
were both Orthodox and spoke Greek, but
from 1830 until 1922, a larger vision prevailed among Greek nationalists that
impelled them to strive for the expansion
of the Greek state to conform more with the
classical boundaries of Hellenic civilization. Such an expanded Greek state would
have included peoples who followed Greek
Orthodox rites but did not speak Greek,
Greek-speakers who were not Orthodox, and
many peoples of presumed Hellenic stock
who were neither Greek Orthodox nor spoke
Greek. This irredentist and expansionist
vision of a Greek state was given its death
blow in the war with Turkey in 1921-22,
which led not to territorial expansion but
to the exchange of Greek and Turkish
populations. Contemporary Greek nationalism
is based on the narrower conception of the
Greek nation consisting of only those who
are both Orthodox and speak Greek. Including
the island of Cyprus within the Greek nation
rests on these grounds rather than on the
recreating of a pan-Hellenic civilization.
      In other instances religious differ-
ences are not a factor in the inevitable
competition for new opportunities in multiethnic modernizing societies and the
principal ethnic differences are based on
caste, tribe, or language. If, in these
cases, the native aristocracy is not collaborationist its leading members may promote
the language and culture of the group, but
if it is collaborationist or has been

imposed or is ineffectual, then the development of ethnic consciousness will depend
upon the creation of new elites and social
classes emerging out of the modernization
process itself as literacy spreads, urbanization takes place, industrialization
begins, and government employment opportunities open up. The development of
ethnic consciousness among Czech middle
class leaders in the industrial centers of
Bohemia in the early eighteenth century
belongs to this type.[33]
     In early modernizing colonial and ex-
colonial societies, government employment
is often the critical factor in the growth
of ethnic rivalries because it provides the
authorities with a means both to reward the
sons of the collaborationist aristocracy
and to create new collaborationist groups
by distributing opportunities unevenly,
whether intentionally or unintentionally.
If government employment expands rapidly
enough and other employment opportunities
keep pace, while literacy and urbanization
are kept relatively low, then such a system
of authority may perpetuate itself for some
time without severe ethnic conflict. However, usually fairly soon, the social
mobilization of backward ethnic groups begins to move more rapidly than the creation
of new job opportunities. At this point,
the classic problem of the developing or
modernizing society occurs, that of the
discontent of the educated unemployed.
Where caste, tribal, or linguistic differences exist to separate ethnically the

relatively disadvantaged, aspirant elite
groups from their competitors in the dominant group, these differences will be the
basis for a special claim for jobs and
other advantages. Such demands are usually
associated with efforts to mobilize the disadvantaged ethnic group and to create a new
sense of identity among its members. At
this point also, the process of intensifying and multiplying the points of difference
between the disadvantaged group and the
cominant group may begin. A disadvantaged
caste group may claim that the dominant
group is really culturally different and
descends from alien intruders and that it
alone represents the true and indigenous
culture.[34] A tribe or linguistic group
may do the same, and those aspirant elites
who manage to find employment in schools
and colleges may strive to assert the
distinctiveness of their mother tongue, may
seek to standardize it, and may uncover
lost or neglected treasures written in
their language to demonstrate its greatness.
If the speakers of the language are geographically concentrated, then a claim
will be made for the dominance of the
language as medium of education in the
schools and the administration in the
relevant territory.
  Although elite conflict and job
competition are common in modernizing
societies, they do not always impel distinctive cultural groups towards ethnic
differentiation. The process of modernization may produce so great an imbalance

between one group and another that many
ethnic groups may become assimilated to
another language and culture. This can
happen, however, only if government policy
also works to favor one group over another,
particularly with regard to the medium of
education in the schools. Such a situation
may arise when speakers of an unstandardized
local dialect or of an old, but non-modern-
ized language are concentrated in a backward
region of a modernizing country. Urbanization and industrialization in the region
are minimal, but educational opportunities
are available in the official language of
the state, which is different from the
local language. Where there are no local
religious elites and relatively few socially
mobilized people are produced from the local
language group, a gradual process of assimilation to the language and culture of the
dominant group will take place. When
modernization and industrialization begin
to affect significantly this area, new
elite groups may arise to mobilize the
remnants of the group more or less successfully, but the size and shape of the group
will have been affected permanently by the
earlier period of assimilation. Areas of
Eastern Europe that conform to this pattern
of development include Macedonia in relation to Bulgaria and Serbia and Montenegro
in relation to Serbia.
　　An alternative situation also favorable
to assimilation and decline in ethnic
identity occurs when differential modernization so favors a minority ethnic group that

it chooses to assimilate to the language
and culture of the ruling ethnic group.
Such a development occurred among the Jews
of Hungary during the middle nineteenth
century, many of whom collaborated with
the Magyar ruling political elite and
aristocracy and played a critical role in
the development of commerce and industry
in Hungary. Their success was such, Barany
reports, that

> before World War I, the
> majority of Hungarian Jews . . .
> managed to achieve economic
> success, social satisfaction,
> and Magyar nationality even with-
> out conversion. Among the
> assimilated Jews, many knew no
> Yiddish at all and took no parti-
> cular pride in developing a
> special Jewish ethos: the Jewish-
> ness of the more traditional-
> minded consisted chiefly of a
> stricter observance of religious
> practices, and this was in no
> way incompatible with loyalty to
> Magyardom during the liberal
> era.[35]

However, such a process of assimilation
may not save an ethnic group from being the
target of the next to rise as education and
industrialization penetrate more deeply into the society. The assimilated group may
remain distinguishable enough by cultural
or religious markers--even when its members

do not choose to use such markers to build
communal consciousness--for it to be
singled out as a scapegoat for the next
group to rise and thereby serve as an
instrument for building communal solidarity
in the newly aspirant Group. Such, of
course, was the case in Hungary when "a
new intelligensia" arose "from the ranks
of the peasantry and Christian small bourgeoisie" to compete for a shrinking number
of government jobs and for economic opportunities with the Jewish middle classes.[36]
Anti-Semitism has been, of course, a common
form in which the ethnic and nationalist
aspirations of the peoples of Eastern Europe
have been manifested at different times and
under different regimes. In contemporary
Eastern Europe, as well as in the Soviet
Union, anti-Semitism has again recurred and
has in part reflected this pattern of upwardly mobilizing ethnic majorities seeking
to exploit cultural differences against a
minority in order to displace the minority
from privileged positions. In several of
the East European Communist states, this
device was used in the 1950s and 1960s to
eliminate Jews from prominent positions in
the state and Communist Party bureaucracies.[37]
     Thus, differential social mobilization
in modernizing, multi-ethnic societies may
favor the differentiation or assimilation
of particular groups and the transformation
of ethnic boundaries, but it nearly always
leads at some stage to some forms and degrees of ethnic conflict and competition,

arising out of elite competition for control over the local society or for new
opportunities in the modern segments of a
developing society. It affects only groups
that either contain threatened traditional
elites or those that benefit by modernization and industrialization sufficiently to
produce an educated intelligentsia or an
entrepreneurial class in a position to
compete for prestige positions and economic
advantages. Most of the members of such
ethnic groups in societies at early stages
of modernization may, however, remain for
decades a relatively unmobilized rural
peasantry or occupy lower class positions
in the cities and towns. They are mobilized
over time, manipulated by contending elite
groups, and taught the language and culture
that the predominant elites determine they
should learn.

Nationality-Formation: From Communities to
Nationalities

Whether or not an ethnic group, mobilized
by its disgruntled elites to a growing sense
of communal solidarity, goes on to make
major political demands and how far it
succeeds depend principally on four fac-
tors--the persistence or the perception of

the persistence of an unequal distribution
of resources either against the advantage
or to the advantage of the group, the degree
to which the process of building communal
consciousness has involved the creation of
the organizational resources necessary to
build a political movement, the response of
the government to the demands and grievances
of the group, and the general political
context.

INEQUALITY, RELATIVE DEPRIVATION, AND ETHNIC DIFFERENCES IN THE DIVISION OF LABOR AND RESOURCES

Many theories of the politicization of
ethnicity or of the development of nationalism in ethnic groups strees the importance
of inequality in the distribution of available resources, social benefits, and opportunities between distinct ethnic groups.
In its simplest form, the argument contends
that nationalism arises in response to objective exploitation of an indigenous group
by an alien group, or of one ethnic group
by another or even of one social class by
another.[38] However, the realization by
many contemporary scholars of ethnicity
and nationalism that the mere existence of
inequality, on the one hand, is not sufficient to produce a nationalist movement
and, on the other hand, that nationalist
movements sometimes arise among dominant
groups has led to somewhat more elaborate
statements of this point of view.

One elaboration of this viewpoint is
the relative deprivation theory, which
argues that it is not objective inequality
as such that precipitates nationalism but
a feeling of frustration or relative deprivation defined as "the balance between the
goods and conditions of life to which people
believe they are rightfully entitled and
the goods and conditions they think they
are capable of attaining or maintaining,
given the social means available to them."[39]
For example, the rise in Croation nationalism in contemporary Yugoslavia in the
face of genuine economic advancement by the
Croats is to be explained, so the argument
goes, not in terms of the persistence of
real inequalities between Croats and Serbs,
but because Croats came to expect the
attainment of economic well-being comparable
to that achieved in West European nations
and they felt this result was not possible
within Yugoslavia.[40]   There are several
problems with this type of explanation.
One is that there is no way of measuring or
even describing adequately the levels of
relative deprivation experienced by different ethnic groups in different societies
to test the basic theory that "those groups
which experience the highest levels of
relative deprivation may be expected to be
most nationalistic."[41] A second problem
is that the theory accepts the arguments
and myths of nationalists as data to demonstrate relative deprivation rather than as
myths themselves in need of explanation.
Third, the deprivation theory cannot explain

the nationalism of privileged groups such
as that of Afrikaaners in South Africa.
        Another elaboration of the theory of
inequality has been presented by Glazer and
Moynihan to explain the politicization of
ethnicity. Their argument is that the
salience of ethnicity is influenced by the
extent to which non-dominant groups fail to
achieve success according to the norms
established by the dominant group, which
may lead to the persistence of status inequalities even in the face of economic
successes. Where there is no single
dominant group, ethnic conflict is even more
likely because there will be competition
between different norms.[42] It is difficult
to see how such an argument can be meaning-
fully applied to many situations of national
or ethnic conflict. For example, Glazer and
Moynihan cite the case of Indian traders
expelled from Kenya because they were better
traders than the Africans. But, what does
this show? Presumably, that African traders
or Africans generally suffered a loss of
status because they were not as good traders
as the Indians and they expressed this feeling in ethnic antagonism and expulsion.
The trouble with this fragment of a theory
is that it is too elaborate to explain a
situation readily understandable in simpler
terms, namely, that Indians controlled a
segment of the economy and attendant resources to which Africans wanted greater
access. When Africans took power in Kenya,
they had the political means to adopt the
easy solution of depriving a culturally

distinct minority group of its economic
control rather than pursuing political and
economic policies that would mediate ethnic
conflict while long-range economic development plans were pursued to create new opportunities for Africans. In other words,
it is a case not of status discrepancies
but of competition for resources valued
equally by two groups. In Eastern Europe,
the comparable case to that of the Indian
traders in Africa is clearly that of the
Jewish commercial, business, and financial
groups in the late nineteenth and early
twentieth centuries who controlled resources and jobs that rising classes from
the dominant nationalities wished to control.

What place, then, does inequality occupy in a theory of nationalism? The
objective existence or subjective perception
of inequality is indispensable to justify
nationalism, but it is not in itself an
explanation for nationalism. The only
certainty is that every nationalist movement has always justified itself in terms
of existing oppression or anticipated
oppression by a rival group. Black nationalists in the United States have been able
to point to objective economic and status
inequalities to justify their demands. On
the other side, Afrikaaner nationalists
will argue that their inequality of numbers
would lead to their suppression by a black
African majority in a system in which blacks
were given equal political rights with
whites and they mobilize nationalist

sentiment to ward off the perceived threat
of inequality and to justify their dominance.
     Most situations of ethnic group
conflict that lead to competing nationalisms fall somewhere in between these two
opposite examples of disadvantaged and
privileged groups. Sometimes rival ethnic
groups face each other directly in ethnically heterogeneous urban areas, but
conflict situations also may arise between
ethnic groups unevenly distributed between
urban and rural areas or between different
regions of a country. Nationalism is most
likely to develop when new elites arise to
challenge a system of ethnic stratification
in the cities or an existing pattern of
distribution of economic resources and
political power between ethnically distinct
urban and rural groups or ethnically distinctive regions. One moment at which such
challenges tend to arise most forcefully is
when industrial development and political
centralization have led to concentrations
of job opportunities in key urban centers
and to the need for trained personnel to
fill the new positions. It is at this
point also in pluralistic societies that
the issue of language becomes critical
because the choice of the official language
and the medium of education determines which
groups have favored access to the best
jobs.[43] Ethnic competition in multi-
national states may focus directly on
specific job opportunities or on the allocation of the investment capital and other

34

resources required to create jobs.

Nationalism may also arise when there is a sectoral division of ethnic groups with one dominant in the countryside and another in the cities. In Deutsch's formulation, one of the typical cases of national conflict occurs when rural groups move into urban sectors dominated by linguistically and culturally distinct urban ethnic groups.[44] In that case, either the newly mobile groups must be assimilated and taught the language of the ruling group or the dominant group itself will be replaced in power by the newly mobilized and culturally different elements or some sort of complex pluralist solution will have to be devised to make multilingualism compatible with the technological and administrative requirements of the modern state. The kind of elite competition that precipitates a major nationalist movement bears a family resemblance to, but is different both in degree and in quality from, the communal job competition engendered in the early stages of modernization. It now becomes a case not merely of competition for a few privileged positions, but of a challenge by one group to the entire distribution of resources or to the division of power between two whole societies or potential societies. It is no longer a question simply of who shall have certain jobs, but who shall determine how jobs and other resources are distributed.

The critical contact points in ethnic nationalist confrontations are the

educational and political arenas--the
schools and colleges, on the one hand, and
the institutions of power and governance,
on the other. A disadvantaged minority
will demand control over the schools first
if it is dispersed, or will contest for the
schools and for local political power in a
particular region if it is geographically
concentrated. The schools and colleges
are a critical contact point for two reasons. They provide a source of high status
employment for new elites and they are also
an instrument of control over the ethnic
group. Whoever controls the schools determines whether or not the ethnic group will
maintain its cultural distinctiveness and
thereby be available for ready political
mobilization on ethnic grounds. Such
conflicts for control over the schools are
endemic in nearly all multi-lingual developing societies where they focus specifically
on the question of medium of education.
Examples abound in the history of Eastern
Europe in such struggles as the Magyar
resistance in the eighteenth century to
Joseph II's efforts to introduce German
language instruction in the schools,[45] or
the conflicts between Germans and Poles in
Upper Silesia in the nineteenth century over
the teaching of German and Polish in the
schools there.[46] If the disadvantaged
ethnic group is a minority concentrated in
a geographical area, its elites will also
demand the use of the regional language
as the principal language of administration
in the area. They will also call for some

form of political-administrative devolution
or decentralization of political power, or,
in some cases, for outright secession. A
disadvantaged majority will, of course,
demand the democratic right of power in the
political system as a whole.

     To return now to the example of the
reassertion of Croatian nationalism in
contemporary Yugoslavia, the Croatian case--
and the whole question of relations between
the nationalities in contemporary Yugosla-
via--can be explained satisfactorily in
terms of competition for economic and
political opportunities and resources without reference to Croatian feelings of
"relative deprivation." In fact, what
appears to be at issue in Yugoslavia--as
in many developing societies--is competition
for economic resources, particularly for
the investment funds needed to promote
economic development and technological
change and to provide employment, and for
political power that crystallized on the
issue of constitutional changes in the
direction of centralization and decentralization.[47] At the same time, the demand
also was made for recognition of Croatian
as an official language of Yugoslavia
distinct from Serbo-Croatian.[48] The explanation for the reassertion of Croatian
nationalism in this form is not that
Croatians are actually deprived or that
they feel relatively deprived, but that
there is advantage to be gained, economically and politically, by emphasizing Croatian distinctiveness. In the contemporary

political context of Yugoslavia, regional
decentralization of both political power and
economic resources serves the interests of
the Croat managerial and professional
strata, who prefer to control opportunities
in Croatia rather than to move to less
developed regions of Yugoslavia.   Croatian
nationalism, therefore, has been articulated
in terms of a demand for regional autonomy.[49]   Serbian interests in Yugoslavia, in
contrast, have been identified more with
centralizing policies and practices because
the Serbian elites are in a position, as the
numerically dominant nationality, to control
more of the political and economic resources
of a centralized Yugoslavian state than any
other nationality.
     Thus, ethnic nationalism and conflict
are most likely to develop when the educational, technological, and administrative
requirements of an industrializing, centralizing state and the democratic demands
of previously disadvantaged mobilizing
groups make it increasingly difficult to
sustain a system of ethnic stratification
or a particular regional or urban-rural
distribution of economic resources and
political power. New elites arise from
culturally distinct, disadvantaged groups
to compete for economic and political
opportunities controlled by the dominant
group. The more widespread the competition
and the more intransigent the dominant
elite, the more likely it is that disgruntled elements from the disadvantaged
group will turn to nationalism. How far

such a nationalist movement will be taken
and how successful it will be depend upon
both the character of internal social and
political communication and organization
within the group and upon the political
interrelations with other ethnic groups.
For an ethnic nationalist movement to
succeed, it is necessary for the elites who
begin the process to be able to pursue or
at least to appear to pursue effectively
the interests of other social classes within the ethnic group. A potential nationalist movement may peter out if the
immediate demands of its elites are satisfied in the political and economic systems.
It may also peter out or remain of marginal
importance if the mass of the people,
whether they are rural peasant or urban
proletariat, find their economic needs
satisfied through the existing system.
Peasants may find that they and their leaders can be elected to positions of power
in the system and that agrarian policy and
rural patronage can be influenced to their
advantage. In such cases, the rural masses
may not find the appeals of their urban
intelligentsia for the protection of their
language and culture of great interest.
Similarly, if the labor market is expanding
in the industrial sector, the urban proletariat and the landless in search of urban
jobs will not be moved by ethnic appeals.
They may be influenced, however, if employment opportunities are not expanding sufficiently rapidly to accommodate new entrants
and if the better positions are held by

persons from different ethnic groups.
     In summary, then, it is not inequal-
ity as such or relative deprivation or
status discrepancies that are the critical
precipitants of nationalism in ethnic
groups, but the relative distribution of
ethnic groups in the competition for valued
resources and opportunities and in the
division of labor in societies undergoing
social mobilization, industrialization and
bureaucratization. The potential for ethnic
nationalism exists when there is a system
of ethnic stratification in which one ethnic
group is dominant over another, but it is
not usually realized until some members
from one ethnic group attempt to move into
the economic niches occupied by the rival
ethnic groups.[50] To the extent that they
fail to do so or have bitter experiences
in doing so, they will protest against the
system of ethnic stratification as a whole
and attempt to mobilize the ethnic group.
Such mobilization may lead either to
communalism involving no more than the
mobilization of one's community for more
effective competition, or it may lead to
nationalism and a more fundamental challenge
to the whole division of labor, resources,
and power in the society. On the other
side, the priviliged group may mobilize
to defend its interests and may also use
ethnic sentiments in doing so. The second
type of situation that may precipitate
competing ethnic nationalisms is one in
which one ethnic group dominates rural
society and another the urban economy. A

third type of situation is that of the
multi-national state in which distinct
ethnic groups occupy compact geographical
regions that are at different levels of
economic development. In either of the
latter two situations there may be intense
competition over the sectoral distribution
of resources by the state, over political
power in the system, and over the languages of education and administration.

POLITICAL FACTORS

Nationalism is a political movement by
definition. It requires political organization, skilled political leadership, and
resources to gain support to make successful demands in the political system.
Moreover, the movement must be able to
compete effectively against alternative
political groups and must be strong enough
to withstand government efforts to suppress
it or to undercut its political support.
Effective political organization and political leadership and the resource base to
maintain them are independent variables
that influence profoundly the outcomes.
Political organizations that can command
some community resources are likely to be
more effective and successful than those
that cannot. Some of the most successful
nationalist organizations have been able to
build and draw upon resources created during
a previous period of communal mobilization.
For example, the NCNC in Nigeria in the
1940s and 1950s based its organization on
the tribal unions created during the

previous decades of Ibo ethnic consolidation
and advancement;[51] the Akali Dal in the
Punjab built an unshakeable base of nationalist support through its ability to call
upon the resources of the SGPC, a body that
manages all the Sikh temples in the province
and that was itself created in an earlier
period of Sikh communal mobilization;[52] the
Zionist movement in Europe and America was
able to call upon, if not command, the
financial resources of its bourgeoisie.
One looks in vain in the history of Eastern
Europe, however, for specifically nationalist organizations with comparable resources. Those nationalist parties that
drew their leadership from the clerics of
the Orthodox and Catholic churches or that
built upon earlier periods of church promotion of ethnic consciousness appear most
comparable to such movements, but there are
hardly any studies of Eastern European
nationalist parties that reveal the structure of their organizations or the sources
of their financial support that would make
it possible to compare them with movements
in other parts of the world.
    A political organization that succeeds
in identifying itself with the community
rather than merely representing the community or pursuing its interests also is
likely to be more effective against external political competition and potential
internal rivals. The Akali Dal in the
Punjab became for many Sikhs equivalent
with the Panth or the Sikh community.[53]
The Zionist movement has so effectively

identified itself with the Jewish community
that to attack Zionism, as the United
Nations did, is considered by many Jews as
well as by many non-Jewish supporters of
Israel as equivalent to anti-Semitism. The
important goal for nationalist movements
in this regard is exclusivity, the drive to
become the sole political representative
of the community so that the community may
act cohesively and unitedly. This is especially important if the group is a
minority, for a cohesive minority may be
able to achieve its goals against a larger,
but more fragmented group, whereas organizational division in a minority ethnic
group may be fatal to its interests.

A third feature of the more effective
ethnic nationalist movements is their
ability to shape the identity of the groups
they lead. Again, the Akali Dal has not
only identified itself with the Sikh community, but has played an increasingly important role in defining what it means to
be a Sikh.[54] The Zionist movement has also
succeeded in redefining for many Jews what
it means to be a Jew; namely, not merely
to be descended from a Jewish mother or be
a follower of certain rituals, but to believe in the right and duty of Jews to
emigrate to Israel or at least to support
the cause of Israel if one does not or cannot emigrate.

Fourth, a political organization, to
be effective in the pursuit of nationalist
goals, must be able to provide continuity
and must be able to withstand changes in

leadership. Most successful nationalist
movements are led by strong, dynamic, and
sometimes charismatic leaders, but such
leadership may not be sufficient to sustain
a movement to the end. Prominent leaders
may die or be killed or may turn away from
nationalism before the group's goals are
attained. There must, therefore, be a clear
successor or a second rung of leaders who
can effect a succession without dividing
the movement. The more successful nationalist movements, such as those of the Sikhs
and Jews, have provided leadership continuity and have coped with succession
problems, but Welsh nationalism ebbed after
Lloyd George became Prime Minister and the
Black community in the United States lost
much of its unity and the momentum of the
movement after the death of Martin Luther
King.
      Finally, it is of critical importance
in the success of nationalist movements
that one political organization be dominant
in representing the demands of the ethnic
group against its rivals. The Muslim
League in preindependence India always insisted, in all its dealings with non-Muslim
political groups, in being recognized as
the sole spokesman of Muslim political
interests. Its leaders knew that to do
otherwise would make it possible for its
opponents to divide and undercut its support. Few nationalist political organizations in Eastern Europe have been able to
achieve such a dominant position within an
ethnic community. More characteristic have

been situations where internal religious and
class differences have undercut the ethnic
solidarity and political cohesion of nationalist movements, which have consequently
either failed to achieve their goals or have
had to rely upon external intervention in
doing so. For example, the dominant position of the Slovak People's Party in expressing Slovak nationalist demands in
interwar Czechoslovakia was undercut by
divisions between Catholics and Protestants
and by the existence of a Protestant-based
agrarian party. The Slovak People's Party
ultimately achieved power in 1939, but only
with the support of Nazi Germany.[55]

Political organization, then, is both
an instrument of an ethnic group in
achieving and evidence of the achievement
of multi-symbol congruence. The most
successful nationalist political organizations have succeeded in shaping the boundaries of their groups to conform to the
political goals they set for them. In
this way, a group becomes defined not only
by its language and/or its religion and/or
its claimed territory, but by the political
organization that pursues its interests.
In Eastern Europe, however, specifically
nationalist parties, taking as their primary
goal the self-determination or liberation
of a single ethnic group have more often
than not taken second or third place to
parties of class interest (peasant or work-
er parties), to parties with foreign support
(Communist and Fascist), or to movements
that have sought to integrate several ethnic

groups (the Yugoslav Partisan movement).
In some cases, class-based and fascist or
clerical parties have been successful in
capturing the nationalist sentiments of a
significant segment of the population, as
did the Fascist Iron Guard in Romania in
the inter-war period or the Slovak People's
Party in inter-war Czechoslovakia. However,
none of these parties achieved such positions of political dominance or public
support that it was able to identify itself
with the community it claimed to represent
and to shape its identity. Nor, of course,
were these parties able to survive the massive disruptions produced by World War II
and foreign intervention.

GOVERNMENT POLICIES

Government policies and institutional
mechanisms may be critical factors in influencing a group's capacity or desire to
survive as a separate entity, its self-
definition, and of its ultimate goals. The
policies available to governments to prevent the maintenance of separate ethnic
identities or to limit the influence of
ethnic groups range from the most extreme
forms of repression, including genocide
and deportation, to policies designed to
undercut potential bases for ethnic group
mobilization through assimilation in the
schools or through the integration or
cooperation of ethnic group leaders into
the structures of power and wealth in the
society. Alternatively, governments may
choose to follow explicitly pluralist

policies and solutions to state-nation relations[56] by establishing political structures such as federalism or by conceding to
different ethnic groups the right to receive
education through the medium of their mother
tongue and to protect, preserve, and promote
their culture in a variety of ways. Governments may also influence indirectly the
development of ethnic conflict through
policies that distribute state resources
and opportunities for government employment.

The whole range of government policies
towards ethnic groups has found expression
at different times in Eastern Europe. At
the most extreme end, several of the East
European states cooperated with the Nazis
in the extermination and deportation of
the Jews. In the post-World War II period,
some of these same states, now under Communist regimes, cooperated with (or submitted
to) the Soviet Union in the deportation of
German minorities.[57] Population transfers
also have been used to resolve ethnic
minority problems involving neighboring
states, as in the Greek-Turkish, Greek-
Bulgarian exchanges at the end of the first
world war.[58] Alternatively, restrictions
on the movement of ethnic minorities have
been used as a mechanism of confining ethnic
groups to particular areas, as in the
confinement of Jews to the Polish Pale by
Catherine II of Russia.[59] Another variant
on this theme of population movement or
restriction is the policy of colonization,
as in the efforts by the German government
to support German movement to and purchase

of lands owned and occupied by Poles in
Posen in the nineteenth century.[60] Less
extreme efforts to deny ethnic minority
groups recognition of separate cultural or
political status through forced assimilation to a dominant language or culture also
have been common in Eastern Europe, such as
the Magyarization policies of the Hungarian
or the Russification policies of Russian
monarchy in the nineteenth century[61] and
the similar attempts of the Soviet Union
under Stalin. Such policies, of course,
often have the contrary effect to that
desired leading frequently to the stimula-
tion of ethnic feelings among the articulate segments of the minorities denied the
right to use their own language or express
their own cultural values in the public
sphere.
     Examples of institutional mechanisms
that may influence the development of
separatist movements are the demarcation
of administrative areas to conform to presumed ethnic boundaries, the establishment
of systems of separate confessional autonomy, and the creation of a federal system
of government based upon cultural-linguis-
tic-territorial groups. It is well known
that, in Africa, the imperial powers often
established local administrative areas
that conformed to tribal boundaries.[62] The
Ottoman millet system, in contrast, recognized the autonomy of religious groups
without reference to ethnic or territorial
boundaries. Among the institutional mechanisms available to multi-ethnic or multi-

national states for satisfying national
demands within a common political framework
is federalism. Federalist solutions to
nationality conflicts are usually viewed
with trepidation by the central authorities in such states who see their primary
purpose as the maintenance of the unity
and territorial integrity of their states
because they fear that federalization is but
a step away from secession and disintegration. On the other side, however, it is
often argued that the failure to grant some
form of political autonomy in a federal
state to aspirant national groups may itself promote secessionist and disintegrative
tendencies that federalism might resolve.
One of the great recurring questions in
this regard, insofar as Eastern Europe is
concerned is, of course, whether or not
Austria-Hungary might have developed into
a viable modern multi-national state had
it established a federal system in 1849.[63]
In contemporary Eastern Europe, only
Yugoslavia and Czechoslovakia have sought
federal solutions to satisfy the national
aspirations of their constituent peoples
within a common political framework.[64] In
the Czech case, however, a highly centralized party structure has been superimposed
upon a federal administrative arrangement.
Moreover, in the Yugoslav case, the devolution of real political and economic power
to the federal units and the decentralization of the party structure in the 1960s was
followed by a revival of nationalist sentiments and demands and by a consequent

reimposition of centralized controls. Consequently, it is clear that the question of
the viability of federalized multi-national
states continues to be a matter of concern
to the authorities in the most ethnically
diverse of the successor states to the
Austro-Hungarian empire.

State-nation relations are often viewed
as a zero-sum game in which state concessions to ethnic nationalist demands are
conceived as invitations or steps on the
road to secession and the disintegration
of the state. In fact, however, there is
a very large range of policy choices that
are available both in federal and in
unitary states for states and nations to
reach accommodations short of secession.
Nowhere is this more clear than in the area
of language policies. Governments may adopt
one, two or many official languages. They
may adopt one or more languages for administrative use at the federal level and
others at the provincial level. They may
adopt special language requirements for
entry into government service or they may
permit the use of several languages as
media of examination and require on-the-
job language training in other languages
after admission. In the schools, government may recognize some languages and not
others either as media of education or as
languages of instruction. For example, the
two components of the Austro-Hungarian
empire followed different policies in this
regard, with the Hungarian government
pursuing Magyarization to the extent of

denying national minorities education in
the medium of the mother tongue whereas, in
Austria, the medium of education was the
mother tongue and German was taught as a
second language.[65] In contemporary Slovenia, an extremely liberal policy of providing bilingual primary education, using
both German and Slovenian as media of
education as well as languages of instruction, has been developed.[66] Government may
recognize the right of a group to control
the public schools in a particular area and
to use its own language as medium of education or it may permit only an individual
choice option, in which the local mother
tongue will be used only if it is requested
by a specified number of parents. Government may choose to follow a policy of
equality with respect to the claims of
competing language groups, enforcing a
state-wide policy of bilingualism for all,
or it may recognize only minority rights
where one language is spoken only in a
particular area or by a dispersed group and
may be used legally only in the area in
question or only for certain purposes.
     The kinds of language policies chosen
may be very important in influencing whether
or not an ethnic group becomes assimilated
or demands recognition as a nationality.
Insofar as language and employment, particularly government employment, are closely
interconnected, groups whose languages are
recognized earlier than others as languages
of administration and media of education
will derive a competitive advantage. Groups

whose languages are not recognized then
have two broad choices. They may give up
their mother tongue or use it only at home
and choose education through the medium
of the language that provides access to
employment, or, if the community has the
resources, it may develop its own network
of private schools to maintain its language
and culture and simultaneously work to
change government policies towards its language. In this interaction between the
variety of government language policies and
community choices, there are many points
at which either conflict or accommodation
may occur. Moreover, the interaction may
lead to the disappearance of some languages,
the loss of numbers of language speakers
over time in the case of others, and the
standardization, modernization, and
consolidation of new speech communities
with recognized cultural and political
rights in the political system for still
other groups. Although government language
policies may influence the course of development of ethno-linguistic movements and
their strength and weakness, mere recognition of an otherwise undeveloped language spoken by a non-modernizing people
will not provide the motive force for
linguistic nationalism nor will any but the
most extreme discriminatory or genocidal
policies destroy the language and culture
of a group that has reached a point of
communal solidarity and determination to
maintain and perpetuate itself.

Another type of government policy that
may influence the development of nationalities from communities is the way in which
the state distributes the economic resources
and public service jobs at its command.
Here, as in the previous two sets of examples, government policies may or may not
succeed and cannot be considered in a vacuum
separate from other motive forces promoting
national differentiation. For example, two
regimes in Czechoslovakia of vastly different political orientation--the parliamentary
regime of the interwar period and the communist regime of the post-World War II peri-
od--pursued the similar policy of diverting
economic resources into the less developed
region of Slovakia in order to rectify the
historical imbalance in industrialization
and general prosperity between the Czech
and Slovak regions of the country.[67] However, neither regime made sufficient
concessions to Slovak desires for political
autonomy,[68] with the result that Slovak
nationalism reemerged forcefully when
political opportunities became available.
However, the form taken by Slovak nationalism in these two periods also differed
significantly according to the different
political contexts in which it operated.
In the interwar period, Slovak resistance
to the centralizing tendencies of the
Czechoslovakian parliamentary regime took
the form of a reactionary, clericalist,
authoritarian movement--the Slovak People's
Party--and culminated in the establishment
of the Slovak Republic, a puppet regime

of the Nazis.[69] When Slovak nationalism
reasserted itself under the Communist
regime in 1968, it took the form of a political alliance with Czech reformists.[70]
Common to both situations is the fact that
economic policies favorable to the Slovaks
failed to prevent the resurgence of Slovak
nationalism in the absence of political
policies to satisfy the desires of Slovak
political elites for regional autonomy and
federalism rather than a centralized state.
Nationalist movements make both economic
and political demands. They cannot be mol-
lified by policies that deal with only one
set of demands.

POLITICAL CONTEXT
The movement from community to nationality
involves inevitable struggle for power between competing ethnic groups. The ebb
and flow of nationalism in an ethnic
community, the intensity of its drive for
power, and the particular form that its
demands take are influenced by the political context. Three aspects of the
political context are especially important--
the possibilities for realignment of political and social forces and organizations,
the willingness of elites from dominant
ethnic groups to share power with aspirant
ethnic group leaders, and the potential
availability of alternative political
arenas.
     In an early modernizing society where
the first groups to organize politically
are ethnic groups, or where the leading

organizations articulate local nationalisms, the question of political realignment may not arise. It becomes important when an ethnic group has made the transition to a community but has not developed its own political organizations. A community may choose not to do so because existing non-ethnic political organizations are so well-entrenched that the only sensible course lies in acting as a pressure group through them, or, as in the East European Communist states, because the formal organization of ethnic movements may simply be prohibited.

Possibilities for political realignment occur when existing political organizations fail to keep in tune with social changes that erode their support bases or in times of revolutionary upheaval. A general political realignment presents new opportunities for nationalist political organizations to arise and to present an effective blend of cultural and economic appeals. The outcome in a situation of this sort cannot be predicted on the basis of cultural differences between rival ethnic groups, but depends upon the patterns of elite competition for power in local party and government structures, upon the ability of competing elites to communicate effectively across class lines and to new social classes, and upon the relative skills and effectiveness of competing leaders and organizations. Once a society has reached a stage of political development in which large-scale political organizations have become entrenched, even dramatic social and

economic changes that, in the early stages
of modernization, would precipitate national conflict may not be sufficient to provide
a basis for an effective nationalist movement unless these social changes also
precipitate a general political realignment.
These remarks apply especially to single-
party states, where nationalist demands
can be articulated effectively only within
the single party and only at moments of
dramatic change in the structure or leadership of the party. Such contextual changes
do occur occasionally even in single-party
states, however, as for example in Czechoslovakia in 1968 when the replacement of the
Novotny regime by that of the reformist
group led by Dubček, presented an opportunity for Slovak nationalist demands to be
articulated.

The second political context variable
that may affect the movement of an ethnic
group from communal consciousness to national status concerns the willingness of
elites from dominant ethnic groups to share
political power. Where that willingness
does not exist, the society in question is
headed for conflict, even civil war and
secessionism. However, where such a willingness does exist, the prospects for
pluralist solutions to ethnic group conflicts are good.

No regime, even the most authoritarian,
can avoid confronting the issues of power-
sharing and pluralism in modernizing multiethnic societies. The Communist regimes of
Eastern Europe, like the Soviet Union, have

had to confront these issues without much
guidance from Marxist ideology which, in
principle, does not regard ethnic differences as desirable bases for social
differentiation in modern societies. In
fact, however, Burks has shown that
Communist Party support in Eastern Europe
in the interwar period relied more on its
appeal to ethnicity than to class aspirations.[71] The success of the Yugoslav
Partisan movement during the Second World
War also depended upon an extremely skill-
ful handling of ethnic and nationality
protests and conflicts.[72] However, once
in power, none of the Eastern European
regimes, anymore than the Soviet Union,
has been able to avoid the recurrence of
ethnic and nationality questions, nor have
the Eastern European regimes followed
consistent policies toward ethnic minorities and distinctive nationalities.
Yugoslavia, like the Soviet Union, has
recognized in principle the right of self-
determination for its nationalities, although in practice it has been assumed that
the right was exercised when the several
nations agreed to the establishment of the
Yugoslav Federal Republic in the 1946 Constitution.[73] In the early years after
World War II, Yugoslavia, again like the
Soviet Union, adopted a federal system in
form, but a centralized system in practice.[74] The regime also permitted the
different ethnic groups and nationalities
in Yugoslavia to retain their distinctive
languages and cultures and tried assiduously

to ensure that all the major nationalities
were represented on most party and government organs--though not the critical decision-making bodies--in proportions close to
their actual distribution in the total
population.[75] However, from the point of
view of power-sharing, the Yugoslav policy
toward the nationality question constituted,
even in the early post-war years, a significant shift away from the Serbian domination that characterized the inter-war
political system. In the 1950s and 1960s,
Yugoslavia experimented with a more genuine
system of decentralization of decision-
making power to workers' councils and
communes.[76] Czechoslovakia also, particularly since the events of 1968, has moved
toward a federal system which, though it
does not provide for full sharing of power
between Czechs and Slovaks, does provide a
good deal more genuine participation in
power by the Slovak minority than is permitted to minority groups in the Soviet
Union.[77] Although such limited policies
in the direction of increased minority
participation in power clearly have not
prevented a new rise in national consciousness in Communist multi-national states in
recent years,[78] the willingness of Communist leaders to provide ethnic minorities
access to positions of power at both the
federal and regional levels has been an
important factor in moderating such movements in the past. The persistence of
demands from ethnic elites in several Soviet
republics to increase their representation

in local decision-making structures[79] and
the reassertion of Croatian national sentiments in Yugoslavia in 1971-72 are, however,
evidence of continuing problems in both
states.

In sharp contrast to the Yugoslav and
Czech efforts to move towards pluralist
solutions to ethnic and nationality policies has been the increasingly repressive
and assimilationist attitude of the Romanian
Communist regime toward its minorities.
In pursuing a policy of "Romania for the
ethnic Romanians," the Romanian government
in the 1950s and 1960s gradually withdrew
the rights of the Hungarian minority in
Transylvania, permitted the emigration of
Germans and Jews, and sought to increase the
proportions of Romanians and decrease the
proportions of minorities in leading positions in the government and in the Communist
Party.[80] However, the assimilationist
and discriminatory policies of the Romanian
government[81] also have failed to reduce the
degree of ethnic and national consciousness
among the minority groups in Romania.[82]

The third political context variable
concerns the availability of and the
relative costs to be borne by an ethnic
group in shifting to an alternative political arena. In unitary, centralized states
that contain geographically concentrated
minorities, it is certain that, at some
point, when the political demands of a
minority are not being satisfied adequately
by the state authorities, the demand will
be made for administrative and/or political

decentralization of power. In multi-ethnic
federal systems, where local ethnic groups
are concentrated regionally, and compete for
power in provincial units, demands often
arise for the reorganization of provincial
boundaries to conform more closely to the
boundaries of ethnic groups. However, it
also sometimes occurs that local minorities, particularly dispersed minorities,
may demand protection from the central or
federal government against provincial
governments dominated by rival ethnic
groups and may orient their own political
activities to an extra-provincial arena.
In pre-modern colonial or imperial systems,
it may also happen that an ethnic majority
in a region dominated by ethnic minorities
will appeal to the central government for
justice, as did the Romanian leaders in
Transylvania in the eighteenth century,
who appealed to the Habsburg Emperor to
grant the Romanian nation political and
religious equality with the three dominant
"nations" of the principality he ruled.[83]
     Federal solutions to the conflicts
of multi-ethnic societies provide considerable political flexibility and present
minority ethnic groups with both the possibilities of demanding the construction of
new or the reorganization of old political
arenas. They also provide simultaneously
alternative arenas in which minority groups
may operate. The use of strategies of
political arena reorganization and multi-
level conflict adjustment work best under
the following conditions: where a relatively

open system of political competition and
bargaining exist; where there is a system
in which the federal and provincial or
local units all have or are granted significant powers such that the capture of power
at one level by one ethnic group does not
close all significant avenues to power;
where there is a multiplicity of ethnic
groups rather than only two or three; where
ethnic conflicts do not run afoul of
ideological disagreements between unitarists
and federalists; and where external powers
are not willing to intervene. Where any of
these conditions are lacking, federalist
and multi-level strategies may fail and
civil war or secession may result. Most of
these conditions have, in fact, been absent
in the Eastern European states where, with
the exception of contemporary Yugoslavia,
federalist solutions to ethnic pluralism
have either not been adopted (as in Austria-
Hungary) or have involved little real decentralization of power. Partly for these
reasons, secessionist and irredentist movements have been recurring and persistent
in Eastern Europe for the past century.

In general, however, the secessionist
strategy is a high-cost strategy that most
political elites will not adopt unless the
significant roads to power in the existing
system appear to be blocked and unless there
is a reasonable prospect of external intervention in their favor. Otherwise,
maximalist programs of national minorities
tend to take the form of demands for
"autonomy," "self-government," or

"confederation" within existing multi-
national states. Even in Eastern Europe,
the leaders of many national movements
have chosen these goals rather than outright secession.[84]
     The most favorable period in modern
times for secessionist strategies was, of
course, the pre-World War I period in the
Balkans when the major powers in Central
and Eastern Europe and in Russia had direct
interests in each other's internal ethnic
conflicts. The consequences of this period
of inter-ethnic international conflict have
produced the term "Balkanization," which has
now become a part of the language of pro-
ponents of national integration everywhere,
who use it as a bad example to be avoided
at all costs. Whatever the moral merits
of this attitude, the free use of the term
has tended to draw attention away from the
great variety of political solutions that
are available in multi-ethnic societies in
between a forced "national integration" and
"Balkanization."

     This chapter has developed an approach
to the study of ethnicity that focuses on
processes of identity formation and
identity change. The approach is designed
to be comparative and universalistic,
oriented to questions concerning the conditions under which ethnic groups, at different times and in different places, undergo
the processes of transformation leading to
subjective self-consciousness as ethnic
communities and/or political significance

as nationalities. Consequently, a set of
definitions is needed that can be used to
analyze groups and processes of change that
have occurred everywhere in the world and
at different historical times. The definition used here of the term ethnic category
is an objective one that implies that one
can, in principle, at any point in time,
divide the peoples of the world or of a
particular society into categories distinguished by cultural characteristics and
symbolic referents. However, in early
modernizing societies where the process of
ethnic transformation has just begun and in
post-industrial societies where considerable
linguistic and cultural assimilation have
taken place among ethnic groups, the division between peoples may not be of such nature as to divide them into clearly compartmentalized groups with sharp boundaries.
Rather, linguistic and other cultural
distinctions may overlap and often are not
congruent with each other, though there
will be differences between some ethnic
groups and others in this regard at any
point in time.

Whether or not a particular ethnic
group's boundaries are sharply defined or
not in its pre-mobilization stage, it is
of the essence of the process of ethnic
transformation that boundaries are made
sharper, that old symbols acquire new subjective significance, and that attempts
are made to bring a multiplicity of symbols
and attributes into congruence with each
other. In this process of ethnic

transformation, which is to be distinguished
from the mere persistence of ethnic differences in a population, cultural markers are
selected and used as a basis for differentiating the group from other groups, as a
focus for enhancing the internal solidarity
of the group, as a claim for a particular
social status for the group, and, if the
ethnic community becomes politicized, as
justification for a demand for either group
rights in an existing political system or
for recognition as a separate sovereign
nation. Although the definition of ethnic
category emphasizes objective rather than
subjective differences and cultural markers,
the argument presented above has been that
such differences are only necessary, but
not sufficient conditions for the process
of ethnic transformation to begin.

Also necessary, but still not sufficient conditions for communal mobilization
are either elite competition for control
over a local society or intra-class competition between competing elites from
different ethnic groups for control over
new opportunities in the modern segments of
a developing society or over prestige and
high-paying positions in an industrial
society. Four characteristic forms of elite
competition for local control are those
between local land controllers and alien
authorities, between competing religious
elites, between local religious elites and
collaborationist native aristocracies, and
between native religious elites and alien
aristocracies. The second general type of

64

elite conflict that may precipitate communal
mobilization arises out of the inevitably
differential character of the processes of
modernization and social mobilization that
typically takes the form in developing
societies of competition for government jobs
and in industrial societies for jobs in
government, industry, and in the universities.

However, the kinds of elite competition
noted above provide only the catalyst for
the symbol manipulation that is involved
in communal mobilization. The sufficient
conditions for successful communal mobilization are the existence of the means to
communicate the selected symbols of identity
to other social classes within the ethnic
group, the existence of a socially mobilized
population to whom the symbols may be
communicated, and the absence of intense
class cleavage or other difficulties in
communication between elites and other
social classes. The means necessary to
promote such inter-class communication are
growth in literacy rates, the development
of media of mass communication, particularly
newspapers, the standardization of the local
language, the existence of texts and other
books in the local language, and the availability of schools or classes in which the
native language and culture can be taught.
The corollary to this condition concerning
means is that, to use Deutsch's terms,
there must be in the local society new
groups of people who are becoming "available" for more intensive communication,[85]

who are demanding education and new jobs in
the modern sectors of the economy. Once
the means and the demand for new opportunities and new forms of communication have
been created, the question arises of which
elites can more effectively capture the
newly mobilizing social groups. A native
aristocracy may manipulate ethnic symbols
in order to provide a justification for
its own privileges, but if it oppresses the
peasantry, the peasant classes and the
sons of the peasantry who move into new
occupations will oppose the continued
dominance of the local landlords, may reject the cultural appeals made by them,
and may look to the state authorities for
support against their local oppressors.
It may also happen that there is no strong
native elite group to promote the local
language and culture, but only a limited
intelligentsia working through literary
societies to standardize the language and
create a new literature in it. Such a
group may transform the native language but
unless its leaders can ensure that the employment opportunities of newly mobilizing
social groups will be enhanced by the
learning of it, their efforts will not
lead to significant communal mobilization.
In early modernizing societies, a high
degree of communal mobilization will be
achieved most easily in two types of situations: a) where there is a local religious
elite in command of temples, shrines, or
churches and the lands and trusts attached
to them and a network of religious schools;

or b) where the local language has been
recognized by the state authorities as <u>both</u>
a legitimate medium of education and
administration, thereby providing the native
intelligensia with both material and cultural rewards to offer to new social groups
aspiring to education and new opportunities.

The necessary and sufficient conditions
for communal mobilization are also the preconditions for the development of a successful nationalist movement. Nationalism as
an elite phenomenon may arise at any time,
even in the early stages of communal
mobilization. However, for nationalism to
acquire a mass base, it must go beyond mere
elite competition for local control or a
narrow range of privileges. The mass base
for nationalism may be created when widespread intra-class competition occurs
brought about by the movement of large
numbers of people from either a previously
overwhelmingly rural group or from a disadvantaged group into economic sectors
occupied predominantly by other ethnic
groups. If such movement is resisted by the
dominant group, supported openly or tacitly
by the state authorities, then the aspirant
group will be easily mobilized by nationalist appeals that challenge the existing
economic structure and the cultural values
associated with it. If the aspirations of
the mobilizing group are perceived as a
major threat to the status and economic
opportunities of the dominant group, then
the groups threatened by such displacement
may become available for a nationalist

movement. (Sometimes, however, the situation of the group threatened with displacement may be too untenable for nationalism
to have any meaning, as in the case of
Indians in East Africa.) The mass base for
competing nationalisms also may be provided
by the uneven distribution of ethnic groups
in urban and rural sectors or in different
regions of a country in such a manner that
there is competition for control over the
state structure and the distribution of
resources for the entire society.

    While intra-class ethnic competition
for economic opportunities or sectorally-
based competition for control over state
power provides the mass basis for nationalism, the demands that are articulated
and the success of a nationalist movement
in achieving them depend on political
factors. Three sets of such factors were
identified above--the existence of and the
strategies pursued by nationalist political
organizations, the nature of government
response to ethnic group demands, and the
general political context. Even when an
ethnic group has achieved a high degree of
communal or political mobilization, it is
far from inevitable that it must then move
to create complete political congruence
with its cultural identity by acquiring a
separate sovereign state. There are a
variety of political goals to be attained
short of sovereignty and a wide variety of
government policies that may be pursued to
undercut, sidestep, or accommodate within
an existing state the demands of an aspirant

ethnic group. Among those goals, and in
the face of the political means and the
power of the modern state as well as the
contemporary aspect of the international
system, secessionism is the least likely
outcome of current conflicts between states
and nations.

CHAPTER II

SOCIAL THEORY AND ETHNOGRAPHY: LANGUAGE AND ETHNICITY IN EASTERN EUROPE

by

Professor Joshua A. Fishman

The study of ethnicity lacks a generally acceptable theory. Most studies rely on objective or external theories that miss the point entirely. Those approaches to an understanding of ethnicity are related to economic, demographic, philosophical, and political factors exclusive of ethnicity per se.[1] The external theories have traditionally been limited to the study of only a few areas of the world and to only a few periods of modern history--yet they purport to be universal.[2] Objective theories mostly ignore Eastern Europe where there has always been an obvious link between language and ethnicity.[3] The continued reliance on these approaches to the study of ethnicity has created two significant gaps that need to be overcome if we are to achieve our goals: understanding ethnicity and its link to language.

First, the study of ethnic groups by external observers focuses on the impact of industrialization, modernization, and

69

political emancipation. That concentration
on comparatively recent social phenomena
generally ignores most of human history and
the bulk of mankind and implies that ethnicity did not exist in earlier periods.
Actually, the study of ethnicity cannot
logically exclude more than half the available data--all of European and Mediterranean
history provides a fertile field for explo-
ration--and still claim scholary respecta-
bility.

Second, an understanding of ethnicity
requires the observer to try and cope with
what it "feels like," with its warmth (and,
for that matter, with the heat it generates),
with its intimacy and its spontaneity. In
short, ethnicity is as much a subjective
experience as it is a matter of objective
specification. No catalog of chronological
detail, exact demography, or eco-political
facts can really convey the meaning of
ethnicity even to external observers, let
alone to people who experience it. This is
not to say that the bio-social or social-
psychological aspects of ethnicity should
be ignored--rather, the point is simply
that there are phenomenological and
cosmological dimensions that merit attention even if they cannot be measured,
quantified, or neatly categorized.

These gaps cannot be bridged in a
single essay, or in a collection of essays.
But, hopefully, this chapter will outline
the importance of alternative approaches
to the study of ethnicity for the benefit
of East European specialists.

Ethnicity in the Classical Hebraic and
Grecian Worlds

The term ethnicity is used here specifically
`-` `-`eference to socio-cultural behavior and
es derived from membership in communi-
of putatively common ancestry known to
s "peoples" or "nationalities." The
vior and values of greatest interest
those linked to the meanings generally
med in explaining such membership; its
`r---`umably unique characteristics; its importance; and how membership in a people
or nationality group compares to other
memberships. Ancient Hebrew and Greek
social theoreticians recognized ethnicity
as a form of extended family feelings and
obligations pertaining to "one's own kind."
They recognized it in themselves and in
their own societies, rather than primarily
in contrast to foreign communities or to
minorities in their midst or elsewhere.
Both cultures were ethnocentric because
their leaders strongly believed they held
pivotal positions in the world and in the
universe. Greeks and Hebrews alike recognized that ethnicity was part of daily
life rather than merely a royal road to
great heights or depths. They recognized
sub-ethnicities within their fold, but
felt that these were subcategories with a
greater, more inclusive, familial bond.
Ethnicity was thought to have various
ramifications and manifestations--without
it they thought life would be dark, impoverished, uncaring, and unloving.

Therefore, they believed that ethnicity
properly spiritualized (among the Hebrews)
and controlled (among the Greeks) would
lead to creative and productive unity.
Otherwise, it would lead to corruption,
injustice, materialism, favoritism and
self-indulging passion. Thus, both cultures
recognized that the benefits of ethnicity--
loyalty, unity, and shared spirituality--
could only be realized through vigilant
struggle. Both of these civilizations recognized a link between language and
ethnicity which is referred to from the
earliest periods. The link was increasingly stressed and culminated in the view that
their God (gods) particularly distinguished
them and their language. They also recognized linguistic uniqueness as an inseparable aspect of all other ethnicities.

Christian Ethnicity

Early and later Christian social theory was
definitely influenced by Hebraic and Greek
concepts of ethnicity. The early church
conceived of Christians as a Third People
(i.e., in addition to Jews and Greeks).
Those who elected to join the Christian
faith were required to renounce other ethnic
ties. Subsequently, as the Eastern and

Western churches became secure, they
both initially found ethnicity to be a
desirable instrument for Church growth and
stability. Thus the Eastern Church's view
that God speaks to each people in its own
language and gave each its own autoceph-
alic church was derived from earlier Hebraic
and Greek thought. That view further entrenched ethnicity as a God-given attribute
that could be put to spiritualized use.
This view is still commonly held in Eastern
Europe. It has passed from Greece to
Bulgaria, into the Slavic world to the north
and east, and to the Hungarians, Moravians
and Bohemians in the northwest.[4] The interrelated sanctity of Church, ethnic collectivity, and language ultimately was a
precursor of Protestantism and modern
nationalist thought.

The Western Church, however, increasingly related ethnicity to the thought and
experience of the Western Roman Empire.
Roman spokesmen recognized the integrative
value of ethnicity as a building-block for
organizing the great multi-ethnic Empire.
However, they distinguished ethnicity from
citizenship; accordingly the Western Church
treated ethnicity as a controllable,
utilitarian characteristic of Christian
life. The Western Church regarded initial
ethnicity as a welcome basis of cooperation,
friendship, altruism, self-sacrifice, and
ultimately as a preparation for an even
higher order of social integration into the
supra-ethnic Empire and Universal Church.
Medieval social and moral philosophy

acknowledged and appreciated ethnicity as
a reliable initial bond that linked human
beings to each other. It was similarly
appreciated during the Renaissance and the
Reformation. However much Church Councils
struggled against exaggerated ethnic claims,
there were no other "natural" modes of
human integration available until the
mercantile and industrial revolutions
transformed Europe and introduced human
experiences and expectations undreamt of
by the Hebrews, Greeks, Romans, the Church
and Humanists.

Mercantilism and Industrialization in Europe

Mercantilism and the industrial revolution
produced new economic elites that eventually
came to political power in Europe. These
revolutions focused on urban locales which
attracted masses of rural folk from
ethnically diverse origins. The masses were
increasingly schooled in selected vernaculars to make them functional in terms of
the needs of the newly developing economic
and political systems. During this period
ethnicity began to be viewed differently
than before, reflecting the political and
economic changes introduced as a result of
the mercantile and industrial revolutions.

These revolutions consolidated the political
and economic systems of countries bordering
on the Atlantic, before reaching those in
central, eastern and southern Europe. The
upper and middle classes of the Atlantic
powers benefited to the disadvantage of the
working and lower classes and the resulting
geographic and social class differences
were subsequently used to evaluate ethnicity
in nineteenth century Europe when modern
mass movements began to crystallize.

The major ethnic threat to peace in
early nineteenth century Europe was the German intellectual revolt against the political, cultural and economic domination of
Central Europe by France. The rights of
disadvantaged ethnic groups were articulated
by Johann Herder and found a responsive
chorus throughout the jumble of principalities and ethnic German colonies in the
Baltic states, Hungary and the retreating
frontiers of the Ottoman Empire in Europe
but also in Ireland ("colonist" Western
Europe), Italy and Greece (Southern
Europe) and the "captive" Slavic states
in the East. Herder's words intensified
the ancient Hebraic and Greek vision of
ethno-linguistic sanctity which recognized
God's glory through the ethnic diversity He
had created. In returning to that vision
Herder related ethnicity to language, folklore, the glorious past, ancestral traditions, and a vision of greatness and unique
destiny. These images of ethnicity continue
to transform indigenous convictions into a
nationalistic awareness in Eastern Europe

to this very day. They are also visible
in Africa and Asia. According to Herder and
his followers God and Nature called for the
protection of ethnic diversity, the cultivation of linguistic differences, and for
the distinctive sanctity and beauty of
various people and their languages. Consequently Herder believed that those political
and economic realities which tended to
weaken them had to be altered. The resulting ideal of the nationality-state threatened the multi-ethnic empires of Central
and Eastern Europe and the seemingly ethnically consolidated polities of Western
Europe. Language was viewed as the key to
unlocking ethnic greatness and the subsequent development of dynamic solutions to
all the problems of the modern era. The
ethnic vernaculars were claimed to be great,
liberating, unifying and authenticizing
phenomena and the validity of these claims
was real and moving despite externalist-
objectivist ideals to the contrary. The
link between language and ethnicity was
experienced most in Eastern Europe, and no
other part of Europe was more deprecated
by the West.

Ethnicity in Modern Europe

THE CIVILITY ROADBLOCK

Three major defenses have been erected
against the recognition of ethnicity as
an enduring dimension of social life in the
West. Each of them assumes that the
mercantile-industrial revolutions have an
objective reality of greater validity than
ethnicity. Thus, Western political
scientists argue that the political stability attained in the West as a result of the
forces set into motion by the commercial
and industrial revolutions is desirable.
Western observers thus have viewed the
ethnic ideologies and movements that spread
from Central Europe throughout the world
as rank disturbers of the peace, dis-
rupters of political rationality, and
perverters of Western civility. In prog-
ressing from the politics of ideology to
the politics of individual liberty Western
"libertarians" were then dismayed to note
that group sentiments, group loyalties,
group bonds, and group passions swayed
masses of people against the established
order. Their own established order was
based on the view that consciously organized and activated ethnic collectivities
or nationalities were results rather than
causes. In the West centuries of shared
political and economic institutions had
consolidated diverse ethnic populations
into peoples with common customs, values,
beliefs and histories within given, traditional, political boundaries. The

nationality movements in the less industrialized and less politically unified
parts of Europe held that people were the
cause and states were the result of their
actions. Lord Acton, J. S. Mill and their
heirs held that view to be an inversion
(perhaps a perversion) of nature and moral-
ity. To those who held this view, the
approach of the Eastern Europeans, late
comers to industrialization and modernization, was proof of barbarism. Westerners
based their judgment on the biased view
that "mobilized," politically conscious
ethnicity required outsiders to hate more
than did such approved loyalties as class,
state, and religion. Westerners did not
understand that people who were belatedly
industrialized and modernized needed traditional bases to achieve ethnic consolidation and self-determination. Those goals--
realized late in an already "modern" world--
meant even more to Eastern Europeans than
they did to Western and Northern Europeans
in earlier centuries. To some Western
Europeans the barbarism of Eastern Europe
is confirmed by technological differences
and by the movements which poignantly link
language and ethnicity. East European
sentiments and movements are viewed by
Westerners as useless remnants of a dark and
distant past, and this bias remains as a
barrier to intellectual cooperation between
social science generalists and Eastern
European specialists.

THE RADICAL ROADBLOCK

Classist Marxist theory evolved as a
counter-reaction to the rest and imagined
evils of economic consolidation produced
by the industrial-mercantile revolutions.
The classical Marxist holds that ethnicity
is unnecessary, undesirable, and a basically
specious fabrication manipulated to delude
and mislead the toiling masses from their
proper concerns. The classist Marxist--
in typical Western fashion--also views
ethnicity as a resultant rather than a
cause, although Marxian weltanschauung
pictures ethnicity as a byproduct of economic forces rather than of political
stability and its socio-economic concomi-
tants. Classical Marxism maintains that
the lives of the masses can be appreciably
improved only by proletarian control of
the basic productive means of modern
economic systems. Consequently, the
classist Marxist maintains that any
attempt to convince the masses that they
can solve social problems on any other
basis of collective action is a misguided
and pernicious attempt to fractionate and
dissipate the potential power of a unified
proletariat. Ethnicity is a diversionary
myth, a barrier on the road leading to the
messianic future and its super-ethnic self-
identification envisioned by the Marxists.
Thus many champions of the disadvantaged
proletariat have come to reject the many
disadvantaged ethnic groups of the world.[5]
    Early Marxists realized that ethnicity
sentiments in Western and Central Europe had

consolidated to such a degree that proletarian organizations had to recognize the
political frontiers between separated ethnic
constellations. However, this artificial
compartmentalization had not yet occurred
in Southern and Eastern Europe, and the
Marxists combatted ethnic consolidation
there in the hope of organizing the growing
proletariat and activated peasantries of
the Austro-Hungarian and Russian Empires on
a supra-ethnic basis to create a universal
brotherhood of workers. Classist Marxists
used research and ridicule unsparingly to
point out the fanciful, anachronistic and
self-seeking basis of ethnic myths and
ideologies involved in countless ethnicity
movements in the "dark part" of Europe.
Economic materialism was incompatible with
the phenomenology and romantic images of
contending and constantly changing ethnic
movements. Classist Marxists joined these
movements only when they triumphed and
then only to capture them from within, since
Marxism failed to destroy them from without.

Classist Marxism has had to accommodate mobilized ethnicity in Eastern and
Southern Europe and Marxists learned to
manipulate it just as the bourgeois nationalists were accused of doing. The neo-
Marxist theories that arose consider
ethno-national consolidation to be the
building block of a new order, much like
that conceived by Roman theorists and the
social/moral philosophers of medieval
Western Christendom. Neo-Marxian schools
also arose among peripheral ethnic

communities that were overlooked or re-
pressed by intellectual elites within their
respective "centers." Nevertheless, "main
stream" Marxism has an established orthodoxy
which is just as entrenched as is that of
capitalism and it continues to express an
unreconstructed bias. To the Marxist the
only fundamental social reality is economic,
and ethnicity is merely a secondary cultural
phenomena. The ethnic dedication and aspirations of politically submerged Eastern
European communities continue to be derided,
attacked, denied and denigrated by Marxists.

THE CONCEPTUAL ROADBLOCK

The civility bias arose in response to the
political consolidation resulting from the
Industrial Revolution. The radical bias,
in turn, developed out of the economic
evils fostered by the Industrial Revolution. Modern sociology has developed a
bias related to the demographic hetero-
genization of urban industrial centers. The
heterogeneity of the modern industrial
center threatens ethnic enclaves in growing
metropolitan areas and raises an issue
concerning the permanence of ethno-cultural
differences in modern technological and
industrial societies. Marx claimed that
economic realities would transform and unify
society and that the proletariat would be
the moving force in the future. Modern
sociologists, before and after Marx,
generally did not ascribe as central a role
to the proletariat. They focused on
technology, the marketplace in particular,

82

and upon industrialization, urbanization and
modernization as major forces that would
lead mankind toward a life style dominated
by impersonalized mass production, distribution, and consumption. These forces swept
across Europe and America, and will ultimately sweep the entire world. Thus
sociologists tend to believe that ethnic
distinctions will diminish and eventually
disappear--to them the touching intimacy of
family and community life is doomed.
     The only sociologist of note to quibble
with that view was Max Weber who disagreed
with Marx that economic realities dictate
cultural behaviors. Weber's brilliant
analyses of society in ancient Israel,
India, China, and during the rise of capitalism in Protestant Europe demonstrated
how ethno-cultural factors resulted in
particular economic practices. Weber
concluded that ethnicity and culture were
themselves causal and not mere byproducts
of economic circumstances. Indeed, Weber
concluded that neither economics nor
culture were exclusive or independent as
causal factors since they were interlinked
in an ongoing chain of interactions. However, despite his analysis Weber agreed
with the general chorus of modern social
theory that society was destined to change
in accordance with the requirements of
technology, efficiency, expertise, and
impersonal objectivity. Like the others
Weber theorized that ethno-cultural distinctions would eventually disappear because of decreasing differences imposed by

ever increasing economic and technological
similarities. Eastern Europe would be no
exception.

American sociology has been particularly influenced by this conceptual roadblock.
The United States is both a country of
immigrants and an industrial giant; its
urban centers are occupied by an unparal-
leled array of ethnic enclaves. Social
theory predicted that those enclaves would
disappear because homogenization was destined to weaken and destroy ethnic differences. American social theory confuses
ethnicity with minority (specifically, with
disadvantaged minority) status. Accordingly, American sociologists (as well as
political scientists and anthropologists)
recognized ethnicity in terms of ethnic
groups and ethnic minorities, that is as
a means of identifying marginal collectivities within the mainstream of society.
American sociologists have almost universally assumed that the mainstream lacked
ethnicity, despite the views to the contrary
of the ancient Hebrews and Greeks, and the
views of the modern Eastern Church, Islam,
and East Europeans. None of the latter
have greatly influenced the constricted
perception of ethnicity held by American
sociologists; they still assume that it is
a minority phenomenon, even in Eastern
Europe, and a blessedly moribund and
patently unnecessary concept to boot.[6]

LANGUAGE AND ETHNICITY

The contempt for ethnicity and its passionate rejection by the bulk of modern Western intellectuals make it imperative that we recognize Herder and the social, cultural, anthropological tradition derived from his seminal contributions. We need to recognize and appreciate that ethnicity is a powerful experience. Sex roles are not the same as sexism; religious beliefs are not the same as religious bigotry; and the phenomenon of ethnicity is not identical to ethnocentrism or racism.[7] Ethnicity must therefore be approached seriously, even sympathetically, as a social dimension that has received too little attention and too much abuse during the past two centuries. That approach will benefit the Eastern European specialist and all of social theory.

ETHNICITY IS "BEING"

Ethnicity in the pre-mobilized state is the untutored and largely unconscious ethnicity of everyday life and ethnographers have catalogued how members of various ethnic collectivities discuss and recognize that phenomenon. The extent to which ethnicity is intuitively defined and experienced as part of an actor's "being" (as distinct from his "doing" and "knowing") is often overlooked in a literal sense. Ethnicity has always been experienced as a kinship phenomenon, a continuity within the self and within those who share an intergenerational link to common ancestors. Ethnicity is partly experienced as being "bone of

ir bone, flesh of their flesh, and blood
their blood." The human body itself is
wed as an expression of ethnicity and
nicity is commonly felt to be in the
blood, bones, and flesh. It is crucial that
we recognize ethnicity as a tangible,
living reality that makes every human a link
in an eternal bond from generation to
generation--from past ancestors to those
in the future. Ethnicity is experienced as
a guarantor of eternity.

The sense of "being" of ethnicity pre-
dates the Hebraic and Hellenic weltanschauung of familial kinship. The externalist
is concerned whether that view of ethnicity
is real and commonly accepted, but the
members of ethnicity aggregates recognize
that it is the view itself that matters,
not its validity according to external
criteria. The feeling of being related to
others as closely as to brothers, sisters,
parents, grandparents, sons and daughters
is one of the most powerful motivations of
humankind. That feeling simultaneously
transcends death and promises eternal life,
while tangibly demonstrating familial roots,
and perpetuation of the lineage. Above
all, ethnicity is a universal mystery to be
shared with other great and powerful forces.

Just as ethnicity is a bodily and
directly experienced reality, language is
also a bodily experience. Language and
speech are elements of identity experienced
in the self and issued from the self.
Speech is fashioned by the tongue and teeth
and other bodily organs. Language is

assumed to be inherited in the same ways as
other physical gifts and capacities. Language and ethnicity are tangible features
of identity related to the other perceived
bodily attributes: sex, intelligence, skill,
strength, wit and temperament. Individuals
belonging to a given ethnic aggregate
supposedly differ from members of other
ethnic groups in physical appearance (although not only on that basis). That
difference together with differences in
language, temperament, and intellect (all
features related to physical attributes),
mark and keep them members of their group.

Exclusively biological interpretations
of human behavior lead to racism, but
ethnicity extends beyond the biological or
"being" dimension. Ethnicity in the modern
era is a consciously manipulated, massive
and dynamic social factor that has resulted in unspeakable racial abuses. However, modern man has perpetrated similar
horrors for philosophical, political,
economic and religious reasons unrelated to
ethnicity. Modern man's capacity for
committing horrible acts is a by-product
of modernity basically unrelated to ethnicity or to the biological assumptions of
ethnicity in particular. Thus, while there
is a racist potential in modern ethnicity,
that potential is not sufficient to damn
the phenomenon. The racist potential in
ethnicity suggests the need to recognize
the emotional investment involved. The
biological component of ethnicity is just
as pliable, escapable, interpretable, and

compromisable as the non-biological bases
of human aggregation. Each folk theory,
whether within or outside an ethnicity
cluster, has escape hatches and allows for
transformation--each has its own rites of
passage and its own supernatural ways of
interpreting paternity and changing the
meaning of "being." Nevertheless, the
biological component is one of the most
powerful features of any ethnicity cluster
and an awareness of this component usually
results in a socio-cultural consolidation
which makes further transformation difficult. The metaphors of blood, bones and
flesh joined by the emotive experience of
tears, pain, joy and laughter produce the
least transient experiences within the
realm of ethnicity. It is significant that
ethnic languages are always thought to
preserve, not merely to evoke, the bio-
emotional experiences of revered ancestors.
Languages link past and present generations
in a peculiarly sensitive web of intimacy
and mutuality. The link between language
and ethnicity in modern Eastern Europe
perpetuates a poignant sense of identity
widely recognized by ethnic collectivities
elsewhere as well. Modern theory may de-
ride the link between language and ethnicity
as irrational and fanciful but that derision
neither explains nor reduces its power.

ETHNICITY IS "DOING"

John Stuart Mill recognized that the modern
polity required a particular kind of civility behavior, "doing," if it was to achieve

stability, and he recognized that ethnicity
was a disruptive rival. Marx also recognized that the modern economy required
proletarian unity, a particular kind of
"doing" to curb the evils of capitalism and
to more widely share the bounty of modern
technology. He also recognized ethnicity
as a disruptive rival. Parsons recognized
that existence in a modern urban society
requires an achieved status, a particular
kind of "doing" unrelated to the principle
of "doing" within ethnicity. The "doing"
of ethnicity is related to the common
paternal lineage shared by all that places
transcendental responsibilities on each
actor. The physical heritage of ethnicity
creates expressive obligations and opportunities for behaving as the ancestors
behaved and preserving their great heritage
by transmitting it to generation after
generation. The "doings" of ethnicity are
thus more meaningful than the goal-directed
behavior theoretically involved through
civility, rationality, or other such mundane
approaches. The "doings" of ethnicity
preserve, confirm, and augment collective
identities and the natural order. Ethnic
"doings" promise solutions to current
problems and to problems yet unstated and
unknown.

Ethnic "doings" are often linguistically encumbered, dependent, and expressable
only within traditional ethnic networks.
Songs, chants, sayings, prayers, invoca-
tions, formulas, rites, jokes, and riddles
are all required, recognized, expected,

rewarded, and undetachable from ethnic communities. They are viewed and fully available only through the linguistic systems to which they are naturally related.

"Doing" is ultimately more negotiable than "being" since behavior and linguistic media are subject to change, but even these changes are subject to authentication before the resulting behavior is justified. The changes are limited to the revitalization and recapture of authentic linguistic expressions. When linguistic shifts occur they will always tend to relate partially and symbolically to the ancestral patrimony befitting the "corpus mysticum."

Obviously, the language component, just as the entire ethnic behavior pattern, tends toward periodic revitalization. Current needs and problems are always a factor in ethnicity. The past always needs to be recaptured, used, interpreted, and exploited to resolve current problems. Thus, ethnicity is more than a means of preserving the past; it also has the potential for giving direction and providing group identity during change. The authentication of behavior has a potential for completing increasingly novel and modern social tasks. Even so, the authentication process increasingly depends upon language. Eastern Europe exemplifies how ethnic authenticity has been used for new "collective" purposes and how language has been used to authenticate those purposes and maximize their attainment.

ETHNICITY IS "KNOWING"

Classical Hebraic and Greek theories stress
ethnicity as "knowing," i.e. they derived
philosophy and even cosmology from an ethnic
basis. However, ethnic "knowing" has deep
roots in all cultures. The physical authenticity of ethnicity requires that we "do"
what is authentic and promises that we will
appreciate infinitely more as a result.
Authentic ethnic responses permit people
to be wise in special ways, more sensitive
to inter-personal vibrations. They allow
people to react to unique stimuli and to
intuit what others cannot grasp. Ethnicity
is a weltanschauung that helps to explain
origins, clarify eternal questions, ration-
alize human destiny, and purports to offer
an entre to universal truths.

Ethnic "doings" and "knowings" are
commonly considered to be impossible in any
language other than the authentic. However,
ethnicity is not necessarily Whorfian[8] since
authentic language is not necessarily an
active agent or a causative factor. Rather,
it is more often a reflective or merely a
traditionally linked factor. In either case
the language of authenticity is a genuine
and altogether frugal route to wisdom
derived from authentic "being" and "doing."
Wisdom requires an authentic medium since
any other mode of expression would be inadequate, shallow, and self-limiting in
expressing the treasures that need to be
enjoyed and sensed. This link between language and ethnic "knowing" is still vibrant
in Eastern Europe where language is a

vehicle of communication, an identifier and
authenticator of individuals within groups,
and of groups in relation to their heritages
of wisdom. Language permits an exquisitely
refined and unique awareness of eternal
verities so it contributes a unique meaning
to life and deserves a unique devotion and
dedication from the living. Since the
wisdom derived from the language of authenticity is unspecified and unlimited it is
likely to provide insights into current
and future problems and salvation, even as
it has so many times in the past. Language
movements are built around this putative
association so that authentic languages
could be more fully established, protected,
and cultivated. The masses in such movements have not been motivated by any
objective "need" to unify modern economies
and polities with their linguistically
embedded school systems.[9] On the contrary,
they are motivated by the subjective need
to unite with their brothers and sisters
in applying their authenticated wisdom to
the solutions of current problems. No
external knowledge or objective scepticism
can replace the validity of language and
ethnicity. Objectivity and external
observation cannot replace the human being's
need to belong intimately, inter-genera-
tionally, authentically. At best, we can
only attempt to understand that need if we
do not experience it ourselves.

ETHNICITY AND IRRATIONALITY

Traditionally Western European intellectuals
have debunked ethnicity--and have tended
to ascribe it to disruptive and disadvantaged peoples. They have never recognized
it in themselves or in their own unmarked
societies. They have denied the mutability,
manipulability, and purposiveness of ethnicity and therefore the functionality of the
link between language and ethnicity. Those
denials need to be examined both with
respect to their validity, as well as to
assist in understanding the subjective
nature of ethnicity. That examination will
emphasize the limitations of modern Western
European social theory as an approach to an
understanding of ethnicity.

MUTABILITY

Western European and American social theories often unwittingly arose from the
changes resulting from the industrial revolution. Of course, the industrial
revolution was itself a by-product of the
prior characteristics and experiences of
Western Europe. Accordingly, those theories are often unjustifiably harsh in their
analysis of the mutability inherent in
ethnicity. Ethnicity is exceptionally prone
to change in terms of membership, content,
and saliency[10] and since ethnicity claims
and stresses authenticity, its mutability
may be viewed as a flaw which invalidates
and discredits it as a social phenomenon.
That critique frequently involves the vul-
garization of ethnicity, a treatment that

would be sharply rejected by the advocates
of other theories. The pristine, unaltered
ethnic nation is a myth, but so is the
notion of a super-ethnic proletariat or
intelligentsia. Furthermore the observations made of a phenomenon in constant
change may still be valid. Theories of
social change should observe changes in
ethnicity with interest rather than citing
change to discredit the validity of its
role. Because political science and sociology tend to reject ethnicity as a causal
factor in social change it is damned if
it does change and damned if it doesn't.
That irrational and infantile rejection of
ethnicity is probably related to its
preverbal-nonverbal origins. The role of
ethnicity in social change has been pre-
maturely denied without having been fully
and constructively examined.

However, those involved in the study of
ethnicity as a legtimate social concern
view the mutability of ethnicity in one
of two ways. It may be viewed as a decline
of interest justifying renewed dedication,
effort, and devotion to pristine authenticity. In this sense, some of the
advocates as well as some of the critics
of ethnicity react similarly by rejecting
mutability. However, their conclusions
differ greatly; the advocates are drawn
to greater commitment and the critics to
greater repulsion. Another kind of "within the fold" reaction to the evidence of
mutability accepts change as the essence
of ethnicity. The mainspring or essence

94

of authenticity is believed to be the pre-
ordained "wisdom" essential to the acceptance of necessary and desirable change,
growth, alteration and self-correction.
This change-accepting rationale belies the
notion that ethnicity is a "backward looking" or "ancestor worshiping" ethos.
Actually, ethnicity is neither, rather it
is an experience of deeply rooted, intimate
and eternal belonging. The operating
principle of ethnicity is authenticity
which operates to reject as well as validate
mutability, depending on the particular
social, historical, and personal environment. Ethnicity movements exploit mutability just as other modern movements do.
        Language academies established to
preserve "the authentic spirit" of particular languages while entrusted with their
modernization exemplify the penchant that
ethnicity systems have for simultaneously
pursuing authenticity and modernization
(mutability). For example, the "great Sun"
theory, which viewed all European languages
as repositories of Turkish genius, and the
exploitation of Graeco-Latin roots in
Talmudic and Medieval Hebrew, make it clear
that authenticity is directional in inspiration and outcome. The desire to be modern
"in an authentic way" (in "our own way"
while remaining "true to our own genius,"
and so as to "preserve our own heritage")
tells us a great deal about the depth of
commitment and adaptability of ethnicity.
That kind of commitment and adaptability
can be studied best in Eastern Europe where

the simultaneous urge toward authenticity
and modernization has been massive and
intensive. Those who sneer at fabricated
peasant costumes, folk songs, folk dances
and folk derivations of communism and
democracy defy understanding the phenomenon
they seek to explain. However, ethnicity
continues to become multi-faceted because
of its ability to indigenize the modern
world.

MANIPULABILITY
The need to belong deeply and intimately to
an ethnic aggregate is a powerful motiva-
tion. Consequently, ethnicity has motivated
movements in all possible directions on
the political compass. Ethnicity has been
unjustly criticized because of its purport-
edly greater manipulability. The anti-
ethnic revulsion that followed the Nazi and
Fascist excesses resulted because those excesses were confused with ethnicity. It
should be noted that ethnicity movements in
the early nineteenth century were largely
moderate and libertarian. The Greek,
Polish, Italian and Irish movements toward
independence all adhered to the kind of
self-respect that permits respectful
acceptance of other nations. This view
was also typical of early South Slavic and
East Slavic ethnicity movements. However,
following the success of the Junkers in
unifying Germany, and that of the Tsarists
in subverting the revolution of 1905 the
manipulation of ethnicity was increasingly
dominated by militant and messianic-

cataclysmic symbols. At the same time
socialist movements also became more
militant, apocalyptic, and cataclysmic in
method and theory. The earlier socialist
tradition of gradualism was paralleled
by the traditional gradualistic approach of
those who advocated ethnicity. The "excesses of ethnicity" have more than been
matched by the excesses of non- or anti-
ethnic modernization and secularization.
Secular messiahs and totalitarian democracies have[11] visited indescribable horrors
upon vast populations without reference to
ethnicity. The clashes between these movements on the domestic and, increasingly on
the international stages, foreshadow greater
dangers ahead. Nevertheless, ethnicity
alone is often the whipping boy.

In everyday traditional life ethnicity
is not nearly as manipulable as it is on the
modern politicist arena. The quiet, self-
defining routines of habitual comfort and
authenticity is the core of ethnicity.
The manipulation of ethnicity to attain
political, economic or cultural goals is
a modern manifestation and is certainly one
of the least unique features of ethnicity.
Indeed, it is often the enemy of unmobilized
ethnicity. The immemorial nature of unmobilized ethnicity and its power when
mobilized are patent and potent in Eastern
Europe. The use of language to achieve
mobilization is clear but the authenticity
of language pre-dates mobilization, manipulation, and that is further subjective proof
of the continuity between authenticity and

modernization.

CIVILITY, RATIONALITY, INDIVIDUALITY

A continuing need of modern man and especially of modern intellectuals is the need
to be free, unbound and unbeholden. This
need is metamorphosed and becomes, among
other things, civility, rationality, and
individuality. The utility of freedom in
modern society is a widely recognized and
primary value. The presumed absence of
freedom in the ethnicity constellation is
often viewed as proof that ethnicity is
undesirable or unsuitable in modern life.
In discussing this issue the extent to
which civility-rationality-individuality
are irrational is often overlooked. Thus
a double standard is employed to evaluate
different value systems.

The recent "rebirth of ethnicity" is
frequently explained in terms of dissatisfaction with the demands of state-aparatuses
for exclusive and overriding loyalty.
This dissatisfaction might be interpreted
as a search for greater individuality in
human affairs or as a search for meaningful, smaller scale communities. Thus, the
"return to ethnicity" may be a long over-
due attempt to achieve freedom and belonging at a manageable, small scale level,
rather than the return to tribalism that
some detractors have suggested.[12] Indeed,
ethnicity suffers from a labeling bias
since the same manifestations considered
to be progressive, modern, and rational
in class-based aggregations are considered

retrogressive, archaic and irrational in
ethnicity aggregations. Ethnicity is thus
stereotyped as a kind of "collective behavior" with all of negative overtones ("group
mind," "blinders," "brainwashing") that this
label has. Nonetheless ethnicity has the
same capacity to organize, select or appoint
leaders, develop loyalties and commitments,
foster identity, combat alienation, create
symbols, provide purpose and direction,
overcome problems and find solutions that
are lauded when they appear in more favored
establishments and bases of aggregation.

The double standard used in evaluating
ethnicity has long been applied by those
who find it does not serve their purpose.
For example, every modern movement has exploited ethnicity to pursue its own advantage and has attacked ethnicity when that
strategy has been advantageous. This has
been true in Eastern Europe. It is also
true that ethnic groups use it to their
own advantage. Such exploitative attempts
are characteristic of societies in conflict,
and neither ethnicity nor anti-ethnicity
is more irrational than the other. Civility, rationality and individuality are not
the exclusive property of one point of view.
The difference between belonging and being
fettered and the differences between individuality and alienation, is primarily in the
eyes of the beholder.

Ethnicity and its recurring link to
language cannot be explained by an exter-
nalist-objectivist approach alone. The

researcher's map of the terrain as "viewed
from above," must be augmented by an internal map that is clarifying, motivating,
and directing to ethnic insiders. The two
maps together are revealing and provocative,
but taken separately they leave the task un-
done. This paper has outlined "the other
map," which is usually overlooked and ridi-
culed, because it is particularly useful in
understanding Eastern Europe. To understand language and ethnicity in Eastern
Europe it is necessary to get into the
experience itself. The researcher who
does so will find a level of comfort,
security, guidance, direction and meaning
to the daily lives of millions of people
that no regime or ideology has succeeded
in rendering elsewhere for any but small
and atypical segments of society. The
reliance on "one's own kind" in Eastern
Europe has derived supremely authentic
beings, doings, and knowings achieved only
via the language of that experience.

CHAPTER III

THE CREATION OF ETHNIC SYMBOLS FROM THE ELEMENTS OF PEASANT CULTURE

by

Tamás Hofer

The traditional peasant culture of the East European people plays a crucial though neither obvious nor self-evident role in their cultural self-identification and in their ethnic symbolisms. In Central and Western Europe peasant culture lacks this ethnic importance, and in Eastern Europe the traditional view of the peasant class was that it was uncouth, unpolished and subservient, with no symbolic importance.

This chapter explains the process that made certain elements of peasant culture symbolically valuable in Eastern Europe during the nineteenth century. The purpose is to illuminate this process and thereby enhance our understanding of modernization and nation building which influenced and was in turn influenced by the creation of ethnic symbols. This chapter will also examine the comparative ethnicity of the various peoples and analyze the content of the ethnic patrimonies of the region. By using certain subjective approaches it is possible to compare the views various ethnic groups

101

have held concerning the world around them.
From the point of view of ethnic-cultural
patrimony there are certain elements in
life that are meaningless, some produce
feelings of belonging, pride and moral
obligation, and others simply evoke aver-
sion.[1] The following pages sketch the
common and diverse features of the "ethnic
world view" (cultural ethnocentrism) of
the people of Eastern Europe.

The peasants, especially in ethnically
mixed regions, have always used cultural
markers spontaneously to express their
ethnic specificity. The region in which
those markers were recognized was generally
narrow. The period of national reawakening
produced a need for markers to integrate
the symbolic referents of the ethnic
community into an image of the national
past. The societies of Eastern Europe that
were developing into nations were highly
stratified. Some of them had their own
elites and elite cultures for centuries as
well as other cultures that ranged from
elite to peasant. During the period that
nations were formed serious efforts were
made to create native intelligentsias and
middle classes out of peasant societies
living under foreign rule. It was at the
level of political leadership, and the
intelligentsia, that the effort to transform some features of peasant culture into
general ethnic symbols had to be made.
(Foreigners played a significant role in
discovering some peasant cultures.) To
make symbols valid for an entire society

and to create a common ethnic awareness out
of newly discovered cultural features, the
institutions of national culture which were
developing simultaneously were indispensable.

The concept of "national culture" is
difficult to define partly because the
political goals, ideals during the period
under discussion were so different. The
concept of national culture subsumes
several factors including the development
of a culture and institutions, such as
schools, academies, learned societies and
journals, that transmit it. The expression
also refers to the content of cultural
material propagated by those institutions
while disregarding structural and class
differences in order to reach the society
as a whole. What the Germans call "Kultur-
träger"--the carriers or propagators of
culture, the guardians of the ethnic patrimony and of the ethnic self-recognition--
play a crucial role in that respect. Jozef
Burszta posits four specific requirements
for a national culture: 1) it is accepted
by the entire nation and all levels of
society as possessing national value; 2) it
is the result of the activity of formal
institutions and is propagated by them; 3)
its various aspects are the domain of well-
defined specialties and specialists; and
4) the basis of its functioning is a common
literary language.[2]

The culture of the people of Eastern
Europe and the ethnic patrimony that under-
lies the development of "national culture"

can be found by taking into account class
differences--the differing life styles of
various social groups, the habits of
consumption, and the various systems of
personal contacts. The recent literature
in the social sciences in socialist countries frequently refer to these problems
by quoting Lenin's view that "in each
national culture two national cultures
are included" (the exploiters and the
exploited). Yet a Soviet scholar, Yu. N.
Bromley, and others, have demonstrated that
class differences never split the totality
of culture. On the contrary, those aspects
of culture are specifically suited to carry
ethnic meaning--religion, language, common
literary language, certain habits in day-
to-day living--produce common characteristics valid for the entire ethnic community.[3] Other common characteristics are
built up through the institutions of each
national culture, but not all of these
features serve as symbolic-ethnic identi-
fiers. Yet among them can be found the
ethnic-cultural patrimony expressed in
different degrees according to the particular social group.

The discovery of peasant culture and
its inclusion in different national cultures
has been studied repeatedly by scholars in
various academic fields, but the conceptual
framework presented here is novel. Peasant
culture is studied in Eastern Europe within
the framework of the home country almost
exclusively for the use of its inhabitants
as part of its national cultural history.

This standard framework is conducive to
learning about the ethnic importance of
peasant culture through the history of
national literature and the work of lin-
guists, yet, it is not enough. Everywhere
in Eastern Europe content and form of various literary movements are based on folk
poetry or folklore, that depict the life of
the peasant. These important literary
works influence the development of national
self-identification and public opinion for
the peasantry. Yet these literary schools
are difficult to describe or generalize
because the East European expressions used
to describe them are diverse.[4] The use of
English exacerbates the problem because
English _termini_ _technici_, e.g., populist
literature, uses associations alien to the
East European contexts from which they were
taken.[5] "Populism in literature" is still
an insufficient explanation of the process
of symbol creation.[6] Furthermore, some
"populist literary movements" use peasant
traditions for purposes that have nothing
to do with the production of ethnic-national
symbols. Similarly, peasant-based stylistic
forms are used in the music, architecture
and fine arts of the various national cultures.

    The growing specialization of scientif-
ic activity in East European societies
created a special discipline for the study
of peasant cultures--national ethnographic
science.[7] (The terms used in Eastern Europe
to describe this science - národopis,
néprajz, ludoznawstwo, etc. - have slightly

different meanings and no exact English
equivalents.) National ethnographies and
folklore studies played an important role
in describing peasant cultures because they
produced material on which symbols could be
based, and because the ethnic self-identification of various peoples is useful in
studying older ethnographic compilations.
Yet ethnographers, because of their scien-
tific-critical bent, were often involved
in debates with important symbol creators.
Consequently the ethnographic histories
of the Eastern European peoples that were
written for "internal consumption" also
describe the development of scientific
methodology and the accumulation of information, but mention only incidentally the
concept of ethnic peasantry.

The Discovery of Peasant Cultures in the Service of National Movements

The people of Eastern Europe who tried to
build their own independent national cultures found that their most important task
was the creation of national languages.
This involved the creation of uniform linguistic norms, notably a reforming of language when there were literary traditions
within the nobility or the bourgeoisie.

The linguistic program also involved the creation and propagation of a national literature, the development of literary institutions, and the education of a reading public. The political importance of language and literature surpassed that of national historiography.[8]

The first goal in the program of the literati was simply to create literature in the national tongue. The next step was an attempt to create literature national in content and genre. The first stage was intended to introduce a "literary life" by translating, transposing, or imitating famous works. In the second stage the collection of ancestral and original traditions, including peasant poetry and folklore, and the cultivation of these traditions became important.

The East European peoples lived under differing political systems and varied social structures so these steps occurred in differing time sequences. There were historiographical dissimilarities between noble, bourgeois and peasant nations, and the people who lived either in their own states or in multinational empires.[9] For example, the Hungarian language reforms completed by 1815-17 were based mainly on existing stems used to enlarge the vocabulary. The study of peasant dialects began later, and the Dictionary of Hungarian Dialect was published in 1838. Where it was necessary to create literary languages out of peasant speech, the study of dialects began earlier. In those cases the study

of folk poetry was entered earlier in an
attempt to achieve literary independence.
For example, the discovery of Hungarian
folk poetry was influenced by early Serb
folk-poetry publications and their reception throughout Europe.[10] Furthermore,
János Erdélyi's Collection of Hungarian
Folk Poetry (1846-48) followed similar
works among the Czechs by František
Čelakovský (1822-27) and among the Slovaks
by Ján Kollár (1834-35).

The views of the East European literati
were initially influenced by Rousseau's
and even more by Herder's opinions, and
later by the writing of the Grimm brothers
and the English collections of Percy. It
is typical of the period that Kölcsey's
enthusiasm for Vuk Kardžić's collection was
greatly influenced by Jacob Grimm who
voiced his opinion of it in Vienna.[11] The
romantic enthusiasm for the simple and
natural and the criticism of contemporary
society typical of English and French
literatures acquired an ethnic, even
national, meaning in Herder's work.[12] East
European readers reacted not to his human-
ism but, almost exclusively, to the ethnic
and national aspects of his work, except
in Russia where people were not forced to
fight for their ethnic independence. Unlike the other East European countries,
literary populism was not a central trend
in Russia, and interest in social problems
remained stronger than interest in national
issues in Russian literature.[13]

The Hungarian example demonstrates
how attention was focused on the oral traditions of the peasantry as a result of the
attempt to find what was old and original;
how those traditions were recognized as
guardians of ancient literature; and how
folk poetry, the concept of peasant culture, and the peasant-centered work program,
emerged to readjust national literature with
folk literature as the model. The developing recognition of folklore worked hand-
in-hand with attempts to raise the
peasantry's social position, something that
did not enter the minds of the early collec-
tors of folk poetry.

Miklós Révai published an appeal in the
journal, Hirmondó, on January 16, 1782, ask-
ing for the development of a national language and for the collection of the remains
of the old Hungarian literature, including
the texts of material that survived among
the common people. His introduction to this
appeal strongly suggests that its author,
Mátyás Ráth, was familiar with Herder's
work. Rath used West European examples to
induce readers to follow the appeal.[14] In
this case references to the work of the
common people was not attributed merely to
the peasantry, but to songs popular within
all social strata. The concept of the
peasantry was delineated in another appeal
published in 1817 by István Kultsár who
again asked for the collection of folk
material. These appeals produced no result
but beginning in the eighteenth century
literature included numerous peasant figures

and works based on folklore. This literature tended to present an ideal picture of
the patriarchal-feudal society and little
attempt to advance social reforms. The
early writers were not opposed to the concept of the "noble nation" and tried to
place peasants peacefully within its limits
by depicting, through literature, a ficti-
tious social symbiosis.[15] Writers who used
popular themes in this manner were primarily conservative and opposed men like
Kazinczy, who participated in the Jacobine
conspiracy, and tried to foster national
literature by introducing the models of
world literature into the country. Some
of these men, for example György Gaál,
Alajos Mednyánszky and János Mailáth, belonged to the Hormayr circle in Vienna and
believed that conservatism was the best
way to achieve national independence. They
were the first to publish collections of
Hungarian folk tales and legends in German.[16]

A new trend of populism emerged in
the 1830s, called "political populism" by
János Horvath, to connect peasant cultures
with national independence and with the
economic and social uplifting of peasants
who were still serfs. This trend prepared
the way for the revolutionary approach
taken in populist literature in 1848-49.
The principles of this movement were tersely
expressed in a letter, dated February 11,
1847, that Sandor Petofi wrote to János
Arany: "Folk poetry is true poetry. Let
us make certain that it becomes dominant!

If the people will rule literature it will
come close to dominating politics too. This
is the task of our century." This generation produced a systematic, scientific edition of peasant works. When the Hungarian
Academy of Sciences held its first plenary
meeting in 1831 it resolved to collect
provincialisms, folk poetry and, above all,
folk songs. The task was entrusted to the
Kisfaludy Circle and the results were
published between 1846 and 1848 under the
editorship of János Erdélyi.[17] The appearance of the last volume was symbolic, it
appeared March 15, 1848, the day the
democratic revolution for national independence erupted in Budapest.

What was at first considered "ancient
poetry" was subsequently divided into peasant folklore and poetry written in a
popular style. After that publications
devoted to peasant texts became philo-
logically exact, verbatim, and linguistically precise. This was different from
the earlier publications in which those
texts were stylistically transformed into
"literary" language. Thus began the
scientific study of peasant texts within
the framework of a developing history of
national literature. Published essays
were devoted to literary forms, stylistic
peculiarities and historical contexts and
became the seeds of the professional,
academic disciplines of folklore and national ethnography.

Beginning early in the nineteenth
century more attempts were made to produce

scientific analytical studies dealing with
other manifestations of peasant culture.
These attempts included descriptions of folk
music, peasant dances, holiday ceremonies--
especially weddings--and peasant costumes.
The German speaking Viennese attorney of
German-Slovak origin from the Zipps dis-
trict, János Csaplovits, produced a volume
dealing with Hungary's ethnography as early
as 1822.[18] Csaplovits believed that Hungarian ethnography meant the characteriza-
tion of the various ethnic groups living
in the country. Besides giving information
about the life style, language, religion
and habits of these groups, his aphorisms
were indicative of their temperaments. To
him Hungary's most striking feature was
its ethnic mosaic. He expressed this in
his famous statement, "Hungary is Europe
in the miniature" meaning that almost every
ethnic group and language existed within
the country's boders. Even if the outlines
were hazy, his work delimited the scope of
the scientific studies of peasant culture
as a feature of ethnicity. By this time
"Volkskunde," national ethnography as an
independent discipline, had assumed a clear
but varied shape in the German-speaking
world and in Eastern Europe.[19]
     The impetus for this development was
based on the general public's growing
awareness of aesthetic values going beyond
folk poetry in the peasant world and peasant art arising from national and international industrial fairs. For instance,
the Hungarian exposition's "suba" (a richly

embroidered peasant coat made of sheepskin
with the wool unremoved) and other pieces
of peasant clothing, had great success at
the London World's Fair of 1851. The organizers of the Paris World's Fair in 1867
purposefully invited the "cottage industries" of numerous European peoples and
several experts consider that this event
marked the discovery of peasant art and
folk craft since the concept of folk art
had not yet been clearly worked out. During
this period, the age of industrial production, the concept of handicraft arts was
born. That concept referred to items
manufactured in peasant households, the
applied arts and crafts, and paid special
attention to distinctive styles of work-
manship. The expositions presented the
products of national handicraft arts and
these arts represented examples of "European exotica" (the peculiar creations of
industrially backward Eastern Europe) to
foreigners. The compatriots of craftsmen
found these works to be inspiring, important, new elements of their ethnic
patrimony. A Hungarian government commission collected--from all counties of the
country--examples of peasant-produced
pottery, carved wooden utensils, fancy
weavings and embroideries for the Vienna
World's Fair of 1873 in an attempt to represent the various regions and nationalities and their spiritual complexions.
Interestingly, a great debate began after
the exposition to decide which of the two
newly organized museums, the ethnographic

or the handicrafts, was to receive the
collection and it was awarded to the
latter. The industrial exposition of 1885
played an important informative and mobilizing role in Hungary. Complete rooms
representing the life styles of various
nationalities, including Hungarians from
different regions, were shown. The result
was commerce dealing in peasant pottery,
textiles and other products, and a systematic attempt to have these goods produced
for the market. Years later articles
appeared that described several middle-
class homes of Budapest as "pottery ware-
houses" because they were filled with rustic
plates and wine jugs.[20] An entire "ethnographic village" was constructed for the
great exposition of 1896, celebrating the
millennium of Hungary's existence. Its 24
houses represented 12 different regions and
12 nationalities living in Hungary. These
presentations influenced the viewers and
Zoltan Kodaly, then 13 years old, was
inspired to devote his life's work to investigating peasant traditions.[21]

Permanent collections of peasant artifacts began to appear in the "national
museums" as early as the middle of the
nineteenth century. The national museum is
devoted to national culture and guards and
presents relics of the national past, language and civilization. The ethnographic
section of the Hungarian National Museum
was created in 1872 but it did not function
systematically or dynamically until the
1890s. By then special museums devoted to

the presentation of local peasant cultures
thrived throughout Europe. Donner organized the collection of peasant artifacts
by students at the University of Helsigfors
in 1874.   Two years later he presented a
comprehensive Finnish exposition that became the basis for the establishment of an
ethnographic museum in 1893.   Ethnographic
museums were opened in Warsaw in 1888,
Lemberg in 1895, Belgrade in 1901, and in
Kraków in 1905.   The Russian Museum in St.
Petersburg was split up, and one part became an ethnographic museum in 1902.   A
Czech-Slav ethnographic exposition was well
received in Prague in 1895 and that collection included Czech, Slovak and Carpatho-
Ukrainian artifacts.[22]
    Professional ethnographers worked full-
time in the ethnographic museums, and today
these institutions are important centers
devoted to investigating national peasantries in Eastern Europe.   The growth of the
profession brought about the establishment
of scientific societies and journals after
1880.   According to Polish scholars the
first systematic university lectures in
ethnography were given in 1851 at Kraków
under Austrian rule.   The first chair in
ethnography was established at the University of Lemberg in 1910 also under Austrian
rule, and by 1925 there were five university chairs in independent Poland.   In
Hungary the first appointment was made at
Szeged in 1933 and Budapest followed a few
years later.

These developments established a place
for the science devoted to the national
peasantry, the carrier of significant segments of the ethnic-cultural patrimony,
among the cultural institutions officially
supported by the state. (Other sciences
dealt with the economic and social problems
of the peasants and was generally recognized
that national ethnography had nothing to do
with solving "peasant problems.") Ethnographers however have often claimed that
their main function is to serve ethnic self-
recognition and that ethnography is therefore "national." Thus, an investigation
of East European national ethnographies
is a good starting point for the study of
ethnicity. Naturally, scientific institutions and universities did not alone
contribute to the acceptance of certain
features of peasant culture as national
symbols. Many other institutions, artistic
schools and movements, and business enterprises were also involved. These groups
either adopted the material and principles
of the "official" ethnographers or attacked
their position. Ethnographic literature
now fills entire libraries and richly
documents the inner conflicts of the various
societies by reflecting those controversies.
National ethnography therefore presents
a changing view of peasant culture and
its significant role in national development. It also reflects, as does the change
in historiography, the fluctuating demands
and goals of national ambitions.[23]

The Ethnic Image of Peasant Culture

European historiography, in the works of
social anthropologists and the interdisciplinary "peasant studies" that have
recently emerged, treats the peasantry as
marginal groups in the cultural systems of
complex societies. According to this view
cultural progress originates in cities and
in the courts of kings and leading nobles.
Professionals in these same circles preserve
and guarantee the literary and scientific
continuity of tradition permitting only
simplified excerpts of their work to reach
the villages. At the village level the
surviving remnants of earlier developments
may assume local colorations due to oral
transmittal. The "great" and "small
traditions" concept propagated by Robert
Redfield expresses this relationship and
the historical validity of his model helps
to explain some peculiarities of peasant
culture.[24]
     A completely different model of peasant
culture can be extracted from the nineteenth
century East European literature devoted to
peasant folklore and art. In this view
peasant culture is greatly original and
creative and it preserves cultural continuity throughout national history. That
continuity is altered by a secondary phenomenon, the court-urban culture that reflects
foreign customs.[25] Therefore, a return to
the peasant culture is needed to renew the
national culture or to rebuild the ethnic
patrimony. This interpretation reflects

historical reality by referring to the
periods when the East European peasant
people were subjected to the "great traditions" of foreign elements. Furthermore,
it shows that the noble nations--in Russia
the court-urban circles--lived according to
foreign models. Finally, during the period
of national reawakening in Eastern Europe
the peasantry had a greater potential to
act creatively and culturally originally
than is usually the case in history. That
assumption rationalizes the introduction of
the concept of "creative peasant culture"
into the science of ethnography.[26]

    According to anthropologists the cul-
tural traits of diverse ethnic groups are
unrelated to ethnicity because the fre-
quency and geographic spread of specific
cultural characteristics are not dependent
on specific ethnic groups. However,
specific cultural traits may acquire secondary functions that create and identify
ethnic symbols recognized by "in" and "out"
groups as belonging solely to a given
group.[27] East European researchers in the
nineteenth century made two diametrically
opposed assumptions. Some assumed that the
structure of the mother tongue and its
vocabulary were an inheritance (i.e. a
patrimony) left by the forefathers and also
assumed that various cultural particulari-
ties were the differentiating and exclusive
inheritance of specific ethnic groups. This
group explained the similarities among
peoples unrelated linguistically and in
origin by assuming cultural traits were

borrowed.   To them diffusion occurred on
a people-to-people basis and they assumed
that some groups were forced to accept the
traits of people who dominated them.   This
explanation led to a clear bias.   People who
tried to get rid of foreign cultural domination became uncomfortable in finding and
acknowledging the influence of dominant
foreign cultures.   On the other hand,
borrowings from people who played positive
roles in national history (usually those
people lived once-removed from neighbors on
the other side of their domain) or those
that could be traced to the influence of
allies and linguistic relatives were presented in a favorable light.[28]   For example,
Hungarian ethnographers gleefully stressed
the connection between the early North
Italian Renaissance and certain motives,
expressions, and architectural styles in
Hungarian folk art, especially in reference
to the glorious period of the Renaissance
King, Matthias.   Hungarians stressed with
similar pleasure the French features of
Hungarian ballads, and they found--at least
in the nineteenth century--similarities between these ballads and those of the Germans
and Slavs less satisfactory.

Other researchers assumed that peasant
culture consists of ballads, fairy tales,
ornamental objects, tools, working habits,
holiday rites, and myths concerning the
origin of the world, and that the past and
origin of each can be discovered indepen-
dently.   Those researchers saw as their duty
the creation out of differing cultural

elements a stratification of cultural traits
corresponding to the various periods of
national history. Antal Herrmann stressed
the importance of developing the Ethnographic Museum by speaking as follows about
peasant objects at the first session of the
Hungarian Ethnographic Society in 1889:[29]

> ... to the most fundamental essence
> of the ethnos belong organically
> all those physical objects that the
> people made for themselves....
> to express ideals living in the
> people's soul. They personify the
> creative spirit's efforts in the
> midst of struggle for survival.
> These objects ... are--in a sense--
> the ossified remains of the people's
> past, the cultural soil, the
> geological strata of development,
> and the archives of cultural his-
> tory, from which, hopefully one day,
> a ray of light will shine through
> the fog covering antiquity. On
> the utensils used in daily life
> people have imprinted indications
> referring to all periods of history
> and prehistory, to all transforma-
> tions and changes of homes, and to
> contacts with other people.

This view of cultural strata especially
valued those features that confirmed "desirable" historical connections for example,
those that established connections between
contemporary and classical Greece, between
Romanian peasant culture and ancient Rome
and Dacia, and between modern Hungarians

and those who conquered the country.

The secondary selectivity stressed by
Frederik Barth was also crucial in creating
ethnic models of peasant cultures. The
images of the peasantry created to serve
the "internal" ethnic needs of each group
stressed elements that served to strengthen
ethnic self-identity. For this reason it
is difficult, even today, to give an overall
picture of European or East European peasant
cultures because in stressing "internal"
needs the interpretation of identical
phenomena differ radically in the ethnographies of peoples living side-by-side.
This problem is also faced in history when
national histories first serve "internal"
needs. It is difficult to construct histories of broader European regions from
national histories.

The selectivity used to define specific
ethnic patrimonies in terms of basically
homogenous East European peasant life was
based on mutual endeavors to underline
contrasts. For example, Franz Tschischka
and Julius Max Schotti published the first
collection of Austrian folk songs in Pest
in 1819 (Österreichische Volkslieder mit
ihren Singweisen). They stressed that
these songs were characterized by a joy of
life, satisfaction, and cockiness and,
Karoly Balla promptly noted that senti-
mentality, inclination to sadness, and
sorrow were the major themes of Hungarian
songs. He explained that those themes were
the result of tragedies in the past, and
added that those traits give the songs (and

nation) nobility and seeds of hope for a
better future. The Austrians and Swiss
stressed the Alpine way of life and Alpine
costumes and, in contrast, the Hungarians--
who were initially enthusiastic about the
hilly region around Lake Balaton and the
mountains of the Carpathians and the Tatra--
turned after 1830 to the Great Hungarian
Plain as the most typically Hungarian region. Pëtofi saw a symbol of freedom in
the endless horizons of this plain. Hungarian ethnographers diligently concentrated
their efforts on such "primitive occupations" as fishing, herding and on those
simple archaic features of life that could
easily be connected with their proud,
nomadic, and conquering forefathers. Their
emphases on that heritage made urban civilization and the customs based on Christianity suspect as "foreign" borrowings. In
contrast, Austrians emphasized Roman
Catholic religiosity, religious pilgrim-
ages, and the urban features of peasant
life.[30]

Contrast and conflicts played a
role in the process of creating symbols.
When János Kriza published his collection
of Székely folk poetry, "Wild Roses," in
1862 he was accused of plagiarism by Julian
Grozescu who noted that several ballads in
Kriza's collection were published in
earlier editions of Romanian folk poetry.
The ballad themes in conflict were widely
used in the region between the Caucasus and
Greece, even penetrating into Central
Europe.[31] However, at that time it was

possible to maintain that any given cultural
feature belonged <u>originally and in fact</u> to a
single ethnic group and that its appearance
in another context could be explained only
through borrowing, or scientific falsifica-
tion.

The Political Use of Peasant Symbols

The following sketch is not a comprehensive
review of this important problem but
specifies certain issues and shows where
additional research is needed.

    The connection between attempts to
discover peasant culture and the various
manifestations of nationalism is still
at issue between scholars, and the issue
illustrates the difficulty inherent in
attempts to separate ethnicity and nationalism. In what follows ethnicity refers
to feelings that produce ethnic self-
awareness and nationalism is defined as a
political movement intended to achieve independence or domination over other peoples.

    The connection is relatively simple
to explain in the case of people who lived
in multinational empires and in the case
of those who lived under several foreign
rulers. For example, the growth of ethnic

124

awareness and the defining of their ethnic
patrimony led the Polish people directly
to the independence movement. The most
striking example of a connection between
ethnicity and nationalism was the publication of the Kalevala that produced a rapid
growth in Finnish ethnic self-consciousness,
and eventually led to the achievement of
national independence.

The issue is more complicated in multi-
national states. In those states organs of
the state often fostered the discovery of
peasant cultures. It was assumed that
this innocent cultural activity would dis-
arm the nationalisms that endangered the
empire. The masters of the state obviously
differentiated between ethnicity and
nationalism but that differentiation was
never clearly stated. They considered that
the discovery of peasant traditions was
compatible with loyalty to the centralized,
imperial state and with the development of
a state-centered nationalism that included
various ethnic units. In fact, even in
these cases the discovery of folk traditions were instrumental in the development
of subsequent national movements.

The circle around Baron Josef Hormayr
in early nineteenth century Vienna is a good
example of how the discovery of folk traditions contributed to nationalism. Hormayr
published Hungarian, Czech, Polish, and
other folkloric texts in various journals
intending to foster loyalty to the empire.
Members of the Hormayr circle György Gaál,
Count János Mailáth, and Baron Alajos

Mednyánszky were inspired to collect and
publish, in German, folk tales and legends
and they maintained close contact with the
conservative Prince Eszterházy and his
family.[32] A few decades later the transformation of Hungarian folkloric research
became an ideological weapon of the anti-
Habsburg Hungarian independence movement.
    Later, in the Hungarian half of the
Austro-Hungarian states, the institutions
interested in Hungarian ethnography made a
similar attempt to discover, present, and
publish the peasant traditions of the non-
Hungarians living in the country. The
Hungarian Ethnographic Museum in Budapest
devoted the same amount of space to exhibits
of materials from various Hungarian peasant
groups as it did to those of the nationalities. The exhibits were equally divided
according to the number of inhabitants
belonging to each group. The ethnographic
village at the millennial exposition displayed as many Hungarian as non-Hungarian
houses. (It is hard to understand, in
retrospect, why the nationalities should
have felt induced to celebrate the Hungarian
conquest.) The first ethnographic journal
of Hungary began publication in 1887--the
German-language review Ethnologische
Mitteilungen aus Ungarn--and its first lead
article described Hungary's population as
the intertwined branches of a mighty tree
representing a very specific and unique
species in the "forest of people."[33] The
author, Antal Herrmann, paid no attention
to the view held outside Hungary that the

Slovak, Serb, Slovene, and Croat branches
belonged to the great Slav tree, and that
the Transylvanian Romanians were considered
to be a branch of the Romanian tree. The
Hungarian Ethnographic Society was founded
in 1889 by ethnographers and folklorists of
the various nationalities living in Hungary.
The society began its activities with specific sections devoted to the Germans of
Hungary, and to Serbs, Bulgarians, Slovaks,
Ruthenians, Poles, Romanians, Armenians,
and Gypsies. Taking into account its multiethnic activity, the society gave its
publication the neutral title Ethnographia
(in constrast to such titles as Česky Lid,
Lud Słowianski and several others clearly
reflecting nationalist goals). Yet, for
example, Gergely Moldován--who wrote in
Hungarian about Romanian folklore in
Ethnographia--became a Romanian national
hero with an august reputation in Romanian
scientific circles.

The development of Polish ethnography
is also typical and it gave preference to
the study of those eastern regions[34] whose
inhabitants (Lithuanian, Bielrussians, and
Ukrainians) had not clearly defined their
ethnic loyalties and who had been subjects
of the historic Polish state in the nineteenth century and even during the interwar
years.[35] These attempts coincided with
the views of Austrian authorities in the
regions inhabited by Ukrainians, and led
to the establishment of the first Polish
ethnographic university chair at Lemberg.
The archeological and ethnographic research

of these lands began soon after the occupation of Bosnia-Hercegovina. The research
was sponsored by the Austro-Hungarian authorities. In 1888 the Landesmuseum was
established in Sarajevo, and in 1891 an
exposition was organized to prove that the
Austro-Hungarian authorities wanted to safeguard and promote the original cultural
structure of the province.

Hungarian literature historiographical-
ly characterizes the period of early populism that developed when the nobiliary
nation was still condescending toward the
peasantry.[36] Condescension and patience
marked the official attitude toward the
nationalities and the discovery of peasant
traditions arising from the search for
Hungarian peasant antiquities.[37] Yet by the
turn of the century some impatient voices
were also heard. An influential ethnographic publication appeared in 1907
supported by the Ministry of Culture under
the editorship of Dezső Malonyay. Its
goal was clearly a strengthening of Hungarian cultural supremacy. This publication sharply criticized the ethnography
supported by the Ethnographic Museum and
tried to enlist the support of young
architects and painters who turned to
peasant art in the attempt to create a
national style. The first lead article
of that publication expressed the view that
the nations with the richest cultural
heritage are the strongest and have a
greater right to survive. It was no longer
enough to build on the historical past and

the language, now it was necessary to
strengthen Hungarianism in the arts. This
was the goal of the publication. The expressed need resulted because "our
independent national individuality is
endangered ... by the circumstance that
pressed several people into the territory
of a small state."[38]

The volumes edited by Malonyay
continued publication following World War I
and were never officially terminated. Then
the Paris peace treaties created a series
of new East European states. The national
delegations who determined the national
borders in Paris used almost the same ideas
that Malonyay presented in his publication
as the conceptual basis for their arguments.
They cited language and the feeling of
popular belonging and repeatedly stressed
arguments based on cultural relatedness.
The delegations used two arguments when
dealing with two borders.[39] The first
stressed that peasant culture guards a
continued belonging to the fatherland and
ethnic unity despite the dominance of
foreign urban ruling classes throughout
history. The second argument was directly
contrary in that it held peasant culture
to be "foreign" while the cultural climate
in the cities, historic monuments and the
old cultural achievements enshrined in "high
culture" proves that the region belongs to
the nation that claimed it on these grounds.
Several delegations had ethnographic and
folkloric sections and the Yugoslav section
was headed by Jovan Cvijić. His

collaborator, Tihomir Georgević, argued
Yugoslavia's claim to Macedonia by referenc-
ing to the importance of Serbian folk traditions:
> Oral folk poetry is a mine of in-
> formation on the subject of Serbian
> national customs, culture, and
> national self-revelation; it is
> also full of references to historic
> events in Serbia's past, and her
> historic locales and personages.
> If anyone were to conceive the idea
> of delimiting the frontiers of the
> Serbian nation on the basis of the
> area over which Serbian popular and
> national tradition extends, he
> would be well on the side of truth.
> Serbian national ballads from the
> Serbian lands outside Macedonia
> always refer to the latter as a
> Serbian land.[40]

Another complicated issue that requires
additional study is the way in which peasant
ethnic symbols became associated with
socially progressive or conservative domestic movements in various countries. Such
ethnic symbols of peasant origin refer to
elements directly connected with popular
culture, e.g., popular songs, heroic ballads, pieces of peasant clothing, ornamental designs, populist literature that
either utilizes the forms of peasant art or
describes peasant life, music, and the fine
arts. This analysis is complicated because
these cultural manifestations may possibly
symbolize ethnicity or the national

130

question, either of which might have
socially progressive or conservative meanings. Yet the relationship of peasant
symbols to the social problems of the
peasantry at various times may have neither
an ethnic nor a national meaning. From
the earliest period it was obvious that the
nationalistic enthusiasm associated with
certain aspects of peasant culture and
folklore had practically nothing to do
with a desire to support attempts to improve the socio-economic position of the
peasantry. The Hungarian populists intended
to create a cultural and social homogeneity,
a "national family life," with the help of
popular culture in which various social
groups could live together as a happy
family. The concept of the zadruga served
as an embodiment of national unity and as
a means of glossing over class differences
for the Serbs and Croats. In many cases a
division of labor, discussions and debates,
developed between intellectuals and writers
who tried to draw attention to peasant problems and those interested in revealing the
treasures of peasant culture. This controversy was exemplified by the debate between
Gergely Berzeviczy, who exposed the economic
exploitation of the peasantry, and the
literary reformer, Ferenc Kazinczy, in the
early nineteenth century.[41] These attempts
to improve the lot of the peasant while
glorifying peasant culture were rarely
compatible in Hungarian history. Sándor
Petöfi led one successful attempt at col-
laboration during the last stages of the
reform period that prepared the ground for

the Hungarian revolution of 1848.

Each succeeding generation found new
historical connotations in the ethnic
materials of peasant cultural origin. The
discoverers of folklore and the creators of
popular music and literature in the nineteenth century were canonized in national
history. The memory of political movements which they fostered through references
to cultural symbols of peasant or populist
origin were associated with their achievements. For example, by 1900 Pëtofi's true
nature was almost totally hidden by the
exigones who followed him and by politicians who referred to his memory while
pursuing nationalistic goals devoid of
social or progressive content.

Finally, the ethnic movement operated
on a purely aesthetic and artistic third
level that had numerous international
ramifications. The first great period of
discovery of peasant folklore and populist
literature had roots in the Romantic Movement, but the earlier revolutionary aspect
of the arts was transformed into conservatism, scholasticism and antiquarianism.
The emerging literary and artistic trends
were at variance with earlier interpretations of popular culture and folklore.
Fortunately, orally transmitted peasant
poetry and the peasantry's creativity
proved to be a rich source of artifacts
which the new artistic schools exploited
to suit their artistic aims. For example,
the "discovery" of Hungarian folk music
in the nineteenth century became known

throughout Europe because the works of Liszt
and Brahms were based on it and because
Ferenc Erkel used the same source for inspiration in his national operas. The
music of interest to these composers included the recruiting music of the military
popular among the lower nobility and peasantry during the eighteenth and nineteenth
centuries; the so-called "new music style"
popular among peasants in the nineteenth
century; the song material of folk-operettas based on peasant themes that followed
the trend of the "new style";[42] and finally
the gypsy music of the coffee houses in the
cities presented for "refined" urban
audiences. In contrast, Béla Bartok and
Zoltán Kodály drew attention to the much
older pentatonic folk music early in the
twentieth century. Their attempts to discover elements of folk music that fit into
the general framework and tendencies of
European music and their compositions based
on the wealth of forms of Hungarian folk
music led the conservative listening
audience to accuse them of being "non-
national" because they presented previously
unknown musical forms instead of traditional, accepted, national and popular
music.

The image that Peter Hanak presented
for turn-of-the-century Hungary can be used
to generalize and describe society in terms
of two pyramids. The first developed in
the feudal period and had landowners on top,
followed by a lower nobility active mainly
as civil servants (they described themselves

as "the historical middle class) with the
majority of the population, the peasantry at
the bottom. The peculiar structure of
Hungarian social development is apparent in
the second pyramid. The capitalist structure which grew outside the feudal system
had the capitalist elite on top, the middle
class just below, followed by the petty
bourgeoisie, and workers on the bottom.
The people within the corresponding levels
of the two pyramids were equal in social
position, but separated by sharply differing ways of life and prejudices.[43] Inevitably these circumstances led followers of
bourgeois radicalism and socialism to
consistently oppose national policies taint-
ed by feudal values and optimistic and
idyllic images of the peasantry.[44] The
radical organizations and organs of the
early twentieth century (e.g., the Social
Science Association and the journal
Huszadik Század) believed that their major
task was to direct attention to the economic and social prostration of the peasantry.
The associated artistic schools either
denied that the popular elements could be
helpful or concentrated, as Bartok did, on
new facets of popular culture.
     The effort, introduced in England by
Ruskin and Morris in architecture and the
applied arts, and to a lesser extent in
the fine arts aimed to illustrate how the
new role of the arts had succeeded in social
life. Their efforts demonstrated how the
"messages" from Western Europe were adapted
in Eastern Europe. Morris and his

134

collaborators advocated revival of the
material environment, which had become
sterile due to industrial mass production,
by turning back to handicrafts. They referred to the impersonal work of medieval
guild craftsmen and to the artistic values
embodied in late medieval English manor
houses. In Hungary Morris and his colleagues were honored as the discoverers of
peasant folk art.[45] (There had been no
peasants in the East European sense for
centuries in England.)

The new approach to art was manifested
by people living in artist colonies like
puritanical monks. They visited villages
in a search for artistic and nationalistic
inspirations from the harmony of peasant
aesthetics. These efforts resulted in a
second wave of populist and peasant-like
architecture. This trend is illustrated
by the work of Jenő Lechner who attempted
to create a national style by decorating
the plain surfaces of large public build-
ings with motifs copied from peasant art.
Aladár Kőrösfői-Kriesch and the younger
Károly Kós introduced several structural
features of peasant architecture following
the English and Scandinavian models, and
the results of their research in Hungarian
villages into their architecture. This
group of artists also collected material
for Malonyay's massive ethnographic
publication. Their work was nationalistic
and intolerant toward the nationalities.

The elements of peasant culture that
were previously replete with specific ethnic

meanings were gradually transformed into
"ethnic banalities" used without rhyme or
reason by all segments of society. A few
samples selected at random will show how
this trend affected peasant costumes. A
lithograph that was very popular in the
Austrian provinces of the Habsburg Monarchy
during the 1850s depicted Emperor Francis
Joseph taking a boat ride on a Bavarian
lake in Tyrolian folk costume, accompanied
by his fiancée Elizabeth, the Bavarian
princess, and her brother Prince Maximilian
wearing Bavarian national dress. The Hungarian politicians demonstrated their
opposition to the Monarch by wearing the
ornate and elaborate felt cloak of the
Hungarian peasants (cifra szür). This
archaic coat had a specially attached,
long, double upper part richly embroidered
in many colors. By the 1870s Alpine national costume associations were formed in
Vienna and the members, usually recruited
from the petty bourgeoisie, met in beer
gardens dressed in the costumes of selected
Alpine regions to celebrate by singing the
songs of that region.[46] Members of the Hungarian middle class thought it was fashionable to appear at balls or festive occasions
dressed in peasant folk costumes and it also
became fashionable to hang peasant pottery
in the entry halls of homes and use curtains
and table clothes decorated with peasant
embroidery. Even Queen Elizabeth had a
"Hungarian peasant room" including furniture
painted with flowery motifs, and pieces of
peasant pottery and embroidery in one of

her Austrian summer homes. Máno Buchinger
recalls that the congresses of the Social
Democratic Party were colorful before World
War I because the delegates of the nationalities usually appeared in folk costumes.[47]
Those delegates were usually miners or
industrial workers so their costumes were
presumably reserved for holidays. The ball
at the opera was one of the most exclusive
and luxurious events of the "season" in
Budapest and in 1912 all of the participants dressed in the costumes of the peasants of Mezőkövesd, a village north of the
Hungarian Plain. Several aristocratic
ladies wore genuine pieces of peasant
clothing while others had ball gowns embroidered at Mezőkövesd.

The Socialist countries found it difficult to determine whether to evaluate
components of the country's ethnic symbol-
ism that were of peasant origin either
positively or negatively. After the October
revolution the Soviets viewed all folklore
as a reactionary symptom of the wish to return to the past, and therefore believed
it should be eliminated. That officially
held view was changed in a speech by Maxim
Gorki at the first congress of Soviet writers in 1934.[48] In this view the people,
whose art was the basis of all art, would
produce art of a higher value, under socialism than they could in earlier periods of
history, he held that the creative activity
of the common people deserved an important
place in socialist culture. Modern Soviet
ethnographers and folklorists consider his

approach to cultural politics overvaluates
folk art. Yet numerous state-supported
institutions have been created in the
Soviet Union and those who performed orally
transmitted folk music, or produced excel-
lent wood carvings or pottery have been
decorated by the state. The Soviet State
Popular Ensemble was founded in 1937 to
produce folk songs, dances and costumes
on the stage. The Ensemble has become an
important representative of Soviet culture
abroad. The state assigned limits to folk
art produced a peculiar development. Russian literature and cultural life never
developed the concept of peasant oral
literature that appeared elsewhere, in
Hungary as early as in the 1830s. Objects
made by peasants or craftsmen and used by
peasants was specifically a part of folk
art in Hungary and such objects embodied
the concept of folk art. On the other
hand, the Russian "narodnoe iskusstvo"
included the products of village industries that the peasants never used, for
example, the lacquered boxes produced at
Palech. The government also sponsored
the development of these products after
1934.
     After World War II, the well-known
political changes in Eastern Europe were
accompanied by the dominance of Stalinist
cultural policies in all the socialist
countries. National institutions were
established to direct the activities of folk
artists and to promote their work. National folk ensembles were established and the

factories, schools and offices organized
groups to perform folk songs and dances.
Huge quantities of folk art were collected
from the socialist countries for Stalin's
seventieth birthday. In Hungary a special
folk exhibit opened on Mátyás Rákosi's
sixtieth birthday (March 9, 1952) to display the products of folk craftsmen made
specifically for the occasion. The press
celebrated the event as the beginning of a
new flowering of Hungarian folk art. One
paper wrote:

> Socialist folk art is the connecting
> link between the peasantry and the
> working class.... The strongly
> evident national style in the
> decorations teaches us to love
> national arts and inspires our
> patriotism.[49]

After Stalin died the centrally sponsored folk art movement declined. The
central "folk ensembles" were retained,
but most of the units established in
schools, factories, and other institutions
were dissolved. Notably the stimulus to
create folk art movements has recently
arisen from the efforts of urban workers
and young intellectuals. These trends
include the "folk beat music" movement in
Poland, and the concept of "dance houses"
in Hungary. The dance houses are club-
like places where young people meet to dance
to the ancient, authentically performed,
folk music. Their aim is to create a
meaningful framework for social gathering
but they were not interested in bringing
folk culture to the stage.[50]

It is interesting to note that international meetings involving socialist
countries treat the "utilization" and present-day secondary "development" of old
peasant art and folklore as an independent
scientific endeavor. These discussions are
intended to establish correct cultural
policies, and were even involved in the debates about socialist patriotism held in
the '50s and '60s. Ethnographers have
also organized specialized meetings to deal
with that topic and ethnographic conference
of the academies of the socialist countries
held in Poznán in 1974 summarized "the
present-day ethnic role of peasant culture"
(the wording used in the conference papers)
as follows: 1) Popular culture satisfies
the aesthetic needs and patriotic feelings
of the members of the ethnic community;
2) It advances the participation of the
masses in the national culture; 3) It contributes to the consolidation and integration of the ethnic unit in the realm of
culture by contrasting the native ethnic
forms and cultural values with the present-
day homogeneous world civilization; 4) It
strengthens the national and cultural belonging in those members of the ethnic
community who live dispersed all over the
world.[51]
These debates and pronouncements hide
the heterogeneous "materials" of the peasant cultures in the East European states.
For example, large segments of the population in Hungary still enjoy the sentimental
songs that imitate folk songs composed at

the end of the century. The schools and
radio programs still frequently use Béla
Bartok's and Zoltán Kodály's interpretations of folk music produced between the
two world wars. In contrast, the young
people who frequent "dance houses" re-
construct the music, using archaic and
peasant instruments. The composition and
harmony of their music is different than
the better known "gypsy" music.

The differing judgments of true "Hungarian" music reflect the values and variations in taste of the different generations.
More importantly, they express the deep
differences of definition of ethnic and
national identities. The official statements and debates dealing with the importance of "peoples' culture" continues
in the socialist states in the attempt to
determine what the "correct," "progressive,"
"retrograde" and "nationalist" interpretations of the legacy of peasant culture
are.[52]

Peasant Culture in the Period of National
Revival

The development in peasant culture during
the period when several of its features and
characteristics gained increasing

significance in national culture need special note. During the period under discussion peasants were an overwhelming
majority in all the East European states.
Folklore, peasant music and creative
craftsmanship were lively and active arts
when they were "discovered" by those who
used them as markers for ethnicity.
     In Hungary, under the influence of
various stimuli, peasant art entered a very
creative period in the nineteenth century.
The rapid industrialization and urbanization of Western and Central Europe created
a great demand for the products of Hungarian
agriculture and the products of peasant
households. The boom in cereal prices made
it possible for land-owning peasants to
accumulate new possessions. This development was paralleled by reforms that eventually led to the abolishment of serfdom.
From the earliest years of the nineteenth
century ostentation was observed in peasant
costumes and in the furnishing of their
homes. At the same time the celebration of
holidays and weddings became more and more
elaborate.[53] In this "representative
sphere of activities" the peasantry imitated
the declining feudal elite and the rural
nobility, not the urban population and
especially not the petty bourgeoisie.
     The various musical and populist lit-
erary trends that originated in other
social strata apparently had a direct influence on the "flowering" of this anachronistic and belated peasant culture. The
Hungarian composers of folk-operettas about

peasants followed the Viennese model and
found inspiration in "new-style folk songs"
that rapidly gained popularity in the
villages at the end of the eighteenth and
during the early nineteenth centuries. The
songs composed for special peasant plays
also became well known and popular in the
villages. The national social dance, the
"csárdás," that emerged during the period
of national rebirth was partly the result
of a new fad of dancing in the villages,
but it was also consciously worked out by
composers and dance teachers who tried to
create a national way of dancing.[54] That
process also explains the simultaneous
emergence of the mazurka and polonais in
Poland. So, it appears that the national
reform movements intended to celebrate
peasant cultures became self-fulfilling
prophecies. The contact between peasants
and non-peasants increased, the relationship between peasants of various regions
became closer, and the connection between
peasant and national cultures proceeded
rapidly during the period of Nation formation. Sándor Petőfi collected folk songs
for the folk song collection edited by
János Erdélyi, and also wrote songs using
the folk song model. Folklorists found
those songs in the villages, together with
new stanzas or slightly altered texts a
few decades later.[55]

All of this leaves the impression that
even the peasants knew that their traditions and utensils had ethnic and national
significance in some circumstances.

Certainly, the wide use of Hungary's coat
of arms as a decorative motif was on
furniture, wine bottles, brandy flasks,
the carvings of shepherds and on
whetstone sheaths made of cattle horns
during the 1870s is noteworthy. Some szűr
coats survived and their applied ornaments
contain as many as ten coats of arms.

Certain peasant groups became markedly
prominent in the elaboration on their
stylized holiday costumes, their material
environment and their habits. By the end
of the nineteenth century the general public associated their regional artifacts
with "peasant art," while the art of other
regions began to fade away. These typically "peasant art" regions emerged in all the
East European countries.

Peasant art expresses both ethnic and
peasant identities and that explains why
peasant costumes survived everywhere in
Eastern Europe among minority peasant
groups and among those who had frequent
contact with urban populations. Bertalan
Andrásfalvy described how interethnic
contact contributed to the spontaneous
growth of peasant ethnic awareness and the
rich flourishing of peasant art. His
example involved the counties of Baranya
and Tolna in southern Hungary where German
villages were established in the midst of
Hungarian villages during the eighteenth
century. During the nineteenth century the
Germans and Hungarians observed each other
and developed peasant cultures in diametrically opposed directions. The Hungarian

costumes became colorful and variegated
and their celebrations became lavish. They
obviously imitated generous Hungarian nobles who enjoyed making impressive gestures
to show their magnanimity. In contrast,
the Germans concentrated on expanding their
holdings and buying additional land. They
lived puritanically, dressed modestly, and
exploited the labor of their own families
to the limit. Their ideal corresponded to
the Protestant work ethic described by Max
Weber and its concomitant attempt to acquire worldly possessions. Due to their
ethnic rivalry the differences in their
ways of life were exaggerated and extremist.
The ostentation of the Hungarian peasants
was in keeping with the national trend,
while the simplicity of the Germans and
their renunciation of folk art stressed
that they were aliens who would remain
aloof from Hungary's national culture and
Hungarian ethnicity.[56]

In summary the people of Eastern
Europe found themselves in a situation
similar to those nations that became
independent after World War II. They, to
quote McKim Marriot, had "the problem of
choosing a suitable past," and they also
had to select "an appropriate cultural
level on a dimension of time,"[57] and the
peasant culture played an important role
in that process of selection in Eastern
Europe. This was especially true of
"peasant nations," and it was also important in the case of "noble" or "bourgeois

nations."

The movements of national rebirth
turned to peasant culture and created
specific institutions, including the all-
important "science of national ethnography" which never developed in Western
Europe.[58] The research based on this
ethnocentric stimulus and the artistic
creativity based on peasant culture
produced results significant for all mankind. It is sufficient to note the heroic
epics of the Balkans,and the Kalevala,as
examples of ethnocentric stimuli--and to
the music of Mussorgskii or Bartók and
the statues of Brancusi as examples of
artistic creativity.

The cultural features of peasant origin
and peasant life play an important role to
the present day in the ethnic self-identity
of the East European people. This historically and culturally significant and rich
material reflects differences in the social
structure of the various social movements
that have taken place in the past. That
is why the study of the cultural symbol-
systems of peasant origin give deep insight into the ethnicity of the East
European people.

CHAPTER IV

THE ETHNOPOLITICAL CHALLENGE AND GOVERNMENTAL RESPONSE

by

Walker Connor

State borders and ethnic borders seldom coincide,[1] and most states contain at least one significant minority. Approximately half of the remaining states are confronted by irredentism because dominant groups within those states extend into adjoining states.[2] The lack of coincidence between political and ethnic borders is a major cause of political instability because people are increasingly convinced that they should not be governed by aliens. The positive corollary of this conviction is that people who believe that they constitute a separate national group also believe that they have the exclusive right to determine their own political destinies. The idea of national self determination has already exerted immense pressure on multiethnic political structures. From the time of the French Revolution until World War II, all but three European states either lost substantial bits of territory or came into being as a result of ethnonational aspirations.[3] Moreover, the decolonial movement

which witnessed the European recession from
Africa and Asia was motivated by the conviction that people should not be ruled by
foreigners.[4]

Ethnonationalism is still ascendant
and approximately 50 percent of all states
have experienced ethnically inspired discord in recent years.[5] Ethnonationalism
currently poses an even greater challenge
to multiethnic states and several governments are confronted by ethnonational
movements. The government of France, for
example, is challenged by Alsatian, Basque,
Breton, Corsican, and Occitanian minorities.[6]

The governments of multiethnic states
generally refuse to recognize the right of
ethnonational groups within their jurisdiction to secede and form separate states.
Secession, no matter what the rationale,
is anathema to national governments.
Lincoln noted in his first inaugural address that "It is safe to assert that no
government proper ever had a provision in
its organic law for its own termination."[7]
Indeed, the American experience is a fasci-
nating illustration of the opposing perceptions of would be secessionists and
governments. The American people acted
upon the presumed right of "one people to
dissolve the political bonds which have
connected them with another," in 1776,
but the government forcibly denied the
Southern states that right less than a
century later. Unionists within the government argued that the Constitution created a

state in perpetuity, and thus adopted
Daniel Webster's view of "Liberty and
Union, now and forever, one and inseparable."[8] The Supreme Court subsequently
upheld that view following the Civil War,
and denied that the Southern states had
seceded since secession was impossible under
the Constitution, which "in all its provisions, looks to an indestructible Union."[9]
Since the Constitution is silent about this
notion of immutability the Court in effect
ruled that statehood implied immutability.

Several governments have been more explicit. The People's Republic of China
(PRC), the Democratic Republic of Vietnam
(DRV), and the Socialist Federal Republic
of Yugoslavia (SFRY) each confronted multiethnic situations and in each case the rise
to power of the Communist Party was accompanied by periodic promises that people
within the states would be granted the right
of national self-determination, specifically
including the right to secede. Once in
power, however, the parties drafted constitutions that forged groups within those
states into perpetual political unions.
None of the post-1949 constitutions of the
CPR reference self-determination, and all
indicate that secessionist tendencies will
not be tolerated. The 1949 provisional
constitution promised (Article 7) "to
suppress all counter-revolutionary elements
who ... commit treason against the mother-
land," instructed the Army (Article 10) "to
defend ... the territorial integrity ... of
China," and warned (Article 50) that

"nationalism and chauvinism shall be
opposed."[10] The same note of irreversible
union appeared in the 1954 constitution
(Article 3) and stipulated that the PRC
"is a single, multinational state ..." that
"acts which undermine the unity of nationalities are prohibited" and that the "national autonomous areas of inalienable parts
of the PRC."[11] The Constitution of 1975
(Article 4) declared that the PRC "is a
unitary multinational state. The areas
where regional autonomy is practiced are
all inalienable parts of the PRC."[12] The
Vietnamese Constitution of 1960 is worded
similarly, "The territory of Viet-nam is a
single, indivisible whole from north to
south" (Article 1). "The Democratic Republic of Viet-nam is a single multi-national
state. Autonomous zones are inalienable
parts of the Democratic Republic of Vietnam."[13]

The Yugoslav Communist Party ingen-
iously informed its citizenry that secession
would not be permitted since they had
exercised their right of self-determination
in the past, and the exercise of that right
was a one time, irreversible action which
created an indissoluble union. In November
1943 the Yugoslav people were informed that
they had already determined to "remain
united":

> On the basis of the right of all
> nations to self-determination,
> including the union with or se-
> cession from other nations, and
> in accordance with the true will

> of all the nations of Yugoslavia
> tested during three years of common
> national struggle for liberation
> which has cemented the <u>indissoluble
> fraternity</u> of all the people of
> Yugoslavia, ... the peoples of
> Yugoslavia ... have proved in the
> common armed struggle their firm
> will to remain united in Yugo-
> slavia.[14]

This assertion that the people of Yugoslavia
had already exercised their right of self-
determination is repeated in Article I of
the Constitutions of 1946 and 1963.[15]
Neither constitution allowed secession,
since secession had, by definition, become
unthinkable.

There are constitutional exceptions
to this refusal of state authorities to
countenance the right of secession on the
part of national groups. The USSR Constitutions of 1924 and 1936 formally declare
that the union republics are sovereign and
have the right to secede from the Union.[16]
Actually, a prerequisite for establishing
an autonomous union republic is a territory
contiguous to the Soviet Union so that the
right of secession is meaningful. Each
Soviet Republic bears the name of a major
national group, so the Soviet authorities
ostensibly acknowledge the right of four-
teen non-Russian national groups to secede.[17] Indeed, the Soviets permitted
secession for a short period after taking
power for several reasons but that power
was rescinded before the Constitutions of

1924 and 1936 were framed.   The Red Army
and indigenous communities combined to re-
absorb most of the seceded regions by
1922.[18] Moscow regained all of the others
with the sole exception of Finland as a
result of World War II.   The emptiness of
the constitutional right of secession has
been periodically evidenced by defendants
found guilty of "counter-revolutionary,"
"anti-state," and separatist activities
despite their attempt to invoke the Constitutional guarantee of the right to secede
as a defense.   Thus, V. Moroz charged that
he was wronged and reported to the Supreme
Soviet of his own Ukrainian Republic that:
"My colleagues and I were convicted for
'propaganda directed at the separation of
the Ukraine from the USSR.' But Article 17
of the Constitution of the USSR clearly
states that each republic has the right to
leave the union."[19]
     The government of the Republic of South
Africa is another possible example of
governmental willingness to countenance
secession. South Africa desires to perpetuate white rule, but whites account for a
dwindling 19 percent of the population, so
the authorities have designated a specific
homeland (Bantustan) for each of the country's major black ethnic groups. In time,
each homeland is scheduled for independence.
But given the forces impelling this
fractionalization of the country, government policies towards the blacks, the
prevalence of apartheid, and the dispro-
portionately small size and disconnected

configuration of the homelands, the degree
of actual independence envisaged by the
government is questionable. Nevertheless,
the authorities can safely challenge detractors of government policies by citing
governments that have surrendered part of
their sovereign domain to ethnic minorities.[20] A few realistic European governments realized that the death knell of the
colonial era had sounded and took the
initiative in surrendering overseas territories that were not part of the emotion-
laden "home country" or "mother country."
Also some governments have recognized faits
accompli perpetuated by secessionist groups
rather than resort to arms. For example
Sweden accepted the Norse defection in 1905
and Denmark recognized the 1944 declaration
of independence by Iceland. The government
of democratic Canada may yet peacefully
acquiesce to the growing demand for independence by Franco-Canadians in Quebec.
But acquiescence is not a positive response
if it is based on the assumption that the
government can do little to reverse the
situation or when a military occupation is
incompatible with the state's democratic
traditions. That kind of acquiescence does
not invalidate the earlier assertion that
governments invariably discourage claims of
secession, whether or not they are predicated upon the right of national self-
determination.
     To the degree that governments act as
free agents they operate on the implicit
assumption that political and territorial

integrity is not a subject for legitimate
debate. Government decisions are normally
made with this usually unstated, perhaps unconscious, but nonetheless real assumption
in mind. As noted elsewhere:

> Against a right of self-determination,
> the authorities raise the right and
> duty to preserve union, to stamp out
> rebellion, to insure domestic tran-
> quility, and to defend the state's
> political and territorial integrity.
> What is a self-evident truth to those
> desiring separation is treason to those
> in authority. In this dichotomic
> atmosphere, "the God-bestowed in-
> alienable right of the nation to
> determine its own destiny" is
> deprecated as "parochialism,"
> "Fascism" or worse. The presumption
> that the state is a given and must
> not be compromised therefore causes
> governments to resist, if need be
> with force, any attempt to dismember
> the state in the name of self-
> determination.[21]

Government resistance to national movements in the homeland should not be confused
with support for national self-determination
in the abstract. Statesmen of diverse political persuasions regularly pay lip
service to self-determination. This exemplifies the righteousness popularly ascribed
to national self-determination, an idea
that has joined motherhood and virtue in the
pantheon of abstractions which politicians
publicly revere. Governments tend to cloak

their real policy by promoting self-determination. That tendency may be legitimate,
devious, or the product of self-delusion.
The American involvement in Southeast Asia
during the late 1960s and early 1970s was
often explained as an attempt to defend
national self-determination for the South
Vietnamese. American spokesmen may have
been sincere but they were at best contem-
plating self-determination for only half the
Vietnamese nation. By aiding the south
Vietnamese, the United States simultaneously
helped them deny self-determination to the
Vietnamese hill people (the "montagnards")
who did not wish to be ruled by either
southern or northern Vietnamese. Similarly,
President Ford explained the U. S. decision
to support black majority rule in Rhodesia
by announcing in a television interview
(May 1, 1976) that this position was consistent with the traditional American
commitment to self-determination. Without
questioning President Ford's sincerity, it
would be interesting to determine how the
President's assertion could be equated with
an American reluctance to support the
Basque, Bengali, Ibo, Mizo, Shan, South
Tyrolean, and other secessionist-oriented
national movements. Even sincere tributes
to the idea of self-determination are not
apt to find a counterpart in foreign policy.
        The abstract support of national self-
determination is reflected in the charters
of interstate organizations, multistate
treaties and resolutions. References to
self-determination have become fashionable

in such documents, but they also customarily
include antithetical references to the
sanctity of national borders. The U.N.
Charter (Article I, paragraph 2) for example
promises "respect for the principle of
equal rights and self-determination of
peoples," but denies (Article II, paragraph
7) the right "to intervene in matters which
are essentially within the domestic jurisdiction of any state." The Charter of the
Organization of African Unity opens with
the conviction "that it is the inalienable
right of all people to control their own
destiny," but it is doubtful whether any
organization is more dedicated to preserving
the borders of multiethnic states.[22] The
Charter acknowledges as much, noting that
the member states are "to safeguard and
consolidate ... the sovereignty and territorial integrity of our States." The
stated purposes of the Organization with
regard to its member states (Article II)
are, among other things "to defend their
sovereignty, their territorial integrity
and independence." The principles of the
Organization (Article III) include "noninterference in the internal affairs of
States [and] respect for the sovereignty
and territorial integrity of each State
and for its inalienable right to independent existence."[23] Still another
illustration of this same tendency to en-
dorse the principle while negating its
effect is offered by the Final Act of the
Conference on Security and Co-operation
in Europe, the so-called Helsinki Accords,

whose principal purpose was to freeze the
existing situation in Eastern Europe.[24]
Consonant with this goal, the signatories
promised to respect each other's "territorial integrity," to regard as "inviolable
all one another's frontiers as well as all
the frontiers of all states in Europe," to
refrain from any action "against the territorial integrity, political independence,
or unity of any particular state," as well
as "from any intervention, direct or indirect, individual or collective, in the
internal or external affairs falling within
the domestic jurisdiction of another par-
ticipating state." Having insured the
sanctity of borders, and thus disavowing
the right of the area's many minorities to
their own state, the Accords proceeded to
eulogize and affirm the right of self-
determination.

> "VIII. Equal Rights and Self-
> determination of Peoples. The
> participating states will respect
> the equal rights of peoples and
> their right to self-determination,
> acting at all times in conformity
> with the purposes and principles of
> the Charter of the U. N. and with
> the relevant norms of international
> law, including those relating to
> territorial integrity of states.
> "By virtue of the principle of
> equal rights and self-determination
> of peoples, all peoples always have
> the right, in full freedom, to
> determine, when and as they wish,

their internal and external
political status, without external
interference, and to pursue as
they wish their political, economic,
social and cultural development.
    "The participating states reaffirm
the universal significance of
respect for an effective exercise
of equal rights and self-determination of peoples for the development
of friendly relations among themselves as among all states; they
also recall the importance of the
elimination of any form of violation
of this principle."
Such documents habitually make no attempt
to explain how to reconcile state integrity
with the right of people, "to determine,
when and as they wish, their internal and
external political status, ..." But it
was apparently clear to the participants
that state integrity was to be respected
in practice while self-determination was
to remain purely an abstract principle.
    Governments frown upon secessionist
movements at home, while often supporting
such movements abroad. Unlike their
generalized statements supporting self-
determination in the abstract, their support
for those movements in practice has been
highly selective. One exception was the
Soviet Union following World War I when the
Soviets indiscriminately viewed all non-
Marxist-Leninist states as enemies of the
same order. In line with Lenin's Theses on
the National and Colonial Questions, the

communist parties of multinational states
were periodically reminded to pursue "reso-
lute and constant advocacy by communists
of the right of national self-determination
(secession and the formation of an independent State)."[25] During the post-war period,
the Soviet government and the Comintern made
direct appeals to minorities in Afghanistan,
China, Czechoslovakia, France, Greece, Iran,
Poland, Romania, Spain, the United Kingdom,
the United States, and Yugoslavia, as well
as, of course, to secessionist sentiment
throughout the colonies. In the post-
Stalinist period, the Soviets were hesitant
to support such movements within non-
Marxist-Leninist states. The few exceptions
(such as support for the Bengali defection
from Pakistan) apparently arose from the
desire to avoid offending third states
(e.g., India) rather than from more direct
objectives. But it is evident that Moscow
still appreciates the Trojan-horse nature
of minorities because the Soviets have not
hesitated to appeal to the ethnonational
sentiments of minorities within other
Marxist-Leninist states, as a cunning
reminder that those governments are vulnerable from within as well as from without. In the case of China, the Soviets
preferred to appeal to the minorities
directly, while in Eastern Europe they often
preferred to work through intermediaries
(e.g., through Budapest in the case of
Romania and through Sofia, and sometimes
Budapest, in the case of Yugoslavia).[26]

160

Unlike the Soviet Union's support of
nationalist movements during the 1920s and
early 1930s, the active involvement of
other governments in such movements usually
concerns an adjoining state, and more
specifically, a group divided by a border
shared with that state. The opportunities
for such involvement are bountiful, since
territories of numerous ethnic groups are
touched by state borders and usually
dissected by them. There have been several
cases of governmental involvement in the
affairs of groups beyond their territorial
boundaries. Northeastern Africa in the
early 1970s is a case in point: the Libyan
government was aiding a separatist movement
within neighboring Chad; Chad's government
was supporting a similar movement within
southern Sudan; Sudan's government was
supporting the movement in Chad and two
others in Ethiopia; Ethiopia was supporting
the movement in the southern Sudan; Somalia
was supporting an irredentist movement in
Ethiopia (and in Kenya); and Uganda was
supporting the movement in the southern
Sudan. The adjoining states undoubtedly
felt that the Organization of African Unity's adjuration concerning the inviolability
of borders and noninterference in the internal affairs of other states was not very
effective.
      Any governmental manipulation of ethnic
sentiments held among transborder segments
of a group may be motivated by defensive
(status quo) as well as by offensive considerations. During most of the late

nineteenth and early twentieth centuries
for example, the Amirs of Afghanistan
fomented unrest among their Pushtu kin on
the British-Indian side of the border in
an attempt to keep the British too preoccupied with this "prickly hedge" to
contemplate further intervention in Afghan
affairs. Prince Sihanouk of Cambodia
pursued a similar policy for years in dealing with his stronger neighbors, South
Vietnam and Thailand. He periodically dis-
avowed irredentist claims toward the Khmers
(Cambodians) living just across the border
within those states, and raged against any
move by those states to evict or assimilate
the Khmers to preserve a buffer responsive
to his appeals.
     It is more likely, however, that
governments which support a transborder
national movement will announce their in-
tention to overthrow the government in the
next state or bring about a change in
political borders to reunify the national
group under their own jurisdiction. The
government may be passionately committed to
either goal or they may be used as an
artificial issue to gain concessions of
another sort. During the 1960s and early
1970s, for example, Iran supported separation of the Kurdish territory within Iraq
to force Iraq to adopt a more friendly
stance on several issues. After the Iraqis
stopped agitating for the separation of
Iran's major oil producing region, which
was populated chiefly by Arabs, the Irani
support for the unfortunate Kurds ceased

abruptly.

In general, however, analysts tend to perceive such movements as being artificially induced, since they receive their major impetus from governments across the border. This may be true with regard to specific situations, but the cause of foment is rarely totally artificial. Government appeals to ethnopolitical yearnings require a popular desire, no matter how incipient. Adolf Hitler, for example, employed the German-speaking people within Austria, Czechoslovakia, and Poland for his own cynical and expansionist ends, and his policies also struck a responsive chord among Germans living outside the German state. If there is no desire for change on the part of its segment of an ethnic group, the resisting government could quickly prove that charges to the contrary are artificial by either conducting a plebiscite or by granting full freedom of expression on the issue. In practice status quo governments rarely do so, but that does not prove that a majority of such groups will favor a change in political allegiance. But it often suggests the presence of sentiments sufficiently strong to be feared by the government. Governments may assist in planting the seed of national awareness among people of another state, they may help nourish the subsequent growth of that awareness, but later attempts to reverse or stop the process are likely to be unavailing, since nationalism is easier to feed than to tame. In

summary, governments can act as a successful catalyst of ethnonationalism only when
the necessary ingredients are present.
Once in flower, ethnonationalism is not
apt to respond to governmental attempts at
curtailment. Thus, the manipulation of
the ethnic desires of minorities played an
important role in bringing the communist
parties of the Soviet Union, Yugoslavia,
China, and North Vietnam to power. But
those parties, once in power, have all
been troubled by the so-called "national
problem," the disunifying force of ethnonationalism.

Governments may take the initiative
in raising an irredentist claim, but most
unionizing movements originate in ethnic
groups on either side of a border, and
those groups then press for governmental
support. If a politically bifurcated
ethnic group within one state is influential, the government of that state
will likely treat the transborder segment
of the ethnic group as one of its legitimate
interests. The Basques of France and Spain
remind us that members of a single but
politically divided nation are likely to
view matters of state as an inferior order
of things in contrast to their ethnic
links. Thus, when a segmented ethnic
group influences public policy, its government will be compelled to advocate or
protect the interests of its transborder
element. Accordingly the relative political influence of an ethnic group is an
essential factor in analyzing a transborder

situation. Political influence may be insignificant or total, not necessarily
related to group size. The form of government within a state is a key variable.

In general, more authoritarian governments are less sensitive to public opinion.
During the 1950s and 1960s, the government
of democratic Austria was often compelled
to protest Italy's treatment of the small,
German-speaking element across the Italian
border, even though the Austrian government
performed that ceremony with little enthusiasm. In that kind of democratic system,
it would be foolhardy for the elected elite
to display disinterest in the plight of
their nearby cousins. In contrast, the
governments of China and the Soviet Union
are relatively immune from domestic public
opinion and they have employed irredentist
campaigns as tools of foreign policy, promoted or discarded according to the strategy
of the moment. Even these governments,
however, are not totally immune to the
opinions of their ethnic minorities, because both Moscow and China have employed
irredentist techniques against each other.[27]

The nuances of the Soviet and Chinese
cases require separate analyses since
numbers even within fundamentally democratic
systems do not necessarily indicate influence. Relatively small groups may be
sufficiently large to affect materially the
balance of political forces within the
state. American politicians are well aware
that small, so-called ethnic groups play a
crucial role in presidential elections

particularly when they are located in states
with large electoral votes. These groups
therefore exert powerful influence on
domestic and foreign policies. Groups in
either authoritarian or democratic states
may be important out of proportion to their
size because of their strategic location.
Indeed, when a group occupies a border region it has a special importance. The
occupied territory may command important
passageways (e.g., the Pushtun control of
the Khyber Pass) or contain key natural
resources (the important oil fields in the
Arab area of southwestern Iran). The
relative influence of groups thus varies
from state to state and, within each state,
from group to group. Generally, however,
democratic governments are less flexible
than authoritarian governments when they
are involved in an irredentist situation.

When a government adopts willingly
or not an irredentist policy, it may or
may not have the means to achieve its end.
Thus the relative strength of states is
another important variable. The pre-World
War II distribution of German-speaking
people throughout Europe clearly constituted
a threat to the continued political viability of Austria, Czechoslovakia, and
Poland, but not to the preservation of Germany because of its disproportionate power.
Logically, a government's willingness to
support an irredentist campaign increases
the probability of adverse consequences,
and if the state's power advantage is un-
certain a policy of irredentism is often

assumed to be an insignificant force in
global politics, because it is limited to a
few situations wherein the state opposed
to the status quo has a favorable power
status relative to its neighbor. In those
cases counteraction is either unthinkable
or unlikely to produce the desired effect.
Yet there are several reasons why irredentism may have an impact. First, governments
may be pressured into dangerous ventures by
segments of their own populations. Second,
it is impossible to measure power scientifically since the concept of power includes
qualitative (e.g., morale), as well as
quantitative components; power is dynamic,
and state secrecy obscures many of its key
components. Third, the relative power of a
state is conditioned by relationships with
other states. Thus, although Afghanistan
has a smaller population, it could conduct
an irredentist campaign against Pakistan
which is sandwiched between Afghanistan
and Pakistan's arch enemy, India. Potential
allies and enemies drastically influence
power evaluations.
     Eastern Europe offers an interesting,
probably unique, example of the restraining
effect that the power of a third state
exerts upon governments disposed to encourage ethnonational unrest in adjoining
states. Changing borders and several new
post-war Marxist-Leninist governments have
not ended interstate frictions caused by
the lack of coincidence between state and
national borders. The unresolved, prickly
issues involving ethnonationalism between

Albania and Greece; Albania and Yugoslavia;
Bulgaria and Greece; Bulgaria and Turkey;
Bulgaria and Yugoslavia; Yugoslavia and
Italy (despite the formal arrangement signed
on November 10, 1975); Yugoslavia and Austria; Yugoslavia and Hungary; Hungary and
Czechoslovakia; Hungary and Romania; and
even between Romania and the Soviet Union
remain very much alive. These issues have
a long history; however, none of these
governments now threaten to support a national segment outside of its borders to
the extent of provoking war. Neither the
comparative strength of any East European
state nor any coalition of these states
can be expected to decide that issue because the Soviet Union remains as the final
arbiter. The Soviet Union would undoubtedly
frown upon open hostilities between frater-
nal socialist states and the Soviets would
likely invoke the Brezhnev doctrine and
intervene. The non-Marxist-Leninist states
in that region, as well as the Marxist-
Leninist states which are signatories to
the Warsaw Pact and COMECON, could not act
without anticipating a Soviet intervention.
Therefore interstate ethnic conflicts within
the region can be expected to remain essentially diplomatic, propagandistic, and
academic issues.
     Even when a state has a clear power
advantage, the government may encounter
barriers in bringing that power to bear.
For example, it may be inconvenient to
resort to force because of the adverse impact on relations with other states. In

sub-Sahara Africa most governments rule pre-
cariously over a multiethnic system and
irredentist claims are met with large-scale
disfavor. The leaders of the Somali Republic have discovered that the state which
too actively pursues irredentist claims
risks political isolation. Geography may
also hamper the application of power. For
example, a common border may be small and
easily immunized against outside irredentist pressure. The border between Algeria
and former Spanish Sahara may prove to be a
case in point. There may also be attitudinal barriers. The concept of power is
effectively dependent upon a state's willingness to use power and weaker states may
question the resoluteness of stronger
states. In this context the key element
of the national concept is psychological
and emotional, not rational. Several
rebellious ethnic groups have fought for
independence against seemingly insurmount-
able odds. The struggle for self-determination waged by the Ibos of Nigeria between
1967 and 1970, despite incredible dispari-
ties in firepower and manpower and massive
starvation was awe inspiring. Therefore it
is quite possible that the ethnonational
urge is not deterred by power ratios at
the grass roots level and at the governmental level, political elites may be as
passionately committed to the unification
of the group as the masses; even if they
are not, governments may have little choice
when there are internal pressures for annexation.

In the case of politically divided
nations irredentism breeds irredentism.
Aggrieved governments naturally respond
with the two-can-play-this-game technique,
countering irredentism by fomenting rebellion and pro-annexationist sentiments
among members of groups under the offending
state's jurisdiction. When more than two
transborder groups are involved, this form
of retaliation may be applied or concentrated upon other ethnic elements. The
Iraqi government beamed appeals to Iran's
Arab minority in 1969 and Iran countered
by aiding the Kurdish revolution in Iraq.
Also, manipulation of ethnonational groups
may escalate when the ethnic map permits as
demonstrated by Iraq's subsequent attempt
to smuggle arms to the Baluchis agitating
against Iranian (and Pakistani) control in
southeastern Iran one thousand miles from
Iraqi territory. The support of ethnonational movements tends to result in
counter campaigns and the evidence suggests
again that it is easier to institute ethnonational movements than it is to resolve
them.
     The issue of governmental support for
ethnonational movements in neighboring
states is stressed because examples frequently occur and because it may increase
a movement's chance for success or failure.
The government normally enjoys an enormously
one-sided advantage when confronting an
indigenous separatist movement. Industry,
the armed forces, communications networks,
and access to external supplies are all

responsive to the government. Without external assistance, ethnonational movements
can muster one offsetting asset, the empathy
of local populaces which may sanction and
support guerrilla warfare. Giuseppi Mazzini
perspicaciously identified guerrilla warfare
more than one hundred years ago as the
"natural" form for a people's war of national liberation.[28] When a movement also has
a nation-bisecting, interstate border that
provides sanctuary, the chance of success
is substantially improved.

A border may provide a sanctuary even
when the government of a state opposes the
guerrillas. Traditionally an aggrieved
government cannot pursue guerrillas across
a common border with complete abandon.
Governments of sanctuarial states are
similarly unwilling to take draconian measures to subdue segments of their own
population similar to those that anti-
insurgency strategists have so often
adopted. Consequently, their actions are
apt to be half-measures which may lead to
acrimony between the two governments which
will further erode coordinated efforts to
eliminate the guerrillas. Recent situations
of this kind occurred on the China-Indochina
border from 1945 to 1949; the Basque sector
of the French-Spanish border; on the borders
between Malaysia and Thailand, Northern
Ireland and the Republic of Ireland; between Iran and Pakistan; between South Tyrol
and Austria; between Burma and India, India
and Bangladesh, Togo and Ghana, and (from
approximately 1954 to 1973) on the border

between South Vietnam and Laos.

   Interstate borders are therefore great
assets even when governments of sanctuarial
states are unsympathetic to the causes of
transborder groups. But when host governments are sympathetic and create safe, fixed
base areas, aid with supplies and equipment
and by training troops, the prospects of
transborder groups are greatly enhanced.
This type of situation occurred on the
Chinese-Indochinese border between 1949-54,
the Cambodian-South Vietnam border between
1954 and 1970,[29] the (French) Algerian
borders with Tunisia and Morocco between
1956 and 1962, the Greek-Yugoslav border
between 1946 and the closing of the border
by Tito in 1948 following his ouster from
the Cominform; the Burmese-Chinese border;
the Laotian-Thai border; the Thai-Burmese
border; the Chinese-Indian border near
Assam; the Iranian-Iraqi border prior to
1975; the Tanzania-Mozambique border prior
to the latter's independence, and the
interstate borders in northeastern Africa
mentioned earlier.[30]

   Two quite distinct conceptions of
borders are discussed here. The traditional
view holds that governments have no right
to take action which affects events on the
other side of a border, and that they are
responsible for preventing internal action
which influence anti-government events in
another country. Yet, the foregoing partial
list of border violations suggests that some
governments have taken a different view;
namely, that governments have the right or

duty, either to assist in the downfall of
a neighboring government or to annex part
of an adjoining country. In either case,
an aggrieved state is normally expected to
abide by the traditional view and it will
invariably be castigated by the government
of the sanctuarial state for any reprisal
that violates the common border. Governments of sanctuarial states therefore
employ both views, i.e., defensive borders
are inviolate and impenetrable; offensive
borders are vulnerable and porous.

Many governments therefore hold transborder causes in more esteem than the
traditions of International Law. Classical
Marxism views the borders of capitalist
states that way and that view is still
officially held by the Chinese People's
Republic. However, the list of border
violations suggests that communism is not
the only factor. Anticolonialism and the
desire to rid non-Arab Africa of white rule
have led to the same low regard for specific
borders. The borders of Angola-South West
Africa and Mozambique-Republic of South
Africa will likely fall into this category.
The urge for annexation also accounts for
certain governmental attitudes toward national boundaries. The desire to dissolve
borders dividing single national groups is
the most common goal and even when it has
not been the principal goal ethnonational
groups and ethnonational aspirations have
been the major vehicles employed to achieve
them. Hanoi and Peking purposefully and
openly supported ethnonational movements

throughout South Asia to ultimately bring
victory to Marxist-Leninist forces.[31]   Ethnic groups within multinational states, and
particularly those <u>partially</u> within a state,
are likely agents of political instability.
    The foregoing discussion establishes
that governments invariably frown upon
secessionist movements in their own
countries. Governments also have to deal
with the problems of ethnic heterogeneity
and their policies vary from state to state
and within a given state from time to time.
It is impossible to catalog all the policy
differences, yet most major policy decisions
made by governments of multiethnic states
have a significant impact on what the
Marxists have termed the "national question." For that reason it is necessary here
to sketch the available policy alternatives.
    Since secession is unacceptable a
government must first decide to permit a
national group(s) to reside within the
state. If not, then the alternatives are
genocide, expulsion, or a combination of
those distasteful techniques which have
long-established historical precedents. The
Ottomans pursued genocidal policies against
the Armenians around the turn of the
twentieth century. More recently, the Germans applied them against the Jews, and
the Croatians used them against the Serbs
in the World War II state of Croatia. Few
modern governments will acknowledge pursuing
a policy of genocide, nonetheless governmental inaction in the face of ethnocidal
activity may accomplish the same result.

The Indonesian authorities, for example,
following the abortive coup of 1965, did
little to prevent the killing of Chinese
inhabitants carried out under the guise of
a grass roots anticommunist campaign. In
Bangladesh, there was a similar lack of
determination on the part of the authorities
to protect the Biharis against Bengalis
during the immediate post-independence
period. The governments of Burundi and
Rwanda have been active participants and
passive onlookers in the massacres of the
Tutsis and Hutus.[32]
     The alternative use of expulsion is
more common and more difficult to disguise.
The expulsion of Germans from Eastern
Europe following World War II resulted in
major changes in the ethnic composition of
several of the states in that region. The
same phenomenon occurred incident to the
well-publicized expulsion of "Asians" from
Uganda in 1972. Sometimes de facto "expulsion" occurs in the absence of formal
policy. In Cyprus, for example, the Turkish
authorities apparently "encouraged" the
Greeks to leave the northern zone; they did
nothing to discourage and everything to
assist the exodus, and did nothing to encourage a return. Israeli policies toward
west bank Arabs after the Six Day War
followed the pattern of expulsion through
inaction. Expulsion can be unilateral or
result from agreements between two states
which become "population transfers." Such
transfers either involve one-way movements
or an exchange of peoples. The one-way

movement is exemplified by India's agreement
to accept limited numbers of Tamils from
Sri Lanka. The exchange of nationals between Greece and Turkey under the Treaty of
Lausanne is an example of an exchange.[33]
     When a government has accepted its
population as a given, it must next decide
whether to favor group diversity or assimilation. Group diversity may then be either
permitted or promoted. In the United
States, the government tacitly approves
diversity by allowing private (group)
schools and churches which use a language
of instruction other than English and in
which diverse cultural traditions can be
nurtured. Some governments may positively
promote diversification by permitting or
encouraging group autonomy; cultural,
political, or both.
     The degree of political and cultural
autonomy granted by governments varies
widely. When the loosest type of political
relationship between ruler and group is
demanded political autonomy may approximate
independence. Multiethnic states such as
Afghanistan, Ethiopia, Iran, and Thailand
did not experience significant levels of
ethnically predicated unrest until quite
recently because the rule of their central
governments was more theoretic than real.
When the governments of such states desire
to intensify their rule in outlying areas,
the absence of roads and communication
networks prevented their control from becoming a pervasive reality. In that
environment, the effective political systems

are small, substate, and ethnically homogeneous. However, as governments acquired
the wherewithal to expand their rule
effectively they do not hesitate to do so
and their resolve is often steeled by external attempts to promote secession. The
presence of "alien" governments is usually
met by increased resentment among ethnic
groups. Paradoxically it is easier to
rule de jure over disparate ethnic groups
before it is possible to rule de facto.
As the prerequisites for de facto rule increase, resistance to both de jure and de
facto rule also increase.

The general unwillingness of governments to grant significant political
autonomy is reflected in the secessionist
struggles of Burma, India and Iraq. These
struggles have been interrupted periodically in response to governmental promises
of political autonomy, then resumed amidst
charges that the governments failed to
live up to their promises. It is, of
course, essential not to confuse form and
content when measuring the degree of
political autonomy permitted by a government. The so-called "autonomous regions"
in the Chinese People's Republic and the
"sovereign republics" in the Soviet Union
may be little more than facades. Similarly,
the already limited autonomy permitted
"states" in the Indian Union further eroded
during the 1970s.

Cultural autonomy is usually closely
interrelated with political independence
and governments may adopt true "hands off"

policies in respect to the cultural manifestations of different ethnic groups when a
loose, tributary relationship is desired.
The millet system of the Ottoman Empire and
the non-Sinified outlying regions of the
Chinese Empire are examples. But state
integration greatly complicates the goal of
cultural autonomy and renders it more difficult to maintain. The government must
formulate policies governing the use of
official and unofficial languages in schools,
business, and government; regulate individual competition versus group quotas for
appointments and advancement in business,
the military and the bureaucracy; and determine allocation of investments and obligations among regionally based ethnic groups.
Those kinds of decisions ostensibly made in
the best interests of the state as a whole
are often perceived by some (sometimes all)
ethnic groups as manifest discrimination.

When the goal of the state is assimilation, governments may elect to reshape the
general population in the image of a dominant group (e.g., to turn Bretons into
Frenchmen, Catalans into Castillians, or
Tibetans into Hans). They may elect to
create ethnically neutral populations as in
the Philippines, Indonesia, or Britain.
Governments must also decide how to mix the
use of persuasion and coercion. Coercive
assimilation can be accomplished through
forced resettlement outside the homeland or
by ethnically diluting the homeland by im-
porting large numbers of other people (e.g.,
the Han Chinese probably represent a

majority in Tibet, Sinkiang (East Turkestan)
and Inner Mongolia). Governments may also
enforce mandatory intermarriage, a practice
reportedly enforced in Zanzibar under Sheik
Aboud Jumbe prior to 1972. The Soviet Union
maintains that the Han Chinese require the
people of Sinkiang to practice mandatory
intermarriage. It is also a common practice
to outlaw the language and other symbols and
characteristics of ethnic groups.

The record of states in promoting
assimilation is the subject of a longstand-
ing debate that resembles the argument over
the chicken or the egg, which came first,
the nation or the state? Lord Acton asserted in 1862: "A State may in the course
of time produce a nationality; but that a
nationality should constitute a State is
contrary to the nature of modern civilization."[34] Sir Ernest Barker disagreed in
1927 by stating that the reverse order of
things was the rule at least since 1800:

> Since the beginning of the nineteenth
> century, it is the nation which
> makes the state and not vice versa.
> The creation of the state by the
> nation was an achievement of the
> French Revolution; it was the
> secret of the unification of Ger-
> many and Italy; it is the basis
> of the "succession" States which
> have issued from the Great War.[35]

Alfred Cobban, in turn, voiced his disagree-
ment with Barker in 1944:

> In historical fact, cultural
> unity has usually followed on

and not preceded political unity.
The cultural nation was more the
creation than the creator of the
political state in France and
England, in the United States,
and the British dominions.[36]
   Neither point of view is totally wrong
nor is it totally correct. Those who maintain that nations have made states evidently
overlook the multinational composition of
most states. Certainly national self-
determination includes the right of nations
to make states but this right is not always
reflected in relationships between state,
divided by ethnonational borders. Yet the
argument that states make nations clearly
exaggerates the record of states.
   States are not successful assimilators.
If they were, the older states would not be
troubled by internal discord. Yet discord
has certainly occurred in such older states
as Afghanistan, Ethiopia, Iran, and Thailand. Obviously, however, none of these
countries were states in the modern sense
until quite recently. That demurrer does
not apply to the states of Western Europe
in which a variety of ethnonational groups
continue to assert their vitality (i.e., in
Austria, Belgium, France, Italy, the Netherlands, Spain, Switzerland, and the United
Kingdom). The scope and increasing mili-
tancy of such groups was demonstrated
during a meeting of some of the groups in
July 1974. Delegates of the Alsatians,
Basques, Bretons, Catalans, Corsicans,
Croats, Flemings, Friesians, Galicians,

180

Irish (of Northern Ireland), Occitanians,
Piedmontese, Sardinians, Scots, and Welsh
attended. The "Celtic League" held another
interesting meeting in September 1975.
Representatives of Alba, Breizh, Eire,
Kernow, Cymru, and Mannin (Scotland, Britta-
ny, Ireland, Cornwall, Wales, and the Isle
of Man) then discussed the creation of a
federation politically separate from France
and the United Kingdom.[37] The attendees
at those conferences do not exhaust the
list of ethnonational groups dissatisfied
with the political structures in which they
have resided for years, some for centuries.
     The tendency of scholars to over-
estimate the record of states as assimilators may be explained by a fallacious
assumption that the states of Western Europe
have successfully assimilated their various
people. Two influential writers on nationalism, Karl Deutsch and Benjamin Akzin,
have perpetuated the notion that several
West European states have achieved assimilation. That idea is central to Deutsch's
theses, in both editions of his well known
Nationalism and Social Communication.[38] He
cited Bretons, Flemings, Franco- and German-
Swiss, Scots, and Welsh (as well as Franco-
Canadians) as examples of totally
assimilated people.[39]His portrayal of
successfully assimilated European states was
repeated in two later works. This faulty
assumption of successful assimilation is
revealed in a passage in which Deutsch
explicitly outlines his view of the European
experience, and enunciates a four-step

process of assimilation. He then continued:
"How long might it take for tribes or other
ethnic groups in a developing country to
pass through such a sequence of stages? We
do not know but European history offers at
least a few suggestions."[40] But despite
Deutsch's implied conclusion and, if European history provides a precedent, it is
still unlikely that other states will
successfully assimilate all of their diverse
people. Benjamin Akzin developed the same
argument as Deutsch in 1964 in State and
Nation.[41] He first notes the dissolving
political significance of the "Welsh, Scots,
Lapps, Friesians, Bretons, Savoyards, [and]
Corsicans," then continues:

> If we look at the modern nation-States
> of Europe we shall see that, except
> for those of the Scandinavian
> peninsula, the population of each
> of them is largely the product of pre-
> existing ethnic groups which have
> integrated into the nations we know
> today. This is true of the French
> nation, consolidated from fairly
> heterogeneous elements between the
> seventh and twelfth centuries ...
> Germans, Italians, Poles, Russians,
> and Spaniards have all become the
> well defined nations we know within
> a century or two of one another....
> Under pre-modern conditions the
> process required a fairly long period
> of gestation ... put into the pot of
> physical proximity, covered by the
> lid of a common political system,

exposed to the heat of cultural
and social interchange, the various
elements will change after a fairly
long time--it took a few centuries
in the past, but may take less in the
future--into a brew. The brew will
not be quite homogeneous. You can
still point to a grain of rice, to a
leaf of onion, to a chunk of meat,
to a splinter of bone. But it will
manifestly be one brew, with its
distinct flavor and taste.[42]

Western European states therefore became
exemplars of something which they were not.

The tendency to exaggerate the record
of states as assimilators may also be explained by the failure to distinguish between trends before and after the turn of
the nineteenth century. Prior to the age
of nationalism which linked political
legitimacy and ethnicity, the trend was
toward amalgamation into larger groups. The
Han, for example, were the greatest assimilators in history, but their assimilation
took place over centuries, and mostly
antedated the modern state-system (usually
dated to the Peace of Westphalia). Since
the French Revolution, contacts between
groups which share a dim sense of a separate
ethnic heritage have tended to cement and
reinforce a sense of group uniqueness.

Finally, an overestimation of the
capabilities of states may be due to the
failure to distinguish between cultural and
psychological assimilation. Comparative
research establishes that an ethnonational

group can lose any of its overt characteristics, including language, and retain a
sense of vital uniqueness. States have many
significant instruments of "political
socialization" at their disposal; for example, public schools and communication networks, including publishing industries.
These and other forces working for overt
homogeneity have permitted certain states
to make great strides in cultural assimilation. It may be difficult for an observer
to note differences between persons of Irish
and non-Irish descent in Northern Ireland
(either may be agnostics or atheists), or
between Scots and Englishmen on the streets
of Glasgow, but the overt similarities have
had little effect in ameliorating the sense
of ethnonational uniqueness which divides
them.

Thus the record of states in assimilating diverse people is poor. The chance
of successful assimilation is demonstrably
greater when the national consciousness of
a people has not yet been formed. Thus,
the chance of propagating a single Yugoslav
consciousness among the Slavic peoples of
the newly formed state was greater in 1918,
and it would have been easier to convince
the Slovaks that they and the Czechs formed
a single nation then than now. It is a rule
of thumb that when scholars and statesmen
make contradictory claims about the national
identity of a people, that people has not
yet adopted an identity. The level of national awareness among Croat, Slovak, and
Slovene was still not fully developed in

1918.[43] The subsequent history of the national question in Czechoslovakia and
Yugoslavia does nothing to indicate that
states are effective assimilators. (See
Chapters II and V).

In this essay assimilation and autonomy
have been treated as exclusive categories,
however, governments may view those factors
as complementary. Thus, the Marxist-Leninist rubric "national in form, socialist in
content," ostensibly promotes cultural and
political autonomy ("the flourishing of the
nations") as a dialectical step toward the
development of a single consciousness.
The Marxist-Leninist strategy is a reminder
that there are a multitude of governmental
approaches to the "national problem" and
the institutions which they have created.
Despite the many variations, no state has
discovered a fully satisfactory response
to ethnic heterogeneity, except such morally
reprehensible acts as ethnocide and expulsion. In addition to the intractable
problems governments would face even if
they could isolate ethnic issues from external considerations, there are often
interstate dimensions to be considered.
Ethnonational groups are more than the
stuff of internal politics; they are also
the tools and targets of foreign policy
because the decisions of one government are
often dependent upon the actions of another.
Indeed, the decisions of a second (or nth)
government may be more decisive factors
than the decisions of a home government.
The varied complexities of ethnonationalism
are seemingly infinite.

CHAPTER V

STATE POLICY, ETHNIC PERSISTENCE AND NATIONALITY FORMATION IN EASTERN EUROPE

by

Trond Gilberg

Professor Brass noted that the formation of community consciousness and the development of a sense of nationality are complex processes which encompass both subjective and behavioral aspects. Objective characteristics such as language and dress further enhance the sense of togetherness of the ethnic group and help set the group apart from other groups or the rest of society. The move toward a sense of nationality is only conceivable, according to Professor Brass, when there is competition for scarce resources and political elites are available to mobilize "their" group for competition for such scarce resources.

Eastern Europe has been an area of unusual ethnic configurations for centuries. Because of its geopolitical position between Russia, Prussia, and the Habsburg Empire most East European political borders did not coincide with ethnic and linguistic boundaries. In southeastern Europe, the Ottoman Empire extended its domination for centuries and the Balkans became an area of fierce religious competition between Muslim and

185

Christian, and political conflict between
Vienna, Budapest, St. Petersburg, and the
Porte. London and Paris entered the fray
on numerous occasions. The state of frequent warfare in Eastern Europe ensured
that almost all ethnic groups in the area
would experience dramatic changes of for-
tune. For centuries following the formation of powerful empires to the west, east,
and south profound socioeconomic and political changes threatened the cultural
stability of virtually all ethnic groups
in the area. Yet scholarly research suggests that ethnicity and national consciousness remained as a commitment to a common
cultural and sociolinguistic heritage and
as a political phenomenon.

Eastern Europe continued to provide a
laboratory for ethnic competition and
conflict during the twentieth century for
several reasons:

1. Ethnic groups were deprived of the
generally required aspects of nationhood,
such as a common language, a common cultural
heritage, institutions, and territory (most
often territory and their own political
institutions). Thus, their sense of ethnic
identity and national consciousness was
not complemented by the organizational
characteristics required for nationhood and
political demands for restoration followed.
This was true of the Poles in Tsarist Russia,
Prussia, and Austria-Hungary, and the Czechs
in the Habsburg Empire. After World War I,
the grievances of these nationalities were
redressed when the Polish and Czechoslovak

states were established, but those new
states included other minorities with claims
similar to those of the Poles and the
Czechs. The national groups hit hardest by
the border settlements in the postwar era
included Germans and Hungarians located as
minorities in the new or expanded East
European states. German minorities were
concentrated in Western Poland and the Czech
Sudetenland, and the Hungarians in Slovakia,
Yugoslavia, and Romania.[1]
     2. The evidence suggests that feelings
of national and ethnic particularism were
enhanced when the ruling political elites
were less socially mobilized than the
minorities. In those circumstances, the
ruling groups (the "home nationality," e.g.,
the Poles and Romanians) enhanced their own
national stature by adopting a policy of
ostensible chauvinism which entailed active
discrimination against ethnic minorities.
Between the two world wars the ruling Polish
elite reluctantly accepted political parties
comprised of minority groups and the Polish
press mostly legitimized the policies of the
ruling groups "in the national interest."
Marshal Pilsudski remained a staunch Polish
nationalist until the end of his reign. The
policies of the Romanians and Serbs were
also chauvinistic during this period.[2]
     The policies of dominant nationalities
in multiethnic societies were overtly chauvinistic emphasizing symbols such as flags,
dress, and language. The political elites
tended to restrict the political power of
minorities or permit access to power only

when minority leaders accepted their political symbols and restrictions. Social
scientists now know that political elites
who refuse significant groups access to
power can expect political instability and
attempts to change the status quo by force.
The policies of the politically
dominant ethnic groups created resentment,
contempt, and a "turning inward" on the part
of the ethnic minorities. This process was
particularly likely when the occupations,
educations, and skills of the minorities
were more highly mobilized than those of the
dominant nationality. Under those circumstances the minority feelings of ethnic
superiority and their strong sense of cultural hierarchy became important politically. This development deterred the
assimilation of minorities into a common
culture for <u>all</u> ethnic groups since most
members of a national group would not
assimilate "downwards," even when a "lower"
group controlled the political institutions
and therefore were in a position to make
important concessions or provide advantages
in exchange for some form of minority
assimilation. On the other hand, ethnic
minorities at a lower level of social
mobilization than the dominant majority
were willing to assimilate; this was a
perceived move "up" and was thus more
palatable, perhaps even desirable. In this
case the dominant group was likely to reject
assimilation (as one East European official
stated to the author: "As you can see, the
Gypsies are assimilating very well in terms

of census classifications. But who wants
Gypsies?")[3]
     Those conditions were all present in the
multiethnic states of Eastern Europe during
the interwar period, and they contributed
to a high level of political tension. In
many cases, policies of the ethnic group
leaders widened the gulf between the groups,
and the political systems took on the
semblance of the Weimar Republic's "lager"
mentality, with ethnicity as a fundamental
basis.
     3. Ethnic particularism was enhanced
when the minority groups focused on ethnic
"homelands" (either adjacent to the territory in which the minority was located or not)
which exhibited their revered symbols of
nationality (e.g., language, dress, flags,
a sense of common heritage). Under those
circumstances, the political leaders of
ethnic minorities became forceful spokesmen for policies of "Heim ins Reich" which
were then adopted by the "home country"
and became the basis of foreign policy
conflicts. Such conflicts occurred frequently in the interwar period, especially
over the irredentist claims of Hungary on
Romania (over Transylvania) and Czechoslovakia; and the German claims on Czechoslovakia (over the Sudetenland) and Poland
(over the former German territories, still
heavily inhabited by Germans, in Silesia
and Pomerania). Nazi Germany's claims on
other countries in Eastern Europe to bring
all Germans back into the Reich had ominous
overtones since Germans were spread all

over Eastern Europe and much of the Soviet
Union.[4]
    4. The ethnic particularism of some
groups was enhanced when a dominant group
maintained differential relations with
various minorities. During the interwar
period, dominant elites discriminated
against some ethnic groups politically
and socioeconomically in practically all
of the countries; in particular the
Ruthenians, Ukrainians, Gypsies, and Tatars.
The level of socioeconomic and political
consciousness in these groups was rather
low (especially the Gypsies and Tatars) and
governmental policies did not directly
effect their national consciousness. Other
groups, Hungarians, Germans, and Jews were
privileged in occupation and education; in
some countries economic activities (e.g.,
banking in Hungary) were dominated by
minority groups while the rank and file of
ethnic majorities lived in relative poverty.
The relative socioeconomic privilege of some
highly developed groups coupled with political underprivilege, created political dissent. Richard V. Burks has shown that
radicalism in the form of communism developed first among these groups, especially
the Jews. Among Germans and Hungarians,
Russian communism prevailed over the radical
tendencies arising from the underprivileged
minorities. The Germans and Hungarians
remained basically anti-communist throughout the entire period.[5]
    5. Economic scarcity and competition
for scarce resources enhanced ethnic

particularism. As noted by Professor Brass,
that competition was one of the prerequisites for the development of nationalism.
Eastern Europe experienced extreme economic
scarcity from the turn of the century to
World War II and is still one of the least
developed regions of Europe although rapid
industrialization has alleviated the problem
during the last two decades.
        During the interwar period, competition
for scarce economic resources exacerbated
the poor relations among ethnic groups.
Politically dominant ethnic groups controlled economic resources and privileges
in many countries, and usually were unwilling to accord minorities full access to
such benefits. Competition for scarce
resources therefore became a minority group
affair and economic improvements could only
be brought about by political struggle which
tended to further group cohesiveness in
opposition to nationalities.[6]
        That pattern was not universal since
some ethnic groups had greater access to
economic privilege notably the Germans and
Jews. The politically dominant groups
tended to consider some German and Jewish
individuals more "palatable," and upward
social mobility was therefore possible, as
long as it did not take on political overtones. Professor Brass quoted Barany to
note that Jews in Hungary, especially prior
to World War I, were totally acceptable
parts of Hungarian economic elites. Many
Jewish individuals became partly Magyarized.
In politics, however, assimilation was

limited, and the limitation resulted in
continued Jewish dissatisfaction, despite
the privileges enjoyed by this group in
several East European states.[7]

Since some minority groups had access
to economic privilege, while others did not,
conflicts among minorities became commonplace. Various groups tried to ally themselves with politically dominant
nationalities to gain economic privileges.
Thus, dominant majorities adopted a strategy
of divide and rule because of their control
over the scarce economic resources.[8]

6. The cohesion of ethnic groups tended to be enhanced when minorities were
concentrated in limited areas, and political
conflict with majority groups and other
ethnic minorities tended to increase.
There is political tension between the political and economic authorities at national, regional and local levels in all
societies. This conflict is increased
when local and regional elites are ethnically different from the central authorities, and when the central elites place
their own representatives in charge of
minority districts. This problem became
important during the interwar period,
especially in Poland, Czechoslovakia,
Romania, and Yugoslavia, where large
concentrations of Germans (Poland and Czechoslovakia) and Hungarians (Romania, northeastern Yugoslavia) were controlled by
officials of the dominant nationality (which
was considered inferior in socioeconomic
and cultural terms). Almost everybody in

Yugoslavia resented the presence of Serb
officials.[9]
    7. Socioeconomic development and
modernization are likely to enhance rather
than reduce ethnic particularism. Despite
the relative backwardness of the East
European states (except for Czechoslovakia)
most were in the process of industrial
development and urbanization by World War I.
In some development was rapid. However,
industrialization proceeded unevenly and
the large industrial cities developed as
modernized "ghettos" in still underdeveloped
countrysides. This process took place unevenly in each country, and with the
distribution of ethnic groups in various
regions, modernization tended to differentiate living conditions and economic
opportunities among ethnic groups. This
process led to increased ethnic particularism. The processes of modernization;
industrialization, urbanization, education,
the spread of literacy, and better communications, did not lead to the assimilation
of individuals into a national, "modern"
culture, but they did tend to expand the
national consciousness of each group. The
educated and socially mobile individuals in
each minority often became leaders of
nationalistic tendencies in their communities rather than spokesmen of integration
and assimilation into "national" cultures.
The East European governments concentrated
on directed industrial development and thus
tended to enhance ethnic particularism
during this period.[10]

Governmental Policies and Ethnic Particularism Under Communist Rule--The Post-War
Period Until the Death of Stalin

When communist parties took power in the
East European countries, nationality
policies took a decisive turn. The policy
of the communist political elites in this
field was a blend of programmatic statements, pragmatism in social and economic
fields, and specific nationality policies,
all designed to further the goals of
communist power and the achievement of
certain specific goals, socioeconomic,
political, and cultural. Since roughly
thirty years have passed since the
establishment of communist-dominated
regimes in Eastern Europe, it is possible
to examine the success or failure of this
complex program, and to explore, in more
general terms, the relationship between
governmental policy and ethnic persistence
and nationality formation in this area of
the world.
        Some aspects of communist nationality
policy in Eastern Europe were ideological.
The people's democracies assumed that the
moving forces in any political system are
classes, not ethnic groups and nationalities, in developing specific programs.
Their main political goals were the establishment of "people's power," the
destruction of bourgeois power, the development of a dictatorship of the proletariat
and the achievement of a socioeconomic base
for the establishment of socialism and later

communism. After 1948, the political
programs were modeled on the experience of
the Soviet Union, and Soviet political and
economic controls were strictly exercised.
Bloody purges were conducted from 1949 to
1953 (in Czechoslovakia even after 1953)
to liquidate any deviations, including
nationalism and domesticism. The new
political masters used these policies to
prove that nationalism was a bourgeois
phenomenon which had no place in a socialist
state. The Marxist political leadership
in Eastern Europe thus set out to prove
that the economic base mattered politically
by restructuring it. They believed that
the most fundamental and persistent ethnic
differences of pre-war Eastern Europe would
then disappear. In the meantime, the
remnants of "bourgeois nationalism" would
be fought to further the inevitable historical process.[11]
     The new leaders expressed the convic-
tion that their new policies would erase
the cultural differences which had existed
between nationalities. From the existing
hierarchy of national cultures they expected
to develop a superior socialist culture
clearly acceptable, indeed desirable, for
all ethnic groups. Thus history was rewritten, and the social sciences and humani-
ties were permeated with ideology. The
heavy Soviet influence also had an effect
on the hard sciences in the countries of
Eastern Europe. Lysenkoism dominated biolo-
gy, and Soviet models were adopted in
chemistry and physics as well as mathematics.

In literature, the deadening effect of "Socialist realism" wiped out the national differentiations which existed previously.[12]

The new regime furthermore instituted economic policies intended to overcome inequality among nationalities. The resulting destruction of the old economic order, the relentless socialization of the means of production, the tempo of industrialization and a reduced standard of living hit all ethnic groups. The accompanying social revolution did not discriminate among majority and minority groups and the privileges of certain ethnic groups all but disappeared, to be replaced by a new privileged class of party apparatchiks and economic specialists with skills necessary for the successful completion of the ambitious social, economic, and cultural programs.[13]

The fundamental rearrangement of political power and socioeconomic standing in the countries of Eastern Europe temporarily rearranged relations between the political elites of each ethnic group. In Romania and Poland the emerging communist elite was recruited from minorities, especially Jews. This phenomenon contrasted sharply with the position of those minorities in the two countries during the precommunist period. Jewish communists also held important positions in the new leadership in Czechoslovakia and Hungary. The Bulgarians and East Germans recruited fewer minority members as leaders. A genuine multinational leadership emerged in

Yugoslavia under Tito, and all major groups
in that country were represented in the new
elite, except the Serbs who held a less
favorable position than before.[14]
    The communist regime in Eastern Europe
therefore had designed policies intended to
remove the preconditions of ethnic particularism which made Eastern Europe a hotbed of
conflict and chauvinism during the interwar
period. The Soviet Union, the dominant
force in the area, intervened to reorder
national borders in terms of "national
self-determination" and in accordance with
Soviet interests. The overwhelming Soviet
presence ended the continuous quarrels which
characterized international relations in
Eastern Europe during the interwar period.
Local elites became totally dependent upon
Moscow and it was crucially important for
them to show that they had decisively shunt-
ed aside their old feelings of "bourgeois
nationalism" and international conflict.[15]
    The ethnic hierarchy which existed in
many East European states was officially
abolished. The new regimes emphasized that
all ethnic groups were to be considered
equal and emphasized that the decisive
differences in society were not between
nationalities, but between socioeconomic
classes. It was dangerous to argue the
superiority of any ethnic group, and the
political purges from 1944 to 1953 decimated
the old nationalist leaders. Thus a native
elite capable of advocating particularist
goals was removed.[16]

The coming to power of representatives
from the most highly mobilized minorities,
particularly Jews, also tended to weaken
ethnic particularism. The socioeconomic
mobilization of Jewish groups in all of the
East European states resulted in considerable radicalism and political protest during
the interwar period, especially when their
path to political power was blocked. Their
radicalism assisted the move of Jewish
communists into top positions in virtually
all of the people's democracies. The party
program required these leaders to emphasize
the equality of all nationality groups, and
precluded them from practicing political
discrimination. The communist parties
carefully recruited members from all ethnic
groups to "balance the ticket" and enhance
their legitimacy.

The Soviet Union's policies in Eastern
Europe tended to reduce territorial claims,
irredentism, and differential political
opportunity as producers of ethnic particularism. There were, however, other potentially important sources of nationalism.
Modernization set relatively static populations into motion, millions of people
flocked to the cities and rapid urbanization led to a breaking down of particularism among nationalities. In many cases,
however, major ethnic groups moved into
cities in their own region and did not
produce a significant intermingling of
groups. Even when several groups moved
into a city, they tended to occupy separate
sections. Thus, modernization and

urbanization did not reduce ethnic particularism by mixing people on a mass scale.[17]
     During the Stalinist period, moderniza-
tion produced a new class of technical and
managerial experts to run the complex
economic system. This process had a somewhat contradictory influence on ethnic
particularism. The possibilities for
advancement were significantly increased
for people with talent, those willing to
work hard, and dedicated to the new regime.
The channels of education and social
mobility, often closed to minority groups,
were now wide open, and this reduced some
of the pent-up resentment which had influenced intragroup relations and feelings
in the past. Yet some newly educated
members of the ethnic minorities refused to
give up their own ethnic heritage, language,
literature, and national symbols. As
modernization encompassed ever larger groups
and literacy and basic education became
widespread, it also became easier for these
leaders to propagate nationalist feelings
in their own groups. Many people must have
experienced the thrill of discovering their
native literature and the historical symbols
associated with it.[18]
     By the end of the Stalin era the
policies of Communist elites in Eastern
Europe had profoundly effected ethnic
consciousness and particularism. The
official denouncing of "bourgeois nationalism" and the purging of former political
leaders was undoubtedly approved by many
minorities. Modernization created

opportunities for increased social mobilization for all ethnic groups, and the old
system of economic and social privilege
which prevented such mobility was destroyed.
The communist political elites provided
increased power and prestige for many
minority individuals, especially those from
groups having relatively high levels of
social mobilization. The tendency of
communist elites to "balance the ticket" of
ethnic group representatives was preferable
(from a minority point of view) to the pre-
war system.

On the other hand, political repression, purges, and the violent social upheavals which resulted adversely affected
the relations between the communist regimes
and the masses of the people. The insu-
larity of the political elites and the
general hatred of party "bosses" became
fundamental problems which cut across
ethnic dividing lines. When a person's
house or farm is expropriated, or they are
shot for "economic sabotage," it doesn't
matter where the order came from. Thus
the policies of the regime unified most
citizens regardless of their ethnic background, in a feeling of alienation.[19]

The policies of the regime had ambiguous results even for upwardly mobile
individuals within ethnic groups. Many
individuals were "assimilated" by the
regime which made it possible for them to
get educations and good jobs while others
used their education to further ethnic
particularism, and become leaders of their

groups. In this way the communist regimes
inadvertently fueled the smoldering fires
of nationalism.
     After Stalin died there were signifi-
cant changes in the socialist states of
Eastern Europe. De-Stalinization resulted
in considerable change among the elite and
the influence of some ethnic minorities was
thus drastically reduced. The purge of
"Zionists and Titoists" removed many Jewish
members of the communist party hierarchies
during de-Stalinization, and the remaining
"Stalinists" in high positions were on the
way out in most countries. A political
leadership emerged in almost all East
European states which was either nationalist
(i.e., made up of individuals once imprison-
ed as "nationalists" and "domesticists") or
primarily attuned to national problems and
the need for autonomy after years of sub-
servience to Moscow. Legitimacy and mass
support for these elites could only come
via renewed emphasis on the national symbols
of the majority population, its history,
traditions, dress, and language. However,
the relative equity in ethnic group relations typical of the Stalinist era, was
again subjected to the nationalism of the
majority group, with increased emphasis on
sovereignty, socialism, and communism. This
trend was not universal, developments in
Poland and Hungary were not copied in the
DDR (the first country to experience political instability after Stalin's death).
Almost a decade passed before the "Czech
road" became perceptible through the

economic and political reforms of 1963.
By 1968 Czechoslovakia outran the others on
this path and was forcibly informed of this
mistake. The "national deviation" in
Albania, seen from Moscow, consisted of a
continued policy of Stalinism even while the
Kremlin was engaged in de-Stalinization.
Bulgaria never strayed from the path of
conformity even during the uneasy years of
Khrushchevism. Ethnic particularism became most important in the post-Stalinist
era in Yugoslavia and Romania. It was used
to legitimize regimes which sought and obtained autonomy from Moscow. Yugoslavia
was a special case, a multiethnic state
based on federalism and decentralization,
its political leadership had rejected
Stalin (or was rejected by him) at an early
stage. Romania was interesting as a test
of state and party policies on ethnic
consciousness in a country with considerable
ethnic differentiation and where centralized
decision making was conducted by a monopo-
listic central party with an orthodox
ideology.[20]

State Policy, Ethnic Consciousness and "National Communism" in Romania

Experts do not agree as to when the Romanian political leadership embarked upon "national communism." Some scholars maintain that it was adopted as early as 1952 while others date its beginning in the late 1950s.[21]
   Most agree, however, that Bucharest had adopted national communism in its domestic and foreign policy by the early 1960s. It was then that relations among ethnic groups in Romania again became a major political issue.
   During the last years of Gheorghe Gheorghiu-Dej's tenure as First Secretary and more strongly during the Ceausescu era the decision making process of the Romanian Communist Party (RCP) profoundly affected the country's national consciousness and ethnic separatism because:
   1. The RCP leadership increasingly conceived of itself as a national political leadership in the tradition of Romanian history, and its main slogans and symbols, especially emphasized by Nicolae Ceausescu, were steeped in Romanian nationalism. Thus Ceausescu never tires of comparing himself with the great heroes of Romanian history, Stephen the Great and Michael the Brave, and his emphasis on national sovereignty and a national road to socialism and communism represents his view that it is a direct continuation of the Romanian people's struggle for independence. Ceausescu proudly notes that the language and culture

of the country were maintained despite the
political supremacy of other groups, and
his speeches hint that such staying power
is only possible for a superior culture and
language. The arts and sciences in Romania
have been mobilized to trace the development
of language, dress, and "Romanian culture"
throughout history, and scholars continue
to research the relationship between the
ancient Romans and their culture and language and that of modern Romanians.[22]

    2. The emphasis on Romanian national-
ism includes veiled (and sometimes open)
criticism of countries in Eastern Europe
which have chosen to stay closer to the
Soviet model in socioeconomic and political
matters. The common argument from Bucharest
is old-fashioned chauvinism; it is a constant reminder that the Romanians constitute
the only Latin element in a "sea of Slavs."
That argument is controversial, and frictions have developed in the socialist camp
as a result. The ancient rivalry between
Hungarians and Romanians is also evident
in the foreign policy rhetoric commonly
voiced in Bucharest.[23]

    The emphasis on Romanian nationalism
involves a certain amount of irredentism.
Romanian politicians, historians, and other
scientists, especially under Ceausescu
have made forceful, if indirect, claims on
Bessarabia which was once Romanian land but
is now mostly incorporated into the Molda-
vian republic of the U.S.S.R. It is said
that Bessarabia belongs to "historic Romania," and the destiny of the Romanians will

not be completed until historic Romania (including Bessarabia) is united. It should
be noted that Transylvania is also considered part of this historic whole, and according to Ceausescu the incorporation of most
of this area into Romania in 1944-45 was
historical justice.[24]
    3. The socioeconomic and political
programs of Romania are executed by a
political elite predominantly made up of
ethnic Romanians. Nicolae Ceausescu is
convinced that the modernization process,
which has been underway for thirty years
will lead to the achievement of a socialist
culture of a higher nature than any of its
national parts; a culture neither Hungarian,
German nor Romanian but socialist. The
General Secretary's discussions of this
culture, however, clearly emphasize Romanian
symbols, adding elements of Marxism-Leninism. The other outward manifestations of
that culture are unmistakably Romanian; for
example, the language of this higher culture
will be Romanian. The Romanian modernization process envisioned and practiced by
Ceausescu therefore has assimilationist
implications for the non-Romanian nationalities.[25]
    4. In developing nationality rela-
tions, several major policies illustrate
the traditional Romanian nationalism embedded in the Bucharest leadership. Various
administrative measures have undermined the
ability of the ethnic minorities to
strengthen or maintain outward manifestations of their nationality. For example

the Hungarian-language university Babeş-
Bolyai was partially dismantled, territorial
reorganization divided the former Magyar
Autonomous Region into several counties with
mixed populations, and there has been a
considerable influx of Romanian officials
at all levels in the new regions. The
administrative reorganization of 1968 reestablished the prewar judet (county)
system, and the RCP aparat was changed at
this level--new, predominantly ethnic
Romanian cadres closely related to Nicolae
Ceausescu, were promoted to the top positions. Judets with considerable minority
populations, e.g., Covasna, Mureş,
Maramureş, Sibiu, Harghita, and Neamt, had
predominantly Romanian second secretaries,
although the first secretaries were mostly
from the largest minority in the area.[26]

The administrative reorganizations
were accompanied by a renewed emphasis on
the Romanian language as the lingua franca.
The General Secretary emphasized that his
regime encouraged national expression,
especially in folk music and art, but made
it clear that the "business language" was
Romanian and every citizen would be required to have a thorough knowledge of it.
The RCP accordingly produced laws which
guaranteed the right to elementary education in the native tongue of all major
ethnic groups, but university education was
more and more conducted in Romanian.[27]

Other somewhat symbolic (but no less
important) policies were undertaken during
the last few years to emphasize the Romanian

aspects of the country. Non-Romanian
names were gradually removed from cities
and streets, in some cases using double
names (in Romanian and in the language of
the largest local minority) and lately, by
completely "Romanianizing" many names. On
the other hand, the regime has emphasized
the need to keep the minority press alive,
and has provided financial support for that
medium, but the stringent political controls
exercised over the papers precluded the
possibility that they would act as spokesmen for the national ambitions of the
minorities.[28]
    In addition to these specific nation-
ality policies the major economic programs
executed by the RCP have had a major impact
on relations among ethnic groups. The emphasis on rapid and sustained industrialization has sent hundreds of thousands of
Romanians into territories predominantly
populated by Hungarians and Germans. The
massive modernization of Romania since
World War II has primarily benefited the
Romanians whose educational/occupational
level was generally below that of the Jews,
Germans, and Hungarians before the war. In
this respect, the economic programs have
functioned to equalize the conditions of
life for the masses of the major ethnic
groups but with considerable relative im-
provement for the Romanians. At the same
time, however, modernization has been
accompanied by stratification primarily
achieved through education and functional
specialization. The Jews, Germans, and

Hungarians are now faced with stiff
competition by a new generation of well-
educated Romanians. The appearance of
Romanians as a socially mobilized group
is perceived as leveling by those groups.[29]
   Two aspects of RCP decision making have
been particularly important to the ethnic
minorities. The party leadership has
consistently recruited members from the
ethnic minorities, and the resulting representation at the lower levels of the
party hierarchy and among the rank and file
roughly corresponds to the proportion of
each group in the general population. At
higher levels of the RCP hierarchy, however,
minority representation falls off sharply,
and the top bodies of the party contain
very few non-Romanians. Ceausescu's closest
advisers and associates now include
Romanians exclusively. Prior to World War
II and/or the past several years the policy
of political recruitment favored the largest
ethnic group. In contrast, the policy of
favoring other ethnic groups was followed
the first few years after World War II.[30]
   Another important political phenomena
in Romania during the last five years has
been the "little cultural revolution,"
manifested as an ideological offensive to
enhance the party's position. By expanding
the party's power and mobilizing the rank
and file Ceausescu evidently hopes to control the technical, managerial, and academic
intelligentsia thereby diminishing the likelihood of increased political pluralization
following the stratification of Romanian

society in the modernization process. The
ideological campaign has increased political
mobilization, and Ceausescu has made it
clear that it is designed to wipe out "bourgeois nationalism" among minority groups.
The nationalistic outlooks of the General
Secretary influence the position of Romanian
ethnic minorities more than ever.[31]

State Policy and Ethnic Consciousness
Among Minorities in Romania

Researching topics as sensitive as the
relations among nationality groups in multiethnic societies, especially when they are
controlled by communist political elites,
poses many problems. Such political elites
are programmed to view conflict among
ethnic groups as a bourgeois phenomenon,
and few members of the elite will admit
failures in policy resulting in continuation
of conflict. At the same time, political
control in those societies effectively
prevents research based on survey data or
any examination of the views of the population. The researcher is therefore forced
to rely upon indirect evidence. There are
three major sources of such indirect
evidence available to Western scholars
interested in Romania. First the speeches,

articles, and political statements of major
elite figures are a source of information,
especially when those political leaders use
their own public statements as major
vehicles of communication. The personalized
style of Nicolae Ceausescu favors a rather
open airing of existing problems in Romanian
society, and his speeches are a major source
of evidence concerning ethnic particularism
and the reaction of ethnic groups to regime
policies.

The general press and the minority
press are sources of limited value. Since
the RCP's control over the press is tight
little controversial material has slipped
through and the minority press is even more
orthodox than publications issued in Romanian. Similarly literature and the performing
arts are of limited research value, especially since the inception of the "little
cultural revolution" in the summer of 1971.
The relative autonomy enjoyed by some of
the best writers in Romania in the period
prior to 1965 was seriously impaired as a
result of the "revolution." Now literature
is securely harnessed to the goals of
"socialist construction."[32] Therefore real
assessments of ethnic relations and statements of group outlooks are rarely permitted
in this medium.

The statistical material published in
great quantity every year is a third source.
Every political and economic elite needs
detailed and accurate information to execute
their policies. Consequently the census
data from 1956 and 1966 and the demographic

yearbooks of the Socialist Republic of
Romania are a particularly valuable source.
The statistical yearbooks contain little
information of direct value for research on
ethnic groups, but the correlation of that
statistical material with census figures
often yields interesting findings. The
following analysis is primarily based on
the sources mentioned.
     Close examination of those sources
yields insight into the reaction of ethnic
minorities to regime policies. It is clear
that modernization and the assimilation
policies of the RCP have not significantly
altered the views of most ethnic minori-
ties--they continue to regard themselves as
Jews, Hungarians, and Germans rather than
citizens of socialist Romania. The General
Secretary frequently complains about the
continuation of "bourgeois nationalism,"
and his emphasis on the need for all
citizens, regardless of ethnic background,
to pull together in the common endeavor of
building socialist Romania clearly suggests
that minority relations are a continuing
problem.
     The General Secretary also complains
about the inadequate party "coverage" of
areas with heavy minority populations. The
party cadres at the central and regional
levels, the youth groups, and the trade
unions, have been roundly criticized for
failing to ensure broader and more enthusiastic political participation by all
groups. The "little cultural revolution"
and the vigorous ideological and

212

organizational campaigns which followed were
mostly intended to achieve a better position
for the RCP among the most important groups,
particularly the Hungarians and the Germans.[33]

It is also important to note that many
members of ethnic minorities have expressed
a wish to emigrate. Those numbers reflect
the lack of minority integration and the
negative reactions to the elite programs
of the regime. During the last decade, an
estimated 17,000 Romanian citizens of
German origin emigrated to West Germany,[34]
and a large number of Jews have been permitted to leave for Israel. The regime
has recently indicated willingness to
grant exit visas for some Hungarians
apparently in return for commercial concessions. Before granting "most favored nation" status to Romania the United States
insisted on the right to free emigration.

More importantly ethnicity is perceived
to be one of several factors which hampers
or prevents fulfillment of Ceausescu's
program of creating "new socialist men and
women." Ceausescu is one of the few leaders
in Eastern Europe who maintains the need
to fundamentally change people's values,
thereby laying the foundation for a new
society. The General Secretary has been
frustrated in this endeavor by such "old-
fashioned values" as egotism, greed, the
primary importance of individual needs
and those of the immediate family at the
expense of the general society, and ethnic
particularism. The ideological campaign,

which has been a major feature of Romanian
political life since the summer of 1971,
is the most recent effort to destroy those
persistent values. The continued criticism
of the party press of failures in ideological work and the admission that there are
continuing problems is evidence that ethnic
particularism persists.[35]
     Other indirect indicators of ethnic
persistence come to light on occasion. For
example, the Hungarian Politburo engaged
in a controversy with the RCP over the
treatment of the Magyar minority in Romania
in the summer and fall of 1971. The
Hungarian Politburo's spokesman, Zoltán
Komocsin, expressed official concern over
the treatment of Magyars in Romania and
indicated that Romania's nationality
policies were detrimental to the maintenance
of ethnic consciousness among Hungarians.
Komocsin hinted that Romanian Magyars were
induced to accept "Romanianization" against
their will. The sharp reaction from
Bucharest reflected in the articles and
statements of Paul Niculescu-Mizil, a ranking member of the RCP Secretariat, are
evidence that real nationality problems
continue to exist.[36] The polemics have
abated since 1971, but there is little
doubt that the Magyar minority continues
to be considered a problem by the RCP
leadership.
     The conversations of some Western ob-
servers with members of ethnic minorities
in Romania have confirmed the strongly
nationalistic, Romanian-oriented policies

of the regime, and its rejection of most
ethnic minorities.

This negative correlation has not
been directly established since the evidence
is indirect and hard to substantiate.
Many visitors to Romania, especially to
ethnically mixed areas, observe that the
residential patterns of most cities, towns,
and villages remain separated, and that
Germans, Hungarians, and Romanians mostly
occupy separate sections. This settlement
pattern may indicate that other aspects
of life are also separate.[37]

Scholars must rely upon statements of
regime leaders to verify the political
aspects of ethnicity, but even so the
available statistics tend to support the
image of ethnic particularism and "separateness" derived from examination of those
indirect sources. The census data for 1966
(the most recently completed census)
provides evidence that the major ethnic
minorities in Romania have not been
assimilated to the dominant Romanian language. See Table 1. Table 1 reveals
large "pockets" of minority language usage
(primarily Hungarian and German) in certain
districts, while speakers of the Gypsy language are scattered throughout the country.
Yiddish is used minimally in all counties.

The census figures for 1966 show that
minority languages are still used in Romania
after three decades of communist-sponsored
modernization and centralized education,
but those data cannot reveal the intragroup dynamics of language usage over time.

Fortunately, the censuses of 1956 and 1966
show that the mother tongue is the chief
means of expression in each ethnic group.
In 1956, 99.4 percent of Romanians spoke
Romanian, and 98.6 percent of the Hungarians
spoke Hungarian. Fully 96.1 percent of the
Germans regarded German as their principal
language. The Jews adopted Romanian as
their main language (57.5 percent) and only
21.9 percent continued to use Yiddish. The
Gypsies adopted Romanian (45.2 percent) and
Hungarian (8.7 percent), while 46.2 percent
continued to speak the Gypsy language.

By 1966, the Romanians, Hungarians,
and Germans had become even more attached
to their native tongue. In 1966, 99.7
percent of the Romanians spoke Romanian,
98.9 percent of the Hungarians spoke Hungarian, and 97.4 percent of the Germans
spoke German. The Jews used Romanian more
heavily than before (65 percent), and
Yiddish was used by only 11 percent. The
Gypsies revered to their native tongue,
58.9 percent used Gypsy, 30.9 percent used
Romanian, and 10.2 percent Hungarian. Data
on the Gypsies, however, are probably
distorted in the census. Many Gypsies
apparently declared themselves to be "Romanian" or "Hungarian" in the census, and
the language figures are therefore inaccu-
rate.[38]

It is difficult to analyze the seeming
linguistic assimilation of the Jews without
some evidence concerning the number of Jewish emigrants and their linguistic prefer-
ences. It seems likely that Jews who

Table 1

The Use of Languages, by Judeţs (Counties), 1966

Judeţ	Total Pop.	Mother Tongue				
		Romanian	Hungarian	German	Yiddish	Gypsy
Romania	19,103,163 (100%)	16,770,628 (87.8%)	1,651,873 (8.6%)	387,547 (2.0%)	5,143 (-)	49,086 (0.3%)
Alba	382,786 (100%)	341,380 (89.2%)	26,710 (7.0%)	12,785 (3.3%)	23 (-)	1,632 (0.4%)
Arad	487,248 (100%)	345,979 (71.9%)	78,294 (16.3%)	43,157 (9.0%)	55 (-)	2,268 (0.5%)
Argeş	529,833 (100%)	528,546 (99.8%)	397 (0.1%)	113 (-)	7 (-)	248 (-)
Bacau	598,321 (100%)	588,996 (98.4%)	7,673 (1.3%)	240 (-)	209 (-)	323 (0.1%)
Bihor	586,460 (100%)	375,348 (64.0%)	198,092 (33.8%)	1,030 (0.2%)	143 (-)	3,133 (0.5%)
Bistriţa-Nasaud	268,600 (100%)	238,750 (88.9%)	21,587 (8.0%)	6,016 (2.2%)	51 (-)	2,001 (0.7%)
Botosani	452,406 (100%)	450,063 (99.5%)	77 (-)	45 (-)	818 (0.2%)	118 (-)

Table 1 (Continued)

Județ	Total Pop.	Romanian	Hungarian	German	Yiddish	Gypsy
Brașov	442,692 (100%)	333,337 (75.3%)	66,545 (15.0%)	41,136 (9.3%)	45 (-)	649 (0.1%)
Braila	339,954 (100%)	335,914 (98.8%)	272 (0.1%)	78 (-)	33 (-)	319 (0.1%)
Buzau	482,784 (100%)	480,111 (99.4%)	137 (-)	45 (-)	16 (-)	2,266 (0.5%)
Caraș-Severin	358,726 (100%)	297,564 (83.0%)	8,787 (2.4%)	26,657 (7.4%)	12 (-)	2,105 (0.6%)
Cluj	631,100 (100%)	459,547 (72.8%)	166,117 (26.3%)	1,681 (0.3%)	138 (-)	2,851 (0.5%)
Constanța	465,752 (100%)	423,811 (91.0%)	851 (0.2%)	414 (0.1%)	65 (-)	345 (0.1%)
Covasna	176,858 (100%)	33,761 (19.1%)	142,327 (80.5%)	254 (0.1%)	1 (-)	17 (-)
Dimbovita	421,557 (100%)	420,216 (99.7%)	154 (-)	69 (-)	7 (-)	885 (0.2%)
Dolj	691,116 (100%)	687,816 (99.5%)	323 (-)	230 (-)	13 (-)	1,756 (0.3%)

Table 1 (Continued)

Județ	Total Pop.	Romanian	Hungarian	German	Yiddish	Gypsy
Galați	474,279 (100%)	471,342 (99.4%)	687 (0.1%)	176 (–)	206 (–)	554 (0.1%)
Gorj	298,946 (100%)	297,801 (99.6%)	264 (0.1%)	43 (–)	2 (–)	566 (0.2%)
Harghita	282,392 (100%)	30,484 (10.8%)	250,679 (88.8%)	210 (0.1%)	7 (–)	568 (0.2%)
Hanedoara	474,602 (100%)	425,375 (89.6%)	40,265 (8.5%)	5,989 (1.3%)	97 (–)	333 (0.1%)
Ialomita	363,075 (100%)	360,665 (99.3%)	148 (–)	38 (–)	1 (–)	1,641 (0.5%)
Iași	617,397 (100%)	615,211 (99.6%)	484 (0.1%)	246 (–)	539 (0.1%)	221 (–)
Ilfov	756,622 (100%)	755,094 (99.8%)	169 (–)	83 (–)	2 (–)	809 (0.1%)
Maramureș	427,645 (100%)	339,361 (79.4%)	55,609 (13.0%)	2,866 (0.7%)	196 (–)	682 (0.2%)
Mehedinți	309,457 (100%)	304.258 (98.3%)	614 (0.2%)	659 (0.2%)	4 (–)	839 (0.3%)

Table 1 (Continued)

Judeţ	Total Pop.	Romanian	Hungarian	German	Yiddish	Gypsy
Mureş	561,598 (100%)	279,784 (49.8%)	252,861 (45.0%)	20,545 (3.7%)	87 (–)	7,967 (1.4%)
Neamţ	471,836 (100%)	470,333 (99.7%)	659 (0.1%)	105 (–)	199 (–)	267 (0.1%)
Olt	476,513 (100%)	475,815 (99.9%)	96 (–)	36 (–)	2 (–)	357 (0.1%)
Prahova	699,224 (100%)	695,504 (99.5%)	878 (0.1%)	542 (0.1%)	24 (–)	1,555 (0.2%)
Satu Mare	359,393 (100%)	198,433 (55.2%)	155,192 (43.2%)	3,859 (1.1%)	51 (–)	698 (0.2%)
Sălaj	263,103 (100%)	195,134 (74.2%)	63,981 (24.3%)	54 (–)	21 (–)	1,438 (0.5%)
Sibiu	414,756 (100%)	295,322 (71.2%)	19,898 (4.8%)	97,355 (23.5%)	70 (–)	1,320 (0.3%)
Suceava	572,781 (100%)	545,922 (95.3%)	582 (0.1%)	3,387 (0.6%)	774 (0.1%)	359 (0.1%)
Teleorman	521,478 (100%)	519,349 (99.6%)	84 (–)	24 (–)	2 (–)	1,848 (0.4%)

220

Table 1 (Continued)

Judeţ	Total Pop.	Romanian	Hungarian	German	Yiddish	Gypsy
Timiş	607,596 (100%)	379,987 (62.5%)	78,758 (13.0%)	110,339 (18.2%)	121 (-)	4,360 (0.7%)
Tulcea	236,709 (100%)	203.095 (85.8%)	107 (-)	84 (-)	55 (-)	33 (-)
Vaslui	431,555 (100%)	430,999 (99.9%)	41 (-)	25 (-)	103 (-)	271 (0.1%)
Vilçea	368,779 (100%)	368,181 (99.8%)	170 (-)	79 (-)	-- (-)	163 (-)
Vrancea	351,292 (100%)	349,833 (99.6%)	135 (-)	37 (-)	38 (-)	1,066 (0.3%)
Bucharest City	1,451,942 (100%)	1,422,207 (98.0%)	11,169 (0.8%)	6,816 (0.5%)	906 (0.1%)	255 (-)

(Based on: Republica Socialiste Romania, Directia Centrala de Statistica, Recensamintul Populaţica si Locuintelor din 15 Martie 1966 Vol. I (Bucharest: 1969) pp. 153-173.)

remained in Romania would be assimilated to
the political system, and thus more would
use Romanian in comparison to those who
left the country. The migration thus probably accentuated the linguistic assimilation of Jews during the decade.

The two largest and politically most
important ethnic minorities (Romanians and
Hungarians) had a "negative" linguistic
assimilation during this period, i.e.,
these groups were less likely to use languages other than their native tongue as
their chief means of expression after ten
years of rapid social mobilization and expanding nationalism on the part of the
dominant Romanian elite.

In 1956, 29.2 percent of the Romanians
lived in urban areas, while the similar
data on Hungarians, Germans, Jews, and
Gypsies were 41.1 percent, 50.1 percent,
95.2 percent, and 17.3 percent respectively.
In 1966, 36.9 percent of the Romanians
lived in urban areas; 47.6 percent of the
Hungarians, 53.8 percent of the Germans,
97.8 percent of the Jews, and 25.6 percent
of the Gypsies were urbanized.[39] Considerable urbanization took place during the
decade, but that process did not mean that
the ethnic minorities moved into Romanian
cities; actually they tended to move into
cities in their own regions. This is
vividly illustrated by the regional distribution of ethnic settlements in 1956
and 1966. According to the 1956 census,
the heaviest concentration of Hungarians
was in the Magyar Autonomous Region, and in

the provinces of Timișoara, Stalin, Oradea, and Baia Mare. The Germans lived predominantly in Stalin and Timișoara. Jews were more evenly scattered in cities throughout the country and the Gypsies in rural regions.

By 1966, territorial reorganizations were completed in Romania. The Magyar Autonomous Region was basically made up of the judets (counties) of Mureș and Harghita as well as part of the judet Covasna. Timișoara had become the judet of Timiș, and partly Caras Severin, whereas the region Stalin was divided into Brașov and Sibiu judets. The region of Oradea was now the judet Bihor, and Baia Mare became Satu Mare and Maramureș judets.

The 1966 census shows that the concentration of Hungarians remained high in the judets which were carved out of the former regions of Timișoara, Stalin, Oradea, Baia Mare, and the Magyar Autonomous Region, ranging from a high of 88.1 percent in Harghita to a low of 2.6 percent in Caras Severin (where Romanian-populated areas had been added in the process of reorganization). The Germans were concentrated in four judets (Timiș 18.0 percent, Sibiu 23.4 percent, Caras Severin 6.7 percent, and Brașov 9.2 percent).[40]

If the census figures are searched for evidence of Romanians moving into urban areas, the picture of this development becomes clear. The Romanians moved into cities all over the country, even into

concentrations, but those two minorities
stayed in their own regions. This conclusion is buttressed when the 1956 and
1966 data are compared. These figures
show that the move of Hungarians and
Germans into Romanian-populated areas was
negligible.[41]
     The modernization process had little
effect upon residential concentrations of
the major ethnic minorities in Romania
and linguistic assimilation made no head-
way at all. It is clear, however, that
industrialization, urbanization, and the
spread of education profoundly affected
all citizens of Romania regardless of
ethnic background. The ethnic minorities
must have perceived this process primarily
as a gigantic move towards leveling,
whereby Romanians caught up with the
privileged Hungarians, Germans, and Jews
in terms of social mobilization. This
process is illustrated by Table 2. The
decade was characterized by a massive
industrialization of Romanians and the
collectivization of practically all
farmers. The move of Romanians into the
industrial working class clearly indicated
that modernization would eventually remove
occupational privileges enjoyed by the more
highly developed minorities.
     The upward social mobility of Romani-
ans during this decade is further illustrated by educational statistics. The
Romanians constituted 85.3 percent of the
total population twelve years or over in
1956 and they comprised 85.51 percent of

Table 2

Occupational Distribution Within Nationalities, 1956 and 1966

All Units 1956	Total Pop.	Workers	Function- aries Intellectuals	Coll. Farmers	Indiv. Farmers
Romanians	14,996,114 (100%)	3,237,850 (21.6%)	1,969,580 (13.1%)	423,713 (2.9%)	8,145,068 (54.3%)
Hungarians	1,587,675 (100%)	517,718 (32.6%)	201,214 (12.7%)	90,129 (5.7%)	636,925 (40.1%)
Jews	146,264 (100%)	37,478 (25.3%)	77,713 (53.4%)	37 (–)	973 (0.7%)
Gypsies	104,216 (100%)	41,738 (40.4%)	574 (0.6%)	7,037 (6.7%)	17,278 (16.4%)
Germans	384,708 (100%)	219,907 (57.1%)	53,110 (13.8%)	41,782 (10.9%)	40,098 (10.4%)
Urban					
Romanians	4,376,247 (100%)	2,044,503 (46.7%)	1,459,392 (33.3%)	23,932 (0.5%)	505,834 (11.6%)
Hungarians	657,368 (100%)	353,081 (53.7%)	155,207 (23.6%)	8,842 (1.3%)	61,470 (9.4%)

Table 2 (Continued)

All Units 1956	Total Pop.	Workers	Function- aries Intellectuals	Coll. Farmers	Indiv. Farmers
Jews	139,232 (100%)	35,420 (25.4%)	75,176 (54.0%)	8 (-)	545 (0.4%)
Gypsies	18,108 (100%)	9,846 (54.4%)	198 (1.1%)	209 (1.2%)	576 (3.2%)
Germans	192,501 (100%)	119,963 (62.3%)	41,153 (21.4%)	5,949 (3.1%)	6,743 (3.5%)
Rural					
Romanians	10,619,867 (100%)	1,193,347 (11.2%)	510,187 (4.8%)	404,781 (3.8%)	7,639,234 (71.9%)
Hungarians	930,307 (100%)	164,637 (17.7%)	46,007 (4.9%)	81,287 (8.7%)	575,455 (61.9%)
Jews	7,032 (100%)	2,058 (29.3)	2,537 (36.1%)	29 (0.4%)	428 (6.1%)
Gypsies	86,108 (100%)	31,892 (37.0%)	376 (0.4%)	6,828 (7.9%)	16,702 (19.4%)
Germans	192,207 (100%)	99,944 (52.0%)	11,957 (6.2%)	35,833 (18.6%)	33,355 (17.4%)

226

Table 2 (Continued)

All Units 1966	Total Pop.	Workers	Function-aries Intellectuals	Coll. Farmers	Indiv. Farmers
Romanians	16,746,510 (100%)	6,507,669 (38.9%)	2,065,083 (12.3%)	6,646,623 (39.7%)	926,911 (5.5%)
Hungarians	1,619,592 (100%)	742,623 (45.9%)	188,215 (11.6%)	553,724 (34.2%)	32,063 (2.0%)
Jews	42,888 (100%)	12,440 (25.0%)	25,496 (59.5%)	142 (0.3%)	71 (0.01%)
Gypsies	64,197 (100%)	30,362 (47.3%)	324 (0.5%)	19,501 (30.3%)	1,670 (2.6%)
Germans	382,595 (100%)	224,264 (58.5%)	52,028 (13.6%)	75,478 (17.6%)	3,772 (1.0%)
Municipalities and Towns					
Romanians	5,707,840 (100%)	3,376,608 (59.2%)	1,568,259 (27.5%)	413,783 (7.3%)	67,336 (1.2%)
Hungarians	718,475 (100%)	461,735 (64.3%)	143,833 (20.1%)	50,298 (7.0%)	3,860 (0.6%)

Table 2 (Continued)

All Units 1966	Total Pop.	Workers	Function-aries Intellectuals	Coll. Farmers	Indiv. Farmers
Jews	42,082 (100%)	12,138 (28.8%)	25,234 (60.0%)	63 (0.1%)	34 (0.1%)
Gypsies	16,240 (100%)	10,686 (65.8%)	204 (1.3%)	1,933 (11.9%)	205 (1.3%)
Germans	173,116 (100%)	114,996 (66.4%)	38,492 (22.2%)	4,768 (2.8%)	942 (0.5%)
Rural Districts					
Romanians	10,384,818 (100%)	2,774,860 (26.7%)	459,088 (4.4%)	6,009,540 (57.9%)	841,272 (8.1%)
Hungarians	859,674 (100%)	259,824 (30.2%)	42,149 (4.9%)	488,763 (56.9%)	26,551 (3.1%)
Jews	757 (100%)	286 (37.8%)	247 (32.6%)	79 (10.4%)	37 (4.9%)
Gypsies	46,439 (100%)	18,608 (40.1%)	111 (0.2%)	17,301 (37.3%)	1,436 (3.1%)

228

Table 2 (Continued)

All Units 1966	Total Pop.	Workers	Function-aries Intellectuals	Coll. Farmers	Indiv. Farmers
Germans	192,220 (100%)	97,782 (50.9%)	12,587 (6.5%)	66,956 (34.8%)	2,730 (1.4%)

Source: Recensamintul 1956, p. 563 and Recensamintul 1966, p. 157.

the enrollment in "higher schools." By 1966,
Romanians constituted 87.25 percent of the
total population (12 or over) and 88.72 percent were enrolled in institutions of higher
learning. In 1906 Hungarians constituted
9.32 percent of the total population and
only 6.07 percent of those were in higher
schools; by 1966, the Magyar share of the
total population (12 or over) was 8.82 percent, but only 6.1 percent were enrolled
in institutions of higher learning. The
Germans were similarly under-represented
although less markedly than Hungarians.
Jews were heavily over-represented in higher institutions in 1956, and remained so in
1966, but the number was drastically reduced.[42]
     The occupational distribution and
access to education suggests that the
policies of the regime favored the Romanians
by giving them a chance to catch up with
more highly mobilized ethnic minority
groups. Those minorities, having enjoyed
relative privilege, must have perceived
those policies as Romanian favoritism.
     The official statistics of Romania no
longer record intermarriage between persons
of different ethnic heritage (although some
such evidence was available in the 1950s
and early 1960s). Consequently there is no
way that this important indicator can be
extrapolated from available figures. The
omission of such data may be an indication
of a low level of intermarriage, an embarrassing statistic for a regime officially
dedicated to assimilating all individuals
within a common culture.

Many Western countries maintain
statistics which show the rate of criminality, alcoholism, divorce, and other social
problems. The figures are often compiled
by region so that the correlation between
census data and figures for "socially
undesirable behavior" may produce an index
of "social dissatisfaction." Unfortunately,
official Romanian statistics do not include
data on criminality and alcoholism since
they would counter the regime's claims that
a higher level of social consciousness had
been achieved. The data on divorce are,
however, compiled by județ. The 1974
demographic yearbook lists the following
judeţs with divorce levels of over 0.70 per
1,000 inhabitants in 1973: Bucharest,
Braşov, Timiş, Arad, Prahova, Argeş,
Constanţa, Gálaţi, Hunedoara, Sibiu, and
Suceava. The judeţs with the lowest levels
(0.40 per 1,000 or below) included:
Bistrita-Nasaud, Botosani, Buzau, Covasna,
Harghita, Ialomiţa, Neamţ, Olt, Vaslui,
and Salaj. Correlating those data with
economic and residential statistics reveals that the high divorce areas were the
most industrialized counties regardless of
ethnic composition. The low divorce rates
were predictably found in the least industrialized and urbanized regions.[43] Thus,
the divorce rate is related to urbanization
and economic activity and not primarily to
ethnic factors.

The professional literature on demography in Romania yields equally negative
results. The "demographic year" in 1973

and 1974 produced many sophisticated and
highly informative articles on demographic
problems but they did not focus on ethnic
minorities as a factor in population movements. Ethnic group relations, indeed anything pertaining to ethnic minorities, is
undoubtedly a nontopic in contemporary Romania.[44]

This evidence outlines the basic nationality policy of the Romanian regime
since the establishment of a communist
political system thirty years ago. There
are also indications that the regime policies have had an impact upon national
consciousness and ethnic particularism.
The regime policies in Romania during the
last generation have favored the socioeconomic development of the country,
albeit as a "socialist development."
Massive industrialization, urbanization,
the rapid spread of education, and a
concentrated effort to break down regionalism in favor of a national political culture have been mainstays of state policy.
Those policies moved the ethnic minorities,
especially those which had a higher level
of social mobilization than the politically
dominant Romanians (i.e., Hungarians,
Germans, and Jews) into a level of mobilization approached by the newly mobilized
masses of Romanians. The Hungarians, Germans, and Jews doubtless considered this a
form of "Romanianization," and the policies
of the regime were not accepted by most of
those groups. The political effect of that

perception was detrimental to the objectives
of the regime since Hungarians and Germans
alike viewed the policies as inequitable.
Ethnic separatism was the immediate outcome.
The "outward assimilation" of the Jews
(through the increasing use of Romanian as
the chief means of expression, and the high
level of mobilization during the entire
postwar period) continued. The internal
status of Jews was significantly influenced
by their migration in large numbers to
Israel.

The fundamental societal changes which
resulted from the modernization program
conducted by the communist leadership failed
to produce mass assimilation to a higher,
socialist culture, especially since that
culture was perceived as basically Romanian
in any case. Linguistic assimilation was
also not forthcoming, at least not during
the period 1956-1966, and ethnic particularism was enhanced because many members of
ethnic minorities tended to cultivate their
national culture rather than a supernatural,
"socialist" culture.

The partial removal of Soviet control
over the foreign policies of the East European socialist states partly resurrected the
old animosities which existed between the
peoples of this area. This seriously
affected the Hungarian minority in Transylvania since the Magyars in that area refused
to be assimilated by a Romanian-dominated
"socialist culture." However, their particularism was enhanced because of Budapest's
renewed interest in fellow countrymen across

the Romanian border. That official concern
strengthened Magyar feelings of separateness, despite exhortations from Bucharest
to accept a socialist culture as defined
by the Romanian government.
     On the other hand, the policies of the
communist regime, especially since 1962-63,
have been a powerful source of integration
and support for the Romanians. The policy
inaugurated by Gheorghe Gheorghiu-Dej and
continued by Nicolae Ceausescu enhanced
Romania's autonomy in the socialist camp
and it has been strongly associated with
traditional Romanian symbols and aspirations. The current leadership has emphasized adherence to Romanian history in the
hope that it will be perceived as a natural
successor to the great heroes and liberators
of the past. At the same time, the social,
economic, and educational policies of the
regime have positively influenced conditions of life for all its citizens, but
especially for the Romanians themselves who
formerly constituted a vast majority of the
uneducated, untrained, and poverty-stricken
masses. Despite the continued lack of
popular response and participation in the
"building of socialism" attested to by
spokesmen of the regime there are elements
of policy which are accepted and supported.
The nationality policy of Nicolae Ceausescu
and his closest collaborators has received
the most support from the Romanians.
     The impact of regime policies upon
ethnic consciousness in contemporary Romania
is similar to the prevailing policies and

perceptions which influenced that relationship earlier. There have been no territorial readjustments since World War II and
irredentism, albeit muted, is still a problem primarily in relations with the
Hungarians. The cultural hierarchies, so
firmly entrenched in the popular mind during
the interwar period, are clearly detrimental
to the RCP's efforts to produce greater
integration of all nationalities. The
process of economic development, which improved the standard of living for practically all citizens is seen to be a fundamental
reordering of economic privilege and it is
thus highly controversial. Access to
political power, especially at the center,
is controlled by ethnic Romanians, and this
is also perceived as a flaw despite the
regime's efforts to politically mobilize
all citizens, especially at the grass roots
level. Thirty years of socialist policy,
therefore, have failed to fundamentally
rearrange the patterns of inter-nationality
relations. Those policies have not bridged
the gap between the political regime and
the minority groups so ethnic particularism
is still a major political problem in
socialist Romania.

The Romanian experience is relevant to
the rest of Eastern Europe yet it should be
noted that many special features pertain
only to Romania in this area. Consequently
a systematic comparison with other socialist
states is difficult. Yet the political regime in Romania has carried out social,
economic, and cultural policies that are

quite similar to those of other regimes in
the area, including one-party monopolism of
political power, a massive mobilization of
the citizenry to achieve the socioeconomic
goals associated with "modernization," and
a quest for fundamental value changes among
the masses which will break down barriers
to elite political control, including ethnic
particularism. These policies have failed
in Romania to the extent that ethnic particularism and ethnic consciousness remain as
important political, socioeconomic, and
cultural factors (indeed they may have been
strengthened) and the Romanian experience
in that sense is typical of the general
East European experience. Marxism-Leninism
and Ceausescuism to the contrary, ethnic
consciousness is still a major political
factor in Eastern Europe and may become even
more important in the future.

CHAPTER VI

ETHNICITY, CULTURE, CLASS AND POWER

by

Ernest Gellner

There is an almost inverse relationship between the importance of nationalism in the
modern world and the scholarly attention
it has received. That lack of attention
may be due to an unseemly modesty in the
presence of an unwelcome, unanticipated
and unforeseen intrusion into both the
liberal and the Marxist accounts of
industrial society.
    Nationalism is explicable as an
inevitable, at least as a natural, corollary
of some specific aspects of modernization.
Modern society is politically centralized
and has little room for private vengeance
or for self-help in maintaining order.
    Monopoly of legitimate violence by a
political center is neither inherent,
universal, nor necessary. On the contrary,
in many, perhaps most, social forms subcommunities are units of defense and
maintainers of order. The essence of a
feudal domain is that it exercises force to
defend itself or to enforce internal
discipline. Tribal segments also exercise
force to defend themselves. The central

237

authority of feudal societies is often unable or unwilling to take on the onerous
task of policing everything, so at least
some of the task may be delegated to local
institutions and communities which have
other functions. That delegation is a
common way of passing some of an otherwise
excessive buck. The modern state, however,
is seldom inclined to do the same for
various reasons.

The preconditions of modern economic
life include a monopoly of legitimate
violence at the center. Modern production
is impressive, it maintains high standards,
and is a full-time business. Consequently
it is difficult for the participants to do
anything else at the same high standard--
they cannot be managers, workers, and soldiers at the same time. Their tasks are
different from the traditional functions of
soldiers, pastoralists, and peasant over-
seers. Those activities--shepherding
flocks, and collecting rents--left time
for military training; indeed they are a
means of training in the exercise of
authority. This is not true of modern
tasks, especially at senior and supervisory
levels. Peasants can raise militias, not
as good as those mustered by pastoralists,
but, depite revolutionary romanticism,
urban industrialism is not a good social
base for military service. The daily tasks
involved and the kind of preliminary training required in industrialized societies
do not appear to be conducive to military
life.

Even when the individual is inclined
to serve and has the free time there are
obvious organizational features which work
against military service. The mobility of
labor, the separation of work place and
home, work place and social loyalties, all
militate against the use of the work
community for defensive or law enforcing
purposes. Clans may work and fight as
units, but the kibbutz, which significantly
doubles as a productive and as a defense
unit, is known to be atypical.

There are apparent exceptions to this
generalization. Nazi Germany and other
Fascist states to a lesser extent were
industrial societies with a military ethos,
but whilst the ethos permeated the total
society and most individuals--it did not
function at the level of productive or
regional units. Actually, the British
military establishment organized into territorial and institutional regiments seems
more suited to adapting communities or
associations for military ends. Englishmen
can go to war not merely in their county
regiments, but also in their guild regi-
ments--e.g., Inns of Court Regiment. But
as Basil Seal, that disreputable character
in Evelyn Waugh's novels, observed, those
regional associations are largely bogus--
and his remark cost him a commission in a
good regiment ("Put out more flags").

There are, however, marginal areas
where law enforcement is weak, and self-help
or spontaneous ad hoc organization has to
take over. The mythology of the American

Wild West struck a deep and near universal
chord of individualism-cum-anarchism and
appealed to much of the world. But, unlike
the tribal dissidence which haunted the
marginal areas of states of the Old World,
the Wild West did not last long.

The recent failure of the modern
industrial state to control some urban
areas is evidence that it does condone private violence despite claims to the contrary. The accompanying rise of private
security agencies is also proof positive of
that dismal fact. The trend is significant,
but has not yet resulted in a situation
in which plunder replaces production.
Happily, the industrial ethos and its organizational sanctions attract gangsters
to legitimate business more often that the
other way around.

Modern nationalism is a phenomenon
connected with the emergence of industrial
society, and it is important to note that
industrial societies are always centralized.
Industrial society most often replaces,
though not always, agrarian societies. But
though agrarian societies are usually
politically centralized it cannot be assumed
that centralization is always advantageous.
Some noncentralized agrarian societies have
been more populous and prosperous than their
centralized neighbors and just as advanced
technologically. But centralization in an
industrial society is no longer optional, it
is more complete and pervasive, qualita-
tively and territorially, and that is an important aspect of understanding nationalism.

Modern society is highly specialized in the economic sense and the division of labor between producers and order maintainers is pervasive. The maintenance of order is left to one or few agencies, and is not conducted alongside the daily work of most individuals or subcommunities. This is not unusual since many societies have a specialized warrior class. But the class engaged in productive activites is extraordinarily specialized. It is hardly relevant to expound on the economic reasons for this specialization; the empirical evidence leaves no doubt. But specialization alone does not make modern society unique.

Industrial society is also occupationally mobile, and that mobility must not be confused with specialization. The most important consequences of specialization and mobility are produced jointly. In Western societies they are often confused, nonetheless, they are very distinct, and it is important that they be conceptually separate. Certain societies possess a complex division of labor, but are not mobile. For example in the caste or millet society the cultural, ethnic and religious images, characterizations, and prohibitions visibly inhibit mobility. Michael Hechter notes that ethnicity is segmental in those societies.[1]

But these cultural inhibitions are not the only reason, nor even the main reason for low mobility. The mobility that does occur leads to a bypassing of cultural stereotypes and requirements rather than to

242

their destruction. A given occupation may
be prescribed for a given social or "ethnic"
category, but if economic realities do not
allow all the members of that category to
be gainfully employed in the prescribed
manner, some will seek other outlets. There
is often a lack of congruence between
social ideal and economic reality in these
matters.
    The real reason for low occupational
mobility is a stable technology and stable
expectations. When there is a degree of
demographic equilibrium, and no violent
extrasocial cataclysms, people go on doing,
roughly, what their fathers were doing previously and heredity becomes a viable
principle in allocating social roles.
Training can be carried out by the communities. By contrast, societies with inherently unstable technologies, or those
habituated to continuous economic improve-
ment (as a right and as a cultural norm)
are fated to experience continuously
emerging new specialisms.
    Most specialisms require a high
technical level and prolonged training
which contrast with traditional societies.
It may be arrogant or unimaginative to
suspect that any fool could serve as a
medieval lord or bishop, but if it is so
there can be no serious objection to the
hereditary principle. The seigneury can
pass to the seigneur's son and the bishopric
could be assumed by the bishop's nephew.
The result of hereditary selections for
high office, when the tasks imposed are not

intellectually complex, are certainly no
worse than any meritocratic procedure.
Such posts may call for "character," but
since it is impossible to select candidates
for that elusive property, the point still
holds.

In contrast, a high proportion of jobs
in western societies are talent-specific.
It is impossible to select a random sample
of the population (by accident of birth)
and turn them, even after training, into
physics professors. Only some people
possess the requisite qualities and they
have to be selected for those particular
aptitudes. The same does not apply to
circus acrobats in Morocco where there is
an acrobat-exporting lineage, which credits
its aptitude to its founding saint and
selects new entrants at least partly by
birth.

This is not to presuppose that special
aptitudes are necessarily genetic, since
they may be accidentally produced by early
events in the development of an individual.
The argument here is based on the premise
that talents be a given as far as the educational system is concerned, and not repro-
ducible at will. Talents can be nurtured
but they must be located first. Thus a
certain proportion of talent-specific roles
are an important factor contributing to
mobility.

In addition to this elite subclass of
talent-specific roles, there is a much
larger class of posts which do not presuppose rare talents or innate abilities but

244

which <u>do</u> require fairly genuine and prolonged training. Prolonged training occurs
in traditional societies with low occupational mobility, but the length of the
initiation may be a manner of controlling
or discouraging entry, rather than a consequence of the skills imparted. Genuine
training tends to be <u>specific</u>. It is not
embedded in training which can be switched
in one of many directions, as with modern
education.
     These obvious properties of the modern
economy and its division of labor are
reflected in the size and nature of educational machinery. Training does not run in
family lines, or in the master-apprentice
lineages of craftsmanship. The selection
for specialization and the training itself,
is in the hands of larger, more complex,
internally specialized institutions, which
comprise the educational system. Nationalism essentially transfers the focus of
individual identity to a culture mediated
by literacy and by extensive, formal, educational systems. In that context it is the
language of the école maternele, and not the
mother tongue that matters. When kinship
and paternity are seen to matter less as
sources of identity, the idiom of nationalism is then used to make a fuss of them.
Hence the rhetoric of nationalism cannot be
taken too seriously, as Joshua Fishman seems
to do--though he does not fully clarify the
extent of his endorsement of this 'inward'
account of nationalism:[2]

It is precisely because language is
so often taken as a biological
inheritance that its association
with ethnic paternity is both frequent and powerful. It is "acquired with the mother's milk."

In contemporary life, language is not
even acquired with the bottle fed milk.
The language which counts comes later in
school textbooks. Julius Rezler's account
best illustrated how folk culture becomes
an object of mystique and vicarious identification at the point when it ceases to be
a reality.

Industrial society is mobile between
generations, and also within individual
life spans and careers. Moreover, just as
specialization is great, so is inter-
specialist cooperation, and that produces
the need to develop communication skills.
Such interaction is extensive, complex, and
unpredictable.

Specialization and cooperation have a
joint impact on the educational system
since a very large part of it is unspecialized. The 'vocational' schools appear
relatively late in the course of an educational career. The American educational
system, part of the most highly specialist
economy ever, is itself highly un-special-
ized! This is not a paradox, rather it is
inherent in the kind of specialization
dealt with here. Americans are not
assemblages of occupational castes or task-
specialized millets; they are a mass of
mobile individuals, cooperating in

diversified ways while engaged in specialized roles. Consequently most essential
training in the United States consists of
acquiring a shared base, which enables
individuals to retrain quickly when they
change jobs, and communicate with each
other when engaged in work.

It should be stressed that "the social
consequences of literacy" are quite distinct, according to whether literacy is
specialized or an universal accomplishment.
The literacy attained by <u>some</u> people has
the social potential for greater centralization, bureaucratism, order both in the
economy and in faith, scripturalism, and
protestantism (i.e., the confrontation of
practice with a written authoritative model).
Universal literacy has the potential for
nationalism.

The connection between industrialization and nationalism has been stressed before,[3] but the problem is to clarify that
connection. Intrapolity diversity, coupled
with the visible inequality, systematically
connected with "ethnic" groups has become
intolerable--yet mankind lived with it
with comparative equanimity in the past.

Modern societies range the gamut from
mild to extreme socialism, and genuine
economic liberalism is no longer an available option. Opposition to government interference in economic affairs is alive and
well and the laissez faire folklore has its
admirers and detractors. There are periodic
political moods and movements that aim to
restore it like those that would recall the

pristine purity of the early church. When
these movements occasionally score political
successes and attain power they are invariably compelled to execute U-turns. Just as
revolutions are invariably betrayed, so the
same fate regularly befalls attempts to restore economic liberalism. It must be
assumed that there are deep structural and
very specific reasons for those betrayals.

The modern ship of state is always
equipped with a steering mechanism--and once
installed it must be used. Even when the
tiller is left to wobble freely a decision
has been made--but in practice, government
leaders cannot really keep hands off. They
must steer the ship in turbulent water and
in proximity of rocks. The visible hand is
essential, and even if laissez faire puritans, of iron will and endowed with a secure
political power base, succeeded in restraining their own hand, that would still be
tantamount to an endorsement of the past
course.

There are other powerful political
constraints, since laissez faire puritans
rarely possess an impregnable political
power base. In other words, rulers cannot
indulge their fantasies, but must act in
a manner that will permit them to remain in
power, and the rulers who monopolize the
means of coercion, and of communication and
association, have more elbow room. Government leaders must attempt to please or
placate interests which might otherwise un-
seat them.

It follows that neither tribalism nor
quietism-on-principle are available options
in modern society. Tribalism involves the
organization of local groups which are
simultaneously productive and defense units;
those groups typically feud with each other
and thereby maintain internal and external
order to the extent that order is kept at
all. This option is not available in modern
society because local instability and the
time and resources for defense are incompatible with modern economic standards.

Quietism is based on the questionable
conviction that any government is better
than none, better than anarchy or tribalism,
and that the sovereign must indeed be
sovereign, because a bound and limited
authority would be contradictory or ineffec-
tive. This attitude seems to have been
widespread in Muslim traditional society
after the decline of the Caliphate. If
government could not be the shadow of God
on earth, if a morally luminous theocracy
was not available, then any effective government was legitimate simply by virtue
of being effective provided it did not
actively go against the precepts of the
Faith.

In practice, quietism requires an
authority to effectively keep the peace,
that is not too arbitrary, extortionate,
or religiously scandalous. This spirit
is positively expressed by Elie Kedourie
in his important book Nationalism:[4]

The only criterion capable of
public defense is whether the

new rulers are less corrupt and
grasping, or more just and merciful ...
The values associated with quietism are
not compatible with modern conditions.
They made sense only when governments lacked
the means and the will to interfere in the
economy.
The intricate modern industrial system
with a central steering mechanism (however
imperfectly used), and especially those
systems wherein economic rates of growth
are dependent upon effective steering,
cannot function merely because the rulers
are merciful and not too grasping. When
the regime permits, the participants with
the greatest economic interest can only
try to influence the leaders whose hands
are on the tiller to act in behalf of that
interest--at least not blatantly against
it. In other words, the organizers of a
modern economic system must be political,
in the modern sense, and organize the system
so that it is responsive to centrally
made economic decisions, and not to local
autonomy.
The striving for participation,
Mitbestimmung, is inherent in modern economic and political life, but not inherent in
some universal moral truths. Quietism
however is a sensible, rational attitude,
when it is feasible. It makes sense when
the general social order is static and
given, and when government is concerned
with the relative detail of who gets what
and how much. Traditional governments may

replace a governor or vizier by another,
vary the taxes, persecute, expropriate
or execute a few people (sometimes more
than a few), but they lack the power to
greatly interfere with the overall social
structure. The majority of people therefore strive to remain unknown to government
and remain apart from the unhappy minority
that is the object of governmental attention. The majority may then embrace
Hobbesian, quietistic, political philosophy.

The contrary view expressed by M.
Ginsberg that "... moral systems may be
judged by the extent to which they permit
or encourage ... self-direction ...."[5] seems
to have little merit. There is a certain
life style, exemplified by some left wing
sects, which consists of virtually uninterrupted participation in meetings, committees,
and discussion groups. But it is absurd
to generalize that style as an ideal for
everyone. Marx's extrapolation, in the
German Ideology, of Bohemian unpunctuality
and wayward mood-switching into the recipe
for the Good Life is equally absurd:[6]

> ... in communist society .. nobody
> has one exclusive sphere of
> activity ... thus makes it
> possible for me to do one thing
> today and another tomorrow, to
> hunt in the morning, fish in the
> afternoon, rear cattle in the
> evening, criticize after
> dinner ...

The kind of nonparticipatory quietism
that accepts a fairly stable social

environment and keeps clear of government
as much as it can seems to be a perfectly
reasonable ideal. "Blessed the man who
does not know government and is not known
to it." But that option is unavailable to
members of a very complex, sensitively
interdependent modern economy, with a modern
government. Those members must combine,
openly or covertly, to ensure that government is not used against them.
      The argument has so far invoked
nothing but obvious, hardly contentious,
features of modern society. People in
that society have acquired an almost
irresistible desire for affluence and they
pay for affluence by endorsing an elaborate
division of labor, combined with intergenerational occupational mobility, rapid
switching of jobs, communication between
occupants of diverse roles, and high technical standards (including literacy as a
minimal precondition). Those conditions
create the need for a near-universal and
thorough educational system. As a result
private and communal warfare and law enforcement is diminished, there is a marked
weakening or erosion of intermediate
communities, and society largely consists
of a mass of mobile individuals. At the
same time, the size of productive units,
technology, and centralized decision
making inevitably imposes a central direction on the whole society. The size and
cost of educational, and other infrastructures then leads to the allocation of
an ever increasing proportion of the total

national income to the state budget.
Those central decisions eventually compel
subsegments of the community to protect
their own interests through overt political
organization (in free societies). The
traditional state, however despotic, was
feeble. It could kill or expropriate its
subjects but it could do little to change
the social structure except by sometimes
destroying the economic infrastructure as
Hulegu is said to have done. Even the
liberal Rechtstaat, hemmed in by the rule
of law, pluralism, and representative
government, is more fundamentally powerful.
Those kinds of governments often make
irreversible and far-reaching decisions
that change the entire form of life of
subsequent generations. That is the kind
of sociopolitical system that has resulted from a collective greed for the
fruits of industrialism. That system is
inevitably nationalist.

The world described above inevitably
comprises strong centralized states which
maintain the expensive functions of order,
complex infrastructures, including elaborate
educational systems, characterized by
considerable occupational and geographical
mobility. Those units are homogeneous internally in the cultural sense because
education is central, prolonged and very
nearly universal. Education must be
conducted in a linguistic and cultural
medium that acquires an importance greater
than ever before. Education is an essential to the social and occupational mobility

which in turn requires communication.

In stable societies communication is
generally contextual. Basil Bernstein[7]
has distinguished the restricted and
elaborated codes of speech (strictly
speaking he deals with styles or sets of
convictions and not "codes") and this distinction applies here. In stable social
environments the meaning of a message hinges
only in small part on when, what and how it
is transmitted, the parties involved, and
the circumstances which occasion it. In
mobile, rapidly changing, single shot
circumstances this is not so. As a girl
on the beach observed while looking at men
in swimming trunks, "the trouble with a
beach is that you cannot tell who anyone
is." The mobile, anonymous, and homogeneous
society is like nudity, a great leveler.
Such contexts cannot convey meaning because
they are unstable and accidental. So meaning is confined to just what is said--the
medium is not the message, the message is
the message--so an effective mastery of the
medium, receiver or transmitter, becomes
important. Therefore in modern national
states with mobile, anonymous populations
(i.e., where membership is by individuals,
because there are no block memberships)
and a homogeneous culture instilled or
transmitted by major industry education has
two jobs: to instill the culture, and to
ensure adequate standards of literacy and
technical competence, adequate for employ-
ability and rapid redeployment of personnel.

This conclusion was reached after
examining the implications of the organizational traits characteristic of modern
societies, without invoking such human
attributes as patriotism, xenophobia, call
of the blood, territoriality, the warmth
of folk cultures, the vernacular, or the
alleged dislike of foreign rule. The failure to invoke these factors does not mean
that they do not exist. It merely shows
that any theory rationalizing the emergence
of the national state as a typical form of
political organization, the normal recipient
of human loyalties, can be formulated without invoking any aspects of nationalist
ideologies themselves.

At this stage it is appropriate to
argue that modern society inherently tends
to provide a fair measure of equality in
style of life. There is no doubt, however,
that there is a lack of equality of ownership, and there is also an unequal distribution of power that stems from certain
obvious traits of modern society. Any
complex and interdependent machine has key
points or levers, and only one hand can
manipulate any one lever at any one time.
This is complicated because different levers
become crucial at different times and the
personnel in control may well rotate. The
question "who wields power" is more complicated than in societies where there are few
levers and where the stationing of personnel
is fairly stable.

Nonetheless there is visible evidence
that there is an equalization of life style

conditions in the modern society. Wage
differentials in the Soviet Union, for
instance, have relatively little effect on
the actual behavior and appearance of people
simply because the pressure of public opinion is against ostentation--to have more
than one servant almost becomes a social
provocation. Similarly, the surviving inequalities of wealth in Britain are not
translated into highly conspicuous differences in life style as they were in Edward-
ian days. Wealth is now discreet. British
gentlemen always <u>said</u> that ostentation was
vulgar, but they actually live up to this
dictum nowadays. The rich may surrepti-
tiously show off to each other, but not to
the public at large. The wife of a knighted
industrialist of a decade or so ago who
habitually showed herself in rich cars and
opulent dresses is now a byword for vulgar-
ity. She would have encountered a great
deal of competition during the <u>belle époque</u>
but these days she has the field virtually
to herself. The only people who are
allowed that kind of display are celebrities
e.g., pop stars, who combine it with such
pedestrian backgrounds and personalities
that their role is to underwrite a general
egalitarianism. Their message is "this
could happen to any of <u>you</u>" and so it is
inoffensive.
    This egalitarianism arises from the
same factors that underlie cultural homogeneity and that homogeneity is probably
part of the same process.

Inequalities of rank conceived to
establish unbridgeable differentiations
between kinds of humanity, are not always
unacceptable. Grown men kissing the feet
of minor chieftains, untouchables in India
picking up warm human excrement--these
inequalities are repulsive for us, but
humanity has lived with them in the past.
They are difficult to sustain in a mobile
society where the countless new encounters
engendered by the needs of economic life,
invoke cooperation. In those circumstances
it is impossible to render the rival
conceptions of status hierarchies congruent.
Situations are bound to occur when two
supposedly high status persons meet with
contradictory expectations of deference.
When this happens frequently it leads to
constant friction. The solution is to
acknowledge that all people are equal.
Then prima facie equality becomes the norm.
Strong centralized states with central
economic steering mechanisms are doomed to
conflict, though not necessarily violent
conflict. Since the steering mechanism can
be directed one way or another and since
the direction taken affects the fortunes of
subgroups within the community they must
struggle to control or influence it.
Mankind as such is not necessarily
doomed to conflict. When land is plentiful
as in premodern Africa for example neighboring agricultural communities were not impelled towards conflict by real economic
interests. Only the desire to acquire
slaves or women, or sheer pugnacity,

impelled them towards it. But interdependence, and the complex, manipulable social
directions of modernity produces interests
that are inescapably in conflict. Conflict
thus generates two important questions.
First, how are the lines of division to be
drawn in this conflict? Second, will
conflict escalate to violence, either total
violence (victory for one side, destruction
for the other) or to the point of fission
within the community?

Marxist theory answers the first question by suggesting that the real conflict
is between social classes defined in terms
of their relationship to the means of
production--not to the means of coercion.
Other conflicts, according to the Marxists,
are superficial, epiphenomenal, or simply
camouflaged or distorted versions of the
"real" conflict. The existence of other
conflicts cannot be denied, and it is also
difficult for the Marxist to deny the
occasional absence of manifest, active
class conflict. Marxist theory holds that
conflicts of interest are nonetheless real
but the participants are not yet conscious
of it. The concept of "consciousness" in
Marxism plays a role similar to "grace"
in Christianity, it accounts for discrepancies between fact and theoretical assertion. At the same time the concept
provides a bridge between the explanatory/
descriptive aspect of theory and its
normative authority. Class conflict is the
key Marxist explanation of history and it
is also a moral imperative. Those who act

in accordance with that concept of history
act in terms of reality (including their
own real interests), while those who act in
other terms merely respond to illusion.
Thus Marxist theory allows for counter-
examples and at the same time accounts for
the failure of people to perceive its truth.
    The major consideration which has
recently dissuaded faith in Marxism is
probably that a given conflict can only be
in the real interest of one class of people
when they succeed in their struggle, they
then recognize that they are better off than
they would have been had the conflict not
occurred, or had not been fought to a conclusion, or not been won. The condition of
victorious proletariats in societies where
victory is said to have been achieved does
not justify emulation by proletarians as
yet unblessed by victory.
    But nationalism is mostly concerned
with the lines of social fission along which
conflict actually occurs.[8] Of course, the
horizontal lines between social classes
envisaged in Marxist theory do appear.
Social strata, defined horizontally, are
mobilized to ensure that national policies
and the central steering mechanism are not
used against them. These "fissions" sometimes transform whole social structures.
The escalation of this conflict is prevented
in those frightening societies which abolish
political competition which they arbitrarily
label redundant, having proclaimed the
elimination of "antagonistic classes." Yet
vertical lines of fission--cultural and

territorial--remain and they are characteristic of nationalistic politics.

Two classes of people are typically
excluded from full citizenship in a modern
society--those who are unable to communicate
in a shared medium at a high level of
literacy, and those who lack a modicum of
technological competence. If they are nonetheless incorporated into the society they
become, at least informally, second class
citizens. Yet, because modern societies
encourage mobility and interdependence they
tend to inhibit inequality--people who are
"less equal" (to use Orwell's phrase) are
now less wiling to accept that status than
in the past when stability somehow compen-
sated for social inferiority or made it
appear "natural." Feudal lords did not
mind being served by filthy peasants or
having their banquet halls warmed up by a
horde of peasants prior to the arrival of
their real guests. Tudor monarchs did not
object to having their beds warmed by a
page prior to turning in.   The modern
privileged classes would consider these
practices unhygienic. The characteristic
lines of fission in modern society follow
the boundaries of the communication media,
or more simply the boundaries of language
and culture. There are boundaries between
the fully enfranchised fluent users of a
medium at the required high level, and
those not so fortunate.

As a result conflict between horizontal
strata, "classes," when it escalates often
terminates in chaos, disintegration and

finally in dictatorship. But conflicts
between social strata can hardly end in
redrawing political frontiers, since that
does not resolve interstratum conflicts.
The threat of physical emigration of a
given stratum may have been feasible in
ancient Rome, but is hardly realistic nowadays. 'Brain drains, the expulsion of an
important proportion of a given class may
seem to constitute an exception, but they
really do not affect the argument.

Escalating conflicts along vertical
frontiers can open other kinds of conflict,
which can be resolved by establishing new
boundaries. Those solutions may seem to be
the least painful and the only permanent way
of terminating conflict. It may be accepted
as such even by those who do not, like
participants in the nationalist vision,
positively desire it as the only legitimate
solution.

It is often said that "nationalism is
strong." But most nationalisms are ineffectual and the majority go down without a
squeak or protest. For every effective
nationalism there are several that are
feeble or dormant. Those that go down are
"objectively" as legitimate as the effective
ones according to the criteria of territoriality, cultural identifiability, shared
roots, and so on. Any historical or ethnographic atlas outlines several possible
nationalities and nationalisms of which only
a few are chosen. That some are chosen is a
sociological necessity, but which ones are
chosen is a matter of historic accident.

The preindustrial world was rich in cultural, religious and ethnic differences
which served as criteria of cultural-
political belonging but the industrial
world only has room for a limited number
of national states. If it is assumed that
the preindustrial world had $\underline{n}$ ethnic groups
and the industrial world has room for $\underline{m}$
national states $\underline{n}$ will be a greater number
than $\underline{m}$ no matter how the counting is done.

In a sense Kedourie put things up-side-
down when he observed:[9]

> To an imperial government the groups
> in a mixed area are all equally
> entitled to some consideration, to
> a national government they are a
> foreign body in the state to be
> either assimilated or rejected.
> The national state claims to treat
> all citizens as equal members of the
> nation, but this fair-sounding
> principle only serves to disguise
> the tyranny of one group over another.
> The nation must be, all its citizens
> must be, animated by the same spirit.
> Differences are divisive and therefore
> treasonable.

It is not so much that nationalism requires homogeneity, as that the objective
social need for homogeneity, for better or
worse, manifests itself as nationalism.
The culture chosen by accident of history
as the medium of homogeneity, then defines
the political "pool" and becomes the object
and symbol of loyalty, rhetoric, and devotion.

Modern egalitarianism and nationalism
are complementary, although modern society
is not necessarily egalitarian in the
distribution of wealth and power. It is,
however, egalitarian in that it requires
its citizens to be of the same kind of
species without deep, overtly symbolized,
caste or estate distinctions. The main
factor making for that kind of equality
is the complex, mobile nature of the
productive process and is in this sense
that homogeneity is used here. Thus
citizens in the modern state become inherently equal and when that equality fails
there is trouble. When friction seizes
on a permanent mark of differentiation
the trouble becomes persistent. When there
are few such marks of differentiation
trouble evaporates.

Traditional societies were different
since they thrived on visible differentiations. When rulers were different from the
ruled, the distinction helped identify them
and habituate the ruled--so all was well.
When the differences ran out they could be
invented. For example, when the supply of
Turkish rulers began to run out in Tunisia
during the nineteenth century Turks were
invented on the spot.[10]

> ... Whenever he saw a young man
> strong of body from the common
> people of the country, he would say
> to him 'Your father was a Turk and
> died without having inscribed your
> name on the register. Why don't
> you come ... and sign your name ....'

The political "pools" must now be politically managed, centralized and effectively governed to assure an easy flow of
fish within them. The cost of the educa-
tional/cultural infrastructure is enormous;
and there technological, administrative and
communication infrastructures are also
needed. The result validates and rein-
forces homogeneity. Since the management
of these services must be conducted in one
language and script, this in turn rein-
forces the importance of the language and
ratifies the personal identification the
irrevocable commitment to it.

In terms of philosophical anthropology
learning to be a human being could at one
time be accomplished on the job. But this
is no longer possible since only certain
human tasks can be learned on the job. A
ballboy may become a tennis player, but
lab attendants cannot become scientists
without additional training. Nowadays,
people can become fully human beings,
citizens in full possession of their civic
rights, only when they complete complex,
formal, and unspecialized training, and
learn the required language.

There is always trouble when homogeneity is imperfect, or where free flow is
impaired and hindered. Either the friction
resulting in the inhibition of free flow
is overcome, or it is not. If it is not,
new "national" boundaries are born. When
this line of fission seizes on deep, ineradicable, at least hard-to-eradicate,
distinguishing signs, the boundaries are

ultimately confirmed and become engrained.

The inhibition of movement during early industrialization created a fission between the active entrepreneurial class and the alienated, passive and culturally disfranchised proletariat. This "class struggle" was eroded when movement across the boundary became easy. Such boundaries however become firm when they are correlated with "ethnic" distinctions. The differential access to power may aggravate differences in access to the modern economy (e.g., in East European peasant nations) when rulers were economically and politically privileged or it may be inversely related (as in the case of the diaspora nationalism of economically effective but politically undominant groups). There are several kinds of nationalism, but that does not contradict the issues involved in understanding national irredentism.[11]

Accordingly, the theory of Marxism needs to be stood on its head. National struggle is not a class struggle which failed, of itself, to reach consciousness. It is instead merely a potential national irredentism which fails to take off for lack of good distinguishing marks.

The theory outlined here hypothesizes the interrelationship of three distinctive boundaries:

1. The boundary between the educated and uneducated. What is meant by this is a boundary between people who are and are not culturally enfranchised in industrial life. That enfranchisement can only be

fully conferred by a modern educational
system.

    2. The boundary between "cultures" is
difficult to define in a way which is
neither nebulous nor circular, because of
the variety of ways that "cultures" become
differentiated. People of different "cultures" recognize each other as being of a
different "kind," and recognize fellow-
members of their culture as being similar.
It is impossible to give a neutral,
universally usable definition of cultural
differentiation because the notion of what
is a "kind" of human being is internal to
various cultures, and that notion varies
from one culture to another. The most important cultural traits of concern here
are those which aid or inhibit easy
communication, most commonly language in
the literal sense. Yet, it is sometimes
more important that people refer to the
same things even if they do it in phoneti-
cally different words. This is the sense
in which fellow Hindus are "of the same
culture," even when one speaks Hindi and
the other Bengali. Genetic differences,
even when culturally irrelevant can become distinguishing marks. If most members
of culture A are blue and those of culture
B green, then people with green skins will
not be admitted as "true A," no matter how
well they internalize the phonetic, conceptual, or behavioral aspects of culture A.
The problem of definition is further complicated because differences (castes, estates)
held to be profound between "kinds" of human

beings often exist inside one culture.

These problems of definition lack a formal solution, because cultural differences are internal to cultures and cannot be defined externally and neutrally. But this does not matter much because in practice it is not too difficult to tell one culture from another and because ethnographic atlases are available. In any case the theory articulated here does not require that the concept of "cultural boundaries" be applicable without ambiguity. The data, in any case, contribute to understanding the situation in which nationalism emerges and brings with it the ambiguity of the cultural material on which nationalism depends. The theory only requires that the concept be applicable, without too much dissent, to an identification of cultures and their carriers.

At the risk of saying the obvious, the distinctions between the boundaries established by education (or its lack), and those of culture, are <u>not</u> the same. But what follows when they overlap is crucial to the theory of nationalism. The boundary between the educated; uneducated occurs in acute form only in early industrial societies. Mature industrial societies incorporate the great majority of their populations in one education-mediated, citizenship-conferring culture. Pre-industrial societies, of course, often have a similar boundary between the educated and those who are not--e.g., between the clerics and the laity--but that usually occurs under

conditions of relative stability, and few
people are impelled to try and cross it.
Under those conditions that boundary does
not generate tension, on the contrary, it
aids in maintaining stability.

3. The boundary between power holders
and "the Rest." (The distinction between
officeholders and those eligible for office
does not matter.) This boundary exists in
most, but not all, agrarian societies. It
is possible to have a well-developed agriculture without a centralized state. However, this boundary is common to all
industrial societies.

Territorial boundaries between political units are implied by strong, pervasive
states. Not all agrarian societies are
centralized states and those that are often
have ill-defined and ambiguous territorial
limits. Border areas may be only nominally
subject to the center. Outlying areas may
be taxed only when royal processions pass
through. Administrative and legal functions may be delegated to local power
holders or assemblies. Boundaries may be
hazy, indescribably complex and tortuous,
hence ineffectual. Some maps of medieval
Europe make ordinary jigsaw puzzles look
like simple grids in comparison. There are
good reasons for this diversity, for when
much of economic and social life is contained within local units, and when the central
state's efforts to monopolize legitimate
violence are relatively feeble, boundaries
do not matter much.

The industrial state, in contrast, has precise boundaries. Any failure to enforce them is exceptional and is considered scandalous. The Chinese once built a road in territory claimed by India without the Indian government even noticing, and this was embarrassing and unflattering to Indian officials. Industrial states tend to effectively control the territories they claim. Government officials must communicate with their administrators, who in turn communicate with the citizens, and administration generally operates in one linguistic medium. The governments of industrial states do their best to ensure effective communications with their populations by fostering effective and linguistically homogeneous education. Consequently universal primary education is implemented with great seriousness. The people receive this particular attention eagerly. After all, education will fit people for places within the bureaucracy. The essence of national sovereignty is to have a national system of education and a national medium of communication.

These concepts are basic to the theory outlined in this essay and articulated in the following propositions:

Proposition 1: Growing, innovative economies require occupational mobility. Moreover, the complexity of technical operations in those societies involves a massive number of encounters between people in which significant information and instructions are passed on. Many of those

encounters are brief and "once-only" so the
resulting communication cannot be achieved
by the kind of tacit understanding conveyed
by grunts between family members. The
technical level of industrial society often
requires complex messages.

From this it follows that the medium
of communication and the level of proficien-
cy of its users is important. Further
there will be tension between any two
populations unable to communicate easily
because of a gap between their respective
cultures.

Proposition 2: Early industrial
societies are characterized by severe gaps
in standards of living, and in moral
participation in effective citizenship
between the class of people fully incorporated in the new economy and those drawn
into it from an agrarian environment. In
liberal societies the culturally incorporated and privileged class will "own" the
means of production and the rest will be
poor. Contrary to Marx who thought this
was the crucial differentia this theory
holds that cultural incorporation is really
the crucial factor, although prior wealth
may be its cause.

Class differences (in the Marxist
sense) do not, of themselves, lead to permanent conflict but class differences
defined in terms of cultural incorporation
or its absence when combined with a pre-
existing cultural boundary, do lead to deep
and often permanent conflicts. Nationalism
is not class conflict that has failed to

reach consciousness, but class conflict is national conflict that has failed to take off for lack of deep cultural, symbolic differentiae.

All industrial and industrializing societies are governed by a central authority, so there is no point in envisaging a confrontation between two uncentralized (and in that sense powerless) communities. There is no industry in a state of nature. Communal hatreds and conflict between two communities in which neither has better access to central authority than the other are ignored here to simplify the argument. If neither wishes to secede the result cannot be called conflict or "nationalism." If one or both secedes the resulting conflict is between the seceding community(ies) and the central power and can be explained in terms of one of the other alternatives.

In our scheme we have two columns:
Power holders versus Those with less power
Into this opposition, _four_ possibilities must be fed covering the alternative conceivable distribution of possessors and nonpossessors of industrially usable education:

Possessors	Nonpossessors
Possessors	Possessors
Nonpossessors	Possessors
Nonpossessors	Nonpossessors

This distinction is quite independent of differences in "culture." We must now also feed in the possibility of the

presence or absence of a cultural boundary.
This will be done by means of the letters A
and B. If, in the same line, the same
letter appears, this indicates that the two
groups are of the "same culture;" if different letters are used the opposite is the
case.
The complete diagram now is:

```
     Power holders      Those holding less power
       Possessors (educ)      Nonpossessors
   1      A                      A     marxist case
   2      A                      B     nationalism E Eur
       Possessors             Possessors
   3      A                      A     harmony
   4      A                      B     mild nationalism W Eur
   Nonpossessors             Possessors
   5      A                      A     colonial homogeneity
   6      A                      B     extreme nat'y scapegoating
   Nonpossessors             Nonpossessors
   7      A                      A     harmony
   8      A                      B     egalitarian deprivation
```

Line 1 depicts the classical Marxian case
in which there is no radical cultural
cleavage. The cleavage is between
possessors of both education and power,
and those with access to neither. (Marxism
holds that each of these forms of privileged access depends on a relationship to
the means of production, which is both
obscure and questionable, and that the
cleavage will aggravate over time, which
is false.)
     Line 2 represents a classical emergence
of nationalism in which cultural differentiation may take a variety of forms--

linguistic or religious. The differentia
may be made permanent, by skin color or
geographic distance. By superimposing these
differences on the cleavage generated by
early industrialism, a powerful form of
nationalism is born.

Line 3 depicts a nonnationalist situation with no radical cultural differences,
and no radical difference with respect to
ease of access to modern education. In this
case some people will have more power than
others but there is no cultural or educational way of identifying them. This case
describes any developed industrial state
with no nationalist problem.

Line 4 represents the relatively bland
West European nationalisms of the nineteenth century, in which two identifiable
cultures faced each other; the members of
each had access to modern economies, the
literacy rates were roughly equal, and
each culture had a recognized script and
an educational infrastructure. The difference in this kind of nationalism lies in
access to power, which could guarantee the
development of a unified single-culture
state and protect the educational apparatus.
The unification-nationalisms of Germany and
Italy in which disunity or actual subjec-
tion meant less power exemplifies this
case, though neither Italian nor German
cultures, as such, were significantly at a
disadvantage.

The difference between lines 2 and 4
corresponds to the late Professor John
Plamenatz's typology of Western and Eastern

nationalisms. By "Western," he referred to
the relatively benigh nationalisms of the
Italians and Germans in the nineteenth
century. "Western" nationalism generally
possessed a viable culture, equal to opposing culture, and merely needed to attain
equality of power and a state machine
capable of protecting and promoting that
culture, while being reasonably coextensive
territorially with it. Plamenatz believed
that "Western" nationalisms were relatively
tolerant and that they were not actually
obliged to invent and impose a culture on
populations previously endowed with
rudimentary and unhomogeneous peasant cultures.[12] These nationalisms later became
nasty only by accident rather than necessity. In contrast Plamenatz feared that the
"Eastern" nationalisms were doomed to
authoritarianism because of the arduous
cultural engineering they were obliged to
undertake. The "Western" nationalisms
merely needed to create state machines to
protect and perpetuate a viable preexisting
culture; the "Eastern" first had to acquire
a state and then impose a new culture.
There is merit in Plamenatz's distinction.

The Plamenatz typology notably ignores
the important alternative schematized in
line 6. That situation depicts two distinct
cultures that coexist, but one has more
political power, while the other, in
contrast, has better access to the kind of
education that permits modern economic
or bureaucratic activity. This situation
arises when a minoritarian or politically

274

subject culture is well equipped and superi-
or to the political rulers educationally
or when it enjoys the advantages of commercial activity, urban living, a high valua-
tion of literacy and learning, or a
combination of these or similar factors at
the start of the race to modernity. This
situation is common in traditional societies, since it is often advantageous for
rulers to encourage, or tolerate, commerce
among politically impotent and excluded
minorities. The accumulation of wealth by
them is less dangerous than it would be in
the hands of equals who could transmute
wealth into power and thus become rivals.
It is also easier to tax or confiscate the
wealth of the politically impotent.
Traders and Palace Guards in traditional
societies are often foreigners, and for the
same reason. (This is far more crucial
than the theoretical prohibitions of usury.)
This pattern is encouraged or initiated
during colonial periods, when less privileged strata of the population may have
more incentive to try their hand at the newly available learning, as for example the
Jews, Greeks, Armenians, overseas Chinese
and Indians, or Ibos.

Elie Kedourie is of course right when
he observes that:[13]

... Greek and Armenian nationalism
arose among populations which were
generally more prosperous and
better able to understand the wealth-
generating economies of modern Europe
than their Ottoman Muslim overlords
....

But the present theory does not require all
nationalists to be economically-culturally
at a disadvantage. Political disadvantage
will do just as well, or better. In a
traditional context, political disfranchise-
ment may be a positive advantage in economic activity; in a modern situation, in which
the entire population becomes mobile and
takes part in economic competition (instead
of being tied to locality and agrarian production) it becomes disastrous. Greater
wealth held by an identifiable community
(i.e., a culturally distinct one) becomes
a permanent provocation, incitement to
envy, and a political temptation. Moreover, the state no longer has much incentive
to protect it, and has a great deal of
incentive to buy the good will of the
envious majority by allowing, encouraging,
and taking part in spoliation of this
minority, which is faced in turn with only
two alternatives--to try and dissolve in
the majority and become culturally in-
distinguishable, or to acquire its own
territory and its own protective state
machine.
    Line 1 describes the classical class
conflict envisaged by Marx but line 5
characterizes the typical revolutionary
situation in Third World countries which
happen to be culturally homogeneous (either
through the historical accident of cultural
unity, or because the only economically
significant culture is the one left behind
by a colonial power, because local vernaculars are too fragmented, devoid of script

or literature, etc.). Here, within a culturally more or less continuous population
the old power holders are less able to
operate a modern division of labor than are
some other segments of the population which
may have been created by the old elite itself (e.g., in providing a modern education
for the officers of crack units of the Army,
so that the first rising is Decembrist in
style, as was the case both in Russia and
in Abyssinia).

The cases where there is no difference
of culture (lines 1, 3, 5, 7) are negative
from the viewpoint of a theory of nationalism. So are lines 7 and 8, where there is
equality in the society from the viewpoint
of access to modernity, no segment having
greater access than any other, none of them
having much. Thus, the situation in line 7
is excluded twice over. Line 8 exemplifies
a kind of traditional conflict between
communities, but does not resemble real
nationalism. The varieties of nationalism
are exemplified by lines 2, 4, and 6:
Eastern (Habsburg), Western (unifactory)
and Diaspora nationalism.

The schematic exposition presented
here is explanatory, not demonstrative.
It is meant to clarify how alternatives are
generated on its own, but it proves nothing.
It is possibly tautological. A typology
(which is all it is) does not establish
that anything historically concrete actually
falls under it. What it excludes it excludes by definition, rather than because
it does not exist. Nevertheless, this

schema is a useful depiction of how the
alternatives, and various patterns of nonnationalist political situations are
generated in the interplay of a limited
number of contrasts. The theory is argued
in the preceding prose, and not in the
schema itself; and it will only stand and
fall if the historical evidence fits or dis-
proves it.

CHAPTER VII

ECONOMIC AND SOCIAL DIFFERENTIATION
AND ETHNICITY

by

Julius Rezler

This paper examines the socioeconomic
differences of ethnic groups in Eastern
Europe during the twentieth century, and
identifies the political, economic and
social factors responsible for those differences. A "differentiation" involves the
study of relationships between at least two
groups related to each other. Accordingly,
this inquiry focuses on the economic and
social relationships of ethnic groups in
Eastern Europe during that period.
    The ethnic group's economic level and
social status are significant indicators
of its position in society or outside of it.
These indicators are important since they
reflect an ethnic group's economic efforts
and social striving as well as the effects
of governmental and noneconomic factors on
their material well-being.
    No other region in our turbulent world
offers a more fruitful opportunity for the
scrutiny of economic and social changes
affecting ethnic groups than Eastern Europe.
For seventy-five years Eastern Europe has
experienced political and economic upheavals

279

of extraordinary magnitude. The multiethnic character of the area has had a far-
reaching even fatal impact on ethnic groups.
The major changes in the ethnic composition
of the countries of Eastern Europe offers
an ideal situation for analysis.

This paper is divided into two parts.
The first part is a conceptual framework
which outlines the historical, political
and economic factors which have determined
the relative economic and social position
of ethnic groups. The second part applies
this conceptual framework to an analysis of
economic and social differences among
ethnic groups in European states during
three consecutive periods.

In the following analysis the term
"ethnic group" is defined as a distinct
social group whose members are identified
by (1) a group consciousness to which all
members owe supreme loyalty,[1] (2) a
distinct culture, a common history, language and literature, (3) their physical
connection to a territory.[2]

The term "social class" is used to
denote a socioeconomic group united by
common economic interests based on the
function performed in the production process, identified by a similar ideology,
income or consumption level.[3] Professor
Brass (Chapter I) relates ethnic groups
to social class and suggests that "ethnicity
is an alternative form of social organization...." The validity of this proposition is questionable since structurally
ethnic groups are related horizontally in a

legal juxtaposition. Classes on the other
hand are vertically differentiated. Ethnic
differences supersede class differences in
Eastern Europe because of a high degree of
ethnic consciousness. Ethnic consciousness
usually prevails over class identity,
particularly when an ethnic group feels
threatened by another ethnic group.

The conceptual framework is a three-
dimensional model with a spatial dimension,
a time dimension encompassing a system of
political, economic, and social parameters.

The spatial dimension is predetermined
by the scope of the topic. The geographical
area examined includes Eastern Europe and
the territories of Bulgaria, Czechoslovakia,
Hungary, Poland, Romania and Yugoslavia in
particular. Albania was intentionally
omitted although some experts consider it
to be part of Eastern Europe. It is a
single ethnic state and has not experienced
the same problem as the other states.

The territorial concept of Eastern
Europe has changed during the past seventy-
five years. The territories which are now
integral parts of the countries in Eastern
Europe, belonged partly or wholly to Central
European states such as Austria-Hungary and
Germany prior to World War I. After 1921
Eastern Europe (as defined in this chapter)
moved eastward due to the annexation of
Russian territories by Poland and Romania
authorized by the Paris peace treaties.
After World War II, the territories of
Eastern Europe expanded westward again with
the annexation of East-Poland, Czechoslovak

Ruthenia, Romanian Bessarabia by the Soviet Union, and because Poland assumed control of former German territories.

This study covers the first three quarters of this century. With the exception of a few references to earlier events of importance because the socioeconomic situation of ethnic groups in Eastern Europe during the second half of the nineteenth century was not significantly different from that in the first eighteen years of the twentieth century. The first three quarters of this century, however, were split by major events into distinctly different historical periods. The contemporary history and interrelationship of ethnic groups in Eastern Europe are distinguished by major, sometimes revolutionary, changes in the political arrangements and ethnic composition of the region.

The first period between the turn of the century and the conclusion of World War I was static and serves as a bench mark to measure later changes. The second period began at the end of World War I and concludes at the end of World War II in 1944-45. The third period encompasses the years from the end of World War II to the present.

The three periods encompass seventy-five years but the major changes in the political, economic and social relationships of ethnic groups in Eastern Europe were compressed within a period of approximately thirty years, between 1918 and 1948. The three periods followed consecutively but the economic and class differentiation of the major ethnic groups did not establish identifiable trends during that period. The major international upheavals which occurred in that era destroyed interethnic relations that were developed in previous periods. Consequently each period must be considered separately. Nonetheless the ethnic groups that inhabited the area continued to exist. Even this connection was broken as some ethnic groups were victimized by expulsion, deportation (Germans, Hungarians), and extermination (Jews). As a result, the area's ethnic makeup was altered particularly after the two great wars.

The factors that affected the economic and social positions of the ethnic groups need to be identified to establish another framework for study. It is emphasized that the socioeconomic status of ethnic groups is not determined solely by such economic and social factors as income and occupational structure. The socioeconomic status of ethnic groups is complex and is affected by several factors: (1) demographic, (2) economic, and (3) political.

The size of an ethnic group related to the total population of a state is the primary demographic factor that affects its economic position. The relative size of an ethnic group may influence political processes which, in turn, relate to its economic well-being. The most important demographic consideration is whether a given ethnic group constitutes a majority of the population of a state or whether it has minority status. The following

discussion of ethnic groups is therefore
based on survey data indicating the absolute size and relative share of ethnic
groups in the several states of Eastern
Europe during the three periods.

The purely economic factors examined
here include the economic indicators, such
as income and consumption, that measure
the relative economic position of ethnic
groups, as distinguished from those factors
that cause changes in their economic level.
The latter factors include the general
developmental level of the state; the
distribution of the ethnic group in each
economic sector and occupational category;
the type of settlement where a majority of
each ethnic group resides; and its opportunity to participate in the economic development of its country.

The general economic level of a state
affects the absolute economic level of its
ethnic groups. In highly developed countries, even minority groups may acquire
economic positions superior to majority
groups in economically less developed
countries. For example, the economic level
of Hungarian farmers in Czechoslovakia was
higher than that of farmers in Hungary
during the interwar period.

The distribution of ethnic groups in
the major occupational categories has a
considerable effect on their aggregate
incomes. When a majority is concentrated
in lower occupational categories, the overall income of the whole group is depressed.
Similarly, when a majority is gainfully

employed in less productive economic sectors
that yield incomes below the national average, the total and average incomes of the
group are reduced. The income level of a
group also depends on its distribution
among the types of major settlements. The
average income in cities and towns typically
exceeds the average in rural areas, and the
quality of life is usually higher in the
cities. Finally, the access of ethnic
groups to opportunities created by economic
development such as industrialization, has
a major bearing on their potential income
level and living standards.

The economic level, however, is determined by a group's own efforts, and by the
political and economic system of the state
in which the ethnic group must operate.
Therefore in determining the relative social
and economic position of a group, political
factors are as important as economic factors. Noneconomic factors affected the
economic level of ethnic groups more decisively than purely economic ones in certain
time periods.

The various branches of government,
particularly the legislative and executive,
have shaped the economic destinies of ethnic
groups in Eastern Europe. The constitutions
and laws either expand or curtail the economic rights and opportunities of ethnic
groups. The interpretation and administration of laws by the executive branch often
modifies the original intent, for or
against,the interests of the ethnic groups.
Government policies often make public

service jobs, the single largest source of
employment in Eastern Europe, accessible or
unavailable to members of certain ethnic
groups. The civil service represents a
stable source of income, a share of political power, and the opportunity to control
and influence others. In socialist states,
where the population is ethnically varied
and the government is controlled by a
majority group, the quantity and quality of
job opportunities available to the minorities may be severely limited.

Government educational policies may
also affect the economic opportunities of
minority ethnic groups particularly in
states where only public education is permitted. There is a well-known correlation
between educational level, occupational
distribution, and size of income. Ethnic
groups which resist assimilation by a
majority may have access to high-level
occupations and corresponding incomes only
when educational opportunities are available
in their own language.

Thus the impact of governmental policies and administration on the relative
economic level of ethnic groups depends on
the political system (democracy - totali-
tarianism); the economic system (market
economy - planned economy); and the government's ideology with regard to nationalities
(tolerance - chauvinism). Those conditions
determine the place of an ethnic group within the power structure of a state, and its
relative economic level and social status.

The political and economic rights of
an ethnic minority in one country, may be
influenced by another state ruled by the
same ethnic group. For example, the power
of Nazi Germany during the 1930s temporarily
improved the position of German ethnic
groups in the countries of Eastern Europe.
The foregoing discussion deals primarily with the causes of economic differentiation among ethnic groups, but those causes
also help to explain social differentiations
in contemporary societies where social
status and economic level are closely interrelated. In East Europe however, historical
factors, such as birth and social origin,
have also affected the process of social
differentiation among ethnic groups. The
effect of historical factors has varied
considerably in the three time periods under
discussion. Social and class origins probably played an important role in establishing a social status until the end of World
War II but since then those factors either
do not matter, or they have an adverse
effect on the individual's status.

Economic and Social Differentiations in
Eastern Europe

SOCIOECONOMIC STATUS OF ETHNIC
GROUPS FROM 1900-1918

Before World War I, the territories that
today comprise Eastern Europe were parts
of the Austro-Hungarian Monarchy, Germany,
Romania, Bulgaria and Serbia. Only three
of the five pre-1918 components of modern
Eastern Europe, Austria-Hungary, Bulgaria
and Germany were multiethnic states, while
Romania and Serbia were single ethnic
states.

Germany contained two major ethnic
groups. The Germans constituted about
92 percent of the population, and the Poles
(5 percent) were included as a result of
the partition of Poland among Prussia,
Austria and Russia in the eighteenth century. Bulgaria's ethnic pattern was more
complex. There Bulgarians comprised 80 percent of the population, but there were
three other distinct groups: Romanians in
Dobrudga, Macedonians in North-Bulgaria,
and Turks in South-Bulgaria. Of the three
multiethnic states only Austria-Hungary
lacked an ethnic group which constituted
an absolute majority. Austria-Hungary's
ethnic composition was kaleidoscopic and
there were eleven ethnic groups which
numbered over one million according to the
1910 census, Germans 23.9 percent, Hungarians 20.2 percent, Czechs 12.6 percent,
Poles 10.0 percent, Ukrainians 7.9 percent,
Romanians 6.4 percent, Croats 5.3 percent,

Serbs 3.8 percent, Slovaks 3.8 percent, Slovenes 2.6 percent, and Italians 2.0 percent.[4]

The Habsburg Empire's two basic components provide an ethnic picture different from that of the Empire as a whole. According to the 1910 census, 30.5 million people in the Austrian half of the Monarchy were divided between the following major ethnic groups: Germans 34 percent, Czechs 21 percent, Poles 18 percent, Ukrainians 11 percent, Slovenes 4.4 percent, Italians 3.6 percent. The 18.3 million people living in the Hungarian half of the Monarchy (without Croatia) were composed of the following ethnic groups: Hungarians 54.5 percent, Romanians 16.1 percent, Slovaks 10.7 percent, Germans 10.4 percent, Serbs 2.5 percent, Ukrainians (Ruthens) 2.5 percent.

The economic differences among the major ethnic groups from 1900 to 1918 was determined primarily by: (1) the general economic level of the state in which a particular ethnic group resided, (2) that group's majority or minority status, and (3) the economic resources of the area inhabited by the ethnic group. Prior to 1918, governments had an indirect effect on the relative economic position of ethnic groups.

1. The varying economic development of the states was primarily responsible for economic differentiations among the major ethnic groups prior to 1918. Germany had attained the highest developmental level, followed by Austria and Hungary. The

remaining states remained at the lowest
economical levels in Europe.

The importance of economic development
is exemplified by the differences experienced by Polish ethnic groups residing in
three states. The Poles living in Germany
enjoyed economic advantages easily surpass-
ing those of Poles who were citizens of
Austria and Russia. The decisive role
played by economic development in determining the status of ethnic groups is
further verified by noting that ethnic
groups constituting a minority in states
with a relatively well-developed system
enjoyed higher economic status than the
same groups in the majority in less developed states. The Romanians in Hungary and
in Romania prior to 1918 are a case in
point. Fischer-Galati observed that

> Rejection of the Rumanians' na-
> tional aspirations by the Austro-
> Hungarian political oligarchy did
> not prevent the gradual evolution
> of an affluent middle class ...
> and a reasonably prosperous peas-
> antry. They enjoyed a much higher
> standard of living than those in
> old Rumania.[5]

South Slavs living in Austria were similarly
advantaged in relation to their ethnic
relatives who constituted a ruling majority
in pre-1918 Serbia.

2. The majority or minority status of
ethnic groups constituted a second major
determinant of relative economic position
prior to 1918. The size of the group in

relation to the population as a whole
generally decided whether a particular
ethnic group was above or below the average
economic level in the country in which it
resided. The size of the ethnic group
affected three important aspects of its
economic position: (1) the share of the
ethnic group in the wealth and natural resources of the country, (2) the distribution of the group among the various sectors
of the economy, and (3) the distribution of
the group among major occupational categories.

a. Majority ethnic groups gained
control over most of the economic resources
of the multiethnic states and, therefore,
succeeded in attaining an above average
economic position compared to the minority
ethnic groups. Large estates mainly owned
by German landlords in the Polish territories annexed by Germany represented 42
percent of the total agricultural area, yet
the Poles who constituted more than 90 percent of the population owned less than 60
percent of the land.[6] According to the 1910
census in Hungary, 91.5 percent of the 1,657
large estates (over 1,400 acres), representing about 30 percent of the total agricultural area, were owned by ethnic Hungarians.
They also owned 80.5 percent of the medium-
sized estates (between 280 and 1,400 acres).
The average size of the estates was directly
correlated with the number of ethnic Hungarian owners--i.e., there were fewer
Hungarian owners of estates, only 39 percent of the owners of dwarf holdings (7

292

acres and below) were Hungarian.

b. The majority ethnic groups in the multiethnic states generally attained a larger than proportionate share of the available jobs in the more productive and better paying economic sectors (manufacturing, trade, finance) and a smaller share of jobs in the less productive and less rewarding economic sectors (agriculture, forestry, construction). Since the more productive sectors of the economy created higher wages than employment in the less productive sectors, more of the individual members of the majority groups had a larger than average income. Members of the minority groups had proportionately lower incomes. The distribution of ethnic groups among the major economic sectors in pre-1918 Hungary illustrates the point. (See Table 3.)

With the exception of the German minority which enjoyed privileged status in Hungary, all the other minority groups had higher than average shares of the less productive sectors and less than a proportionate share of the more productive sectors. Accordingly, the average income of Romanians, Slovaks, Serbs and Ukrainians was adversely affected.

c. The distribution of ethnic groups among major occupational categories similarly effected their economic levels. Members of comparable occupations drew the same or similar incomes regardless of ethnic origin, but the majority ethnic groups generally enjoyed larger than proportionate

Table 3
Percent Distribution of Ethnic Groups in the
Hungarian Economy (1910)

	Hungarians	Germans	Slovaks	Romanians	Ukrainians	Serbs
Agriculture and Forestry	51.79	47.21	69.13	84.32	87.10	81.54
Manufacturing and Mining	21.23	27.60	16.00	6.41	4.18	7.84
Trade	4.71	5.40	1.26	0.64	0.18	2.17
Transportation	3.60	1.56	1.18	0.64	0.49	0.67
Government	4.73	2.46	0.88	1.18	0.48	1.89
Service	5.99	4.24	4.60	2.22	2.86	0.83
Others	7.95	11.53	6.95	4.59	4.71	5.06

Source: Dr. László Katus. Der Donauraum und seine Völker, Vol. III, Oesterreichische Akademie der Wissenschaften, Vienna (under publication).

shares of the higher ranking and better paying occupations, and the minority ethnic
groups obtained more than proportionate
shares of jobs at the lower end of the occupational ladder. Consequently, income
level of the majority groups exceeded the
average prevailing in the economy of the
respective multiethnic states while the
relative economic level of minority groups
were below the national averages. The
distribution of ethnic groups among the
major occupational categories in pre-1918
Hungary exemplifies the above point. (See
Table 4.)

The position of ethnic groups shown by
the data deviates from our model because of
the disproportionate share of Germans in
the higher ranking occupations. Germans
were a minority ethnic group in pre-1918
Hungary, but they escaped the economic
disadvantages of other minority groups because of their privileged status in the
Monarchy. Therefore they enjoyed a greater
share in most higher ranking occupations
than the Hungarians who constituted the
majority ethnic group. This anomaly dis-
appears when the percentage of Hungarians
in each occupational category is compared
to that of non-German minorities. The
Hungarians enjoyed a larger share of the
more prestigious and better paying occupations, while the non-German minorities
had a lesser share except that there was a
greater percentage of Hungarians working
in agriculture. Agriculture had the lowest
average income, yet there were more

Table 4

Occupational Distribution of Ethnic Groups in Hungary in 1910
(in the percentage of the respective ethnic group)

Occupation	Hungarians	Germans	Slovaks	Romanians	Ukrainians	Serbs
Owners and managers of estates over 140 acres	0.52	0.48	0.11	0.12	0.06	0.34
Owners of farms below 140 acres	27.89	35.39	48.10	60.00	61.50	66.29
Owners and self-employed persons in industry and trade	13.83	21.39	8.32	4.06	2.18	6.18

296

Table 4 (Continued)

Occupation	Hungarians	Germans	Slovaks	Romanians	Ukrainians	Serbs
Profes-sional and clerical employees	5.96	3.60	0.53	1.23	0.32	1.79
Agricul-tural workers	27.63	15.86	25.47	26.76	24.62	17.93
Non-agri-cultural workers	16.23	17.69	12.77	4.40	3.04	3.94
Service	4.59	3.28	2.82	1.42	1.43	1.25
Others	3.46	2.40	1.88	2.25	1.85	1.85

Source: Dr. László Katus. Der Donauraum und seine Völker, Vol. III, Oesterreichische Akademie der Wissenschaften, Vienna (under publication).

Hungarians engaged in that activity despite
their status as a majority group.

3. Significant differences also occur
when the relative economic levels of minority ethnic groups, residing in the same
country, are compared. Those differences
can be explained in terms of historical
developments and availability of the
natural resources in the regions inhabited.
The experience of the five main minority
groups in pre-1918 Hungary illustrates those
differences.

Historically the Slovaks were subju-
gated by the Hungarians following their
occupation of Hungarian territory in the
ninth century. That subjugation permanently
affected the economic position of Slovaks
in comparison to the four other groups
which later settled in Hungary under different circumstances. Most Germans and Romanians, and the Serbs, settled in former
Hungarian territories incident to the Turkish occupation of the southern half of
Hungary. Those large areas, previously
inhabited by ethnic Hungarians, were de-
populated due to almost uninterrupted wars
for 150 years, and because of the continuous
Turkish incursions which decimated the
Hungarian population to obtain slaves and
recruits for the army. Most of the Germans and Serbs were settled by the Habsburg
monarchs in the devastated territories of
Hungary regained from the Turks and both
groups enjoyed the protection and support
of the Austrian emperors long enough to
become established as economically viable

in their respective territories.

The Germans and Serbs were also favored
by the wealth of natural resources in their
new homelands, and by their proximity to
important markets.[7] In contrast, the
Romanians, Slovaks and Ukrainians lived in
mountainous areas on mostly barren lands
with poor transportation. Prior to the
period of industrialization those lands
were considered poor in natural resources,
so those three ethnic groups existed at an
economic level far below that of the Germans and Serbs.

The economic differentiation among
ethnic groups in the Austrian half of the
Monarchy was less extreme than that in
Hungary. In Austria the Germans, Czechs
and Slovenians enjoyed similar standards
of living. The economic level of the Poles
was considerably lower than that of the
three other groups.

The governments of Eastern European
countries had the least impact on the
relative economic position of ethnic groups
during the pre-1918 period because political
democracy mostly prevailed in Germany and
Austria-Hungary and the minority ethnic
groups were represented in the legislative
assemblies of those states. In the territories comprising the present Eastern
Europe, before 1918, ethnic groups possessed
more local autonomy than in the interwar
period, or in the period following World
War II. As a result of that local autonomy
minority ethnic groups were protected
against assimilation by majority groups.

The pre-1918 economic system was characterized by laissez-faire so the governments generally refrained from interfering
in the economic relations and activities
of its citizens. The adherence to the
doctrine prevented governments from using
economic power to oppress minority ethnic
groups and permitted such groups to utilize
their resources, meager as they may have
been, to full advantage. The spirit of this
era was exemplified in Transylvania (formerly a province of Hungary) where banks
residing in Romania purchased lands from
impoverished Hungarian gentry for distribution among Transylvanian Romanians without
interference on the part of the Hungarian
government. That kind of transaction was
impossible after World War I.
        Even prior to 1918 governments initi-
ated economic policies to advance industrialization, but those policies were not
intended to destroy ethnic minorities.
The Hungarian industrial policy before World
War I is a case in point. Industries were
developed with government subsidies wherever
natural resources were found regardless of
ethnic considerations. As a result, industrial establishments were built in mountainous regions populated mainly by minorities.
"The presence of abundant resources ...
automatically designed Slovakia as the chief
centre for Hungary's primary industry....
The highest subsidies went to non-Magyar
counties."[8]
        The government educational policies in
the multiethnic states did, however,

adversely affect economic levels of ethnic minorities in the pre-1918 era. With few exceptions, secondary and university education was conducted in the language of the majority ethnic group, particularly in Hungary and Bulgaria. Jobs in government service and the professions required at least a secondary education and since the minority ethnic groups lacked access to higher education in their own language their economic development and income levels were retarded. There were exceptions in the Austrian half of the Monarchy where Czechs and Poles had access to higher education in their own languages. Poles were also free to use their language in public administration and in schools in Russia and, to lesser extent, in Germany.

Social differentiation among the ethnic groups of Eastern Europe was primarily determined by their relative economic status in the pre-1918 period. In addition economic factors, social factors (such as the prestige of the respective ethnic group), birth and origin, contributed to social differentiation among the ethnic groups. The structure of the East European societies prior to 1918 consisted of: an upper class (primarily aristocrats); an upper middle class (landed gentry, wealthy industrialists and bankers, high ranking government officials); a middle class (middle layer of government officials, including army officers, professionals, nongentry owners of medium-sized estates, managers of business enterprises); a lower middle class (clerical

staff of government, prosperous freeholding
peasants, owners of small industrial and
trade enterprises, upper level of skilled
workers); and the lowest social class (semiskilled and unskilled industrial workers,
small landholders, agricultural laborers).

In Germany, the German and Polish ethnic groups were led by their own aristocracies. Differences in their economic
levels, placed a larger share of the German
ethnic group in the upper middle and the
middle classes, and more Poles were to be
found in the lower middle class and the
proletariat.

There were considerable differences in
the pattern of social stratification within
the Austro-Hungarian Monarchy. In the
Austrian part, the stratification of Germans, Czechs and, to lesser extent, of the
Slovenians showed a similar pattern. There
was no significant difference in the distribution of these ethnic groups among the
major social classes. Yet the Austrian
Poles and particularly the Romanians living
in Bukovina, tended to be found toward the
lower end of the class structure. In
Austria there were more Poles and Romanians
in the proletariat than any of the other
ethnic groups.

There were greater differences in the
social structure of the various ethnic
groups in Hungary. Aristocrats of Hungarian
and German origin formed the upper class.
The upper middle class consisted mainly of
Hungarians (government officials, landed
gentry) and Hungarian Jews (owners of large

business enterprises), and to lesser extent,
of Germans. Few members of the other ethnic
groups achieved upper middle class status in
pre-1918 Hungary. There was a larger proportion of Hungarians and Germans in the
middle class than their share of total
population. The other ethnic groups were
underrepresented in the middle and lower
middle classes (except for the Serbs in
Southern Hungary) and the great masses of
Slovaks, Romanians and Ukrainians were to
be found in the agricultural proletariat.

The stratification of ethnic groups,
however, varied in the major regions of
Hungary. Hungarians generally constituted
a majority of the middle class in the
country as a whole, but there was almost no
established Hungarian middle class in
Southern Hungary. Hungarians formed the
upper and upper middle classes, separated
from the majority of Hungarians, who were
mostly laborers and dwarf landholders
considerably lower in social status than
the prosperous Germans and Serb peasants.[9]

Social stratification in Transylvania
before 1918 was patterned on nationality.
Hungarians and Hungarian speaking Jews made
up the middle class, but Romanians succeeded
in developing a small middle class and lower
middle class by 1900 even though most were
part of the agricultural proletariat in that
region. The social structure of the Slovaks
in Northern Hungary was similar to that of
the Romanians, with even smaller middle and
lower middle classes than those of the
Romanians, primarily because many Slovakian

businessmen and professionals were voluntarily assimilated into Magyardom.

The Interwar Period (1918-1944)

The defeat of the Central Powers in 1918 shattered the ethnic mosaic of Eastern Europe and redesigned it in a different pattern. The peace treaties which concluded World War I radically changed political boundaries, some of which had existed for centuries. Consequently, the political, economic and social interrelationships among the ethnic groups of the region, were fundamentally altered.

The resulting shifts in the relative economic and social position of ethnic groups in Eastern Europe become apparent by examining the quantitative changes which took place in the absolute and relative size of the ethnic groups composing the population of East European states established after 1918.

Ethnic Composition of Eastern Europe Between
1918 and 1944

The territories of the East European states
which emerged after 1918 previously belonged
wholly or partly to Austria-Hungary, Germany, Russia, Bulgaria, Romania and Serbia.
The Paris peace treaties broke Austria-Hungary into three separate states (Austria,
Hungary, Czechoslovakia). Germany and
Russia lost the territories which connected
them to the present Eastern Europe before
1918. Poland reappeared as an independent
state after nearly 150 years of partition.
The boundaries of Romania and Bulgaria were
radically altered and Serbia became the
nucleus of the newly formed Yugoslavia.
    The changes in the territories and
political boundaries of East Europe resulted in a massive transfer of ethnic
groups between national jurisdictions.
Hungary and Bulgaria were no longer multiethnic states since 90 percent or more of
their post-1918 populations belonged to the
ethnic majority. Romania and Serbia became
multiethnic states. Czechoslovakia and reborn Poland also became multiethnic during
the interwar period.
    The nature of ethnic relations was
also fundamentally changed after 1918.
Before 1918 the Poles, Czechs, Slovaks,
and Croats existed entirely as ethnic
minorities despite their large numbers.
Other ethnic groups constituted minorities
in some countries and majorities in others
(e.g., the Romanians and Serbs). Hungarians

were concentrated mainly in prewar Hungary,
and only about 80,000 Hungarians were
settled outside the Carpathians in Romanian
Moldavia.

After World War I, many former minority
groups (Poles, Czechs, Slovaks, Romanians,
Serbs, Croats, Slovenians) assumed majority
status, while significant segments of some
majority ethnic groups (Hungarians, Ukrainians and Germans) were separated and transferred to other jurisdictions as minorities.
According to official censuses circa 1930,
25.5 percent (23 million) of about 91 million persons living in non-Russian Eastern
Europe belonged to minority ethnic groups
in their respective countries. Of that 23
million people there were over seven million Russians and Ukrainians, six million
Germans, over four million Jews, 2.7 million
Hungarians, one million Albanians and nearly
one million Turks.[10]

According to some demographic experts,
official census figures underestimated the
size of minority ethnic groups. According
to the Polish census taken in 1931, there
were 741,000 ethnic Germans in Poland, while
Germany claimed that the actual figure was
over 1.7 million.[11] Similarly, the 1930
Czech census showed 690,000 Hungarians,
while demographic experts in Hungary estimated their number at over one million.[12]

Economic Differentiation 1918 to 1945

After the political boundaries of East
European states were redrawn, the situation
of ethnic groups was drastically changed.
Most of them remained in the territories
where they lived before the peace treaties,
but their status changed from majority to
minority or vice versa. This basic shift
profoundly affected their economic levels
in absolute and also in relative terms.
The change was caused by economic and political factors.

The difference in the economic development of their past and present countries
was an essential factor in determining the
economic status of the ethnic groups.
Those ethnic groups transferred from countries with higher levels of economic
development suffered from the difference.
The transfer of territories from Hungary
to Romania, and the annexation of former
German territories by Poland are cases in
point. The transfer of territories from
countries with lower developmental levels
generally benefited the minorities involved. The economic position of ethnic
groups in the Hungarian territories was
improved when the territories were attached
to Czechoslovakia after 1918.

After World War I the economic position
of ethnic groups in the successor states
reflected their pre-1918 status. They retained the economic assets and income
sources they possessed before their transfer. The initial pattern of economic

differentiation among those ethnic groups,
however, changed radically. The majority
groups, formerly minorities, used their newly gained power, primarily their control
over their new governments, to redistribute
the economic assets and income. This process created shifts in the economic levels
of the ethnic groups involved--the positions
of the majority groups improved and those
of the minority groups declined.

The economic policies of governments
controlled by majority groups were instrumental in rearranging economic relationships among the nationalities of Eastern
Europe during the interwar period. Most of
the population in the East European
countries (with the exception of Czechoslovakia) were engaged in agricultural production so the redistribution of assets and
income logically began in that sector and
agrarian reforms were instituted to achieve
that objective.

Four states, Czechoslovakia, Poland,
Romania and Yugoslavia, initiated and
executed large-scale agrarian reforms
directed primarily against minority ethnic
groups. The Romanian land reform of 1921
especially affected the minorities.[13] The
magnitude of that reform can be appreciated
by considering the prereform situation.
Most of the minority ethnic groups resided
in Transylvania before 1921 and members of
minority ethnic groups held almost 6.5 million of the 8.6 million hectares of the
agricultural area and the Romanians held
2.1 million. By the end of 1929, almost

1.75 million hectares were expropriated
and another 121,000 formerly owned by the
Hungarian state, were ceded.[14] Most of the
expropriated lands had been owned by members
of minority ethnic groups. The recipients
of the expropriated lands were 73 percent
Romanians and 27 percent members of minorities. The previous owners were almost exclusively members of minority ethnic groups,
so the Romanian land reform adversely
affected the non-Romanian nationalities,
particularly since ethnic minorities constituted more than 27 percent of Transylvania's
total population.

The land reform in Yugoslavia was
slightly less severe from the viewpoint of
the minorities. The Yugoslav reform was
also essentially national and political in
character. The architects of the reform
declared: "The national purpose of this
measure was the destruction of the big
landed proprietor," and since the landed
class was almost exclusively comprised of
minority ethnic groups, they were the target
of reform. The land reform also covered
areas populated by majority ethnic groups,
but it was not as harshly executed in those
areas. The agrarian reform expropriated
751,000 out of a total area of 2 million
hectares in Vojvodina, which previously belonged to Hungary.[15]

Members of minority groups were victims
of discrimination when the expropriated
lands were distributed. For example, the
government decreed that members of minority
groups could not even buy land within 50

kilometers of the northern frontier. The
land reform also affected agricultural
laborers, who were mostly (75 percent) from
minority ethnic groups. The breakup of the
large estates deprived them of their job
opportunities and livelihood. In addition
between 80,000 and 120,000 agricultural
laborers, mostly Hungarians, were adversely
affected in Vojvodina. Land reform was
also used by the Yugoslav government to
weaken the cohesion of the minority ethnic
groups and more than 17,000 families from
Serbia were resettled in expropriated lands
amidst minorities.[16]

The agrarian reform of 1921 in Czechoslovakia followed a similar pattern and
heavily affected the Slovak half of Czechoslovakia, formerly the northern part of
Hungary. The estates in the Sudetenland
were not large enough to be affected by reform so the German minority did not suffer
much. However, 1.4 million of 4.9 million
hectares in Slovakia were expropriated.
Most of those landowners were Hungarians and
Jews. Of the 185,000 beneficiaries of land
reform, 6.2 percent were Hungarians who
constituted 23 percent of Slovakia's population. As in the other successor states,
Czechoslovakian minority groups lost heavily
as a result of land reform and the economic
position of their landed upper and upper
middle classes was practically ruined.

The Czechoslovak government, however,
adopted an autarkist policy that benefited
wheat producing areas in Southern Slovakia
mainly inhabited by Hungarians. As a result,

lower middle class Hungarians were materially better off than before World War I, and
in comparison to Hungarian farmers across
the border.[17]

The land reform in Poland was less extensive and in 1921 and 1925 over 6.5 million acres of land were distributed (i.e.
one tenth of the cultivated land).   In the
Western provinces, ceded by Germany, more
than one third of the cultivated land
belonged to big estates owned mainly by
Germans who suffered considerable losses.[18]

The minority ethnic groups in the
successor states also suffered great economic losses in the public sector.   East
European governments adversely affected the
relative economic position of minorities
by controlling jobs in the civil service
and in government owned enterprises, such
as railroads and postal services.   Professor
Brass observed " ... government policy that
may influence the development of nationalities ... is the way in which the state
distributes ... its own public service jobs."
The way the successor states, particularly
Czechoslovakia, Romania, Yugoslavia and
Poland, distributed jobs in the public sector favored members of the majority ethnic
groups and economically damaged the minorities.   In Czechoslovakia, for example, the
number of Germans in the administrative
services was reduced by 25.3 percent between
1921 and 1930 and German railway clerks and
postal employees were reduced by 37 percent.
Between 1921 and 1930 the number of Hungarians in government administration declined

by 59.4 percent, in the railways by 55.9
percent and in the postal service by 57 percent.[19]
     Although Hungarians constituted 5 per-
cent of Czechoslovakia's population in 1930,
their share of postal jobs was only 0.9 percent, and their share of railway jobs was 2
percent.[20] Similar patterns developed in
Romania and Yugoslavia. In Yugoslavia
minorities were actually excluded, almost
without exception, from public careers when
Serbo-Croatian was declared to be the sole
language of administration.[21]
     The governments of East European states,
however, were not satisfied with the virtual
exclusion of minorities from public employment. They limited the job opportunities
of the minorities in the private sector
through legislative acts, and by direct
pressure. A Romanian law passed in 1934
decreed that every enterprise operating in
Romania had to have a quota of ethnic
Romanians on its staff. That law resulted
in a mass dismissal of Hungarian, Jewish
and Russian employees.
     Fiscal and monetary policies, particu-
larly in Romania and Yugoslavia, also
effectively weakened the minority groups.
The tax laws were strictly applied to
business enterprises owned by members of
minorities, and leniently applied when
businesses were owned by members of the
majority. In Romania, firms which displayed shop signs in non-Romanian languages
were taxed and a 12 percent surtax was
charged to firms which kept their books and

accounts in languages other than Romanian.[22]
The most vigorous economic assault was
directed against Jews as a result of an
ancient tradition of anti-Semitism in the
old Romanian kingdom (Regat).

Because government policies seriously
affected their economic position the right
of the minorities to participate in government became increasingly important to them.
They could only exert influence on governmental policies which threatened their
economic existence by becoming participants
in the political process and the degree of
participation allowed was determined by the
political system of the country. During the
interwar period only Czechoslovakia had a
democratic political system in a West-
European sense. There minorities were
allowed to form political parties, and
elections were held by secret ballot. But
even in Czechoslovakia, electoral districts
were gerrymandered to reduce the voting
power of minorities.[23]

The political rights of minorities in
the other successor states were severely
limited. Hungarian electoral laws deprived
a majority of the lower classes of the
franchise regardless of ethnic background.
Romania practiced democracy in name only.
Representatives were elected, but the exercise of political rights by the minorities
was curtailed. Members of the Hungarian
minority were especially pressured and
during the first election after World War I,
30 of the 33 candidates nominated by Hungarian parties were disqualified. Only one

was elected. The ethnic Germans fared
better politically than either the Hungarians in Transylvania or the Russians in
Bessarabia because they willingly cooperated
with the Romanian government.

The political representation of minority ethnic groups in Romanian local governments was as inadequate as in the national
government. The Romanian system reduced
the autonomy of the counties and municipal
councils in Transylvania so that real power
was wielded by prefects appointed in
Bucharest who were, without exception, ethnic Romanians. The mayors in large towns
were also government appointees, and the
notaries who administered the villages were
appointed by the prefects.[24]

The worst political oppression of ethnic minorities occurred in Yugoslavia during
the interwar period. This state completely
disregarded the provisions of the St. Ger-
main Peace Treaty with regard to the political rights of minorities.[25] Germans and
Hungarians were not permitted to vote during
the election of the Constitutional assembly.
The Hungarian Party pressured by the government had to withdraw all of its candidates
in the 1923 elections. The German party was
more leniently treated and elected seven
representatives. The half million Hungarians in Vojvodina finally attained political
representation in the Yugoslav Assembly, but
it lasted only until 1929 when all political
parties were dissolved and an authoritarian
government took over in Yugoslavia.[26]

Minority ethnic groups were also gross-
ly underrepresented in the local governments

of Yugoslavia. The communal elections of
1927 were considered quite liberal by
Yugoslavian standards and several Hungarian
and German candidates were elected, only to
be annulled later. In Vojvodina, where
Hungarians and Germans constituted a
majority of the population, only ten Germans
and six Hungarians were among the 130 village leaders. After 1929 officials of local
governments were appointed by the central
government.[27]

After World War I Poland functioned as
a parliamentary democracy and 87 of 410
seats in the Sejm were occupied by representatives of the German, Russian and
Ukrainian minorities. After the coup d'état
of Marshal Pilsudski in 1926, however,
Poland became an authoritarian state and the
political participation of minority groups
was diminished. The position of the ethnic
Germans in Poland improved as a result of
Germany's growing power.[28]

In summary the relative economic position of the ethnic groups in Eastern Europe
during the interwar period was adversely
affected by government policies particularly
in the public sector and agriculture. But,
the quasi-capitalistic economic system of the
East European states allowed the minorities
to pursue their economic activities. That
economic independence permitted them to
preserve their ethnicity and resist the
assimilative efforts of the majority ethnic
groups.

Social Differentiation During the Interwar
Period

The changes in the social structure of ethnic groups after 1918 requires a review of
the general structure of the East European
societies.
     The East European countries achieved a
measure of industrialization during the
interwar period but their economies remained
predominantly agricultural, and this was
reflected in their social structure. In
those countries where the upper class
survived land reforms (Hungary, Poland), it
consisted of a small number of titled landowners and the proprietors of large-scale
industrial and financial establishments.
Between the upper class and the masses of
the lower middle class there was a thin
middle class, made up of government officials, professionals, and owners of medium-
sized business enterprises. The vast
majority of the lower middle class was
formed by peasant farmers, railway and
postal employees in lower job classifications, the owners of small trade and industrial shops, and a group of skilled
industrial workers. The proletariat including the landless agricultural laborers
and a growing number of semiskilled and unskilled industrial workers comprised the
lowest class in the East European societies.
     The class structure in Hungary was
typical of the stratification of East European societies. There the upper and upper
middle classses constituted 6 percent of

the society; the middle class 8 to 10 percent; the lower middle class 33 percent; the proletariat 43 percent (23 percent industrial workers and 20 percent agricultural laborers). The remainder were pensioneers and the institutionalized population.[29] The middle class in Hungary was proportionately larger than middle classes in other East European countries with the exception of Czechoslovakia and its growth was caused partly by an influx of government officials of Hungarian origin from the successor states.[30]

According to Heltai, "In only one East European country did the social structure resemble the structure of the Western industrial countries--Czechoslovakia." While in all the other countries, the share of farmers and agricultural laborers ranged between 53 percent (Hungary) and 80 percent (Bulgaria), in Czechoslovakia they constituted only 34 percent of the population, and the relative majority of the population was engaged in industry and trade. But even in this country "striking dissimilarities existed between industrialized Bohemia and Moravia ... and the agrarian Slovakia."[31]

The social structures of East European countries was slowly transformed due to industrialization during the interwar period, but major changes occurred for non-economic reasons. As a result of the economic policies pursued by East European governments, the social stratification of ethnic groups in each country reflected

differing patterns. As a rule of thumb,
social descendency was the pattern among
those ethnic groups that changed from
majority to minority status, i.e., their
upper classes contracted and their lower
classes expanded. The class structure of
ethnic groups which either became a majority
or joined existing majority groups reversed
that process. The shifts in class structure
are described below.

As a consequence of agrarian reform in
the six East European countries after 1918
the upper class minorities were practically
eliminated. The Hungarian upper class in
Czechoslovakia, Romania and Yugoslavia, and
the upper class German group in Poland
(mostly titled owners of latifundia) were
economically destroyed. The Polish, Czech
and Hungarian upper class groups survived
when they were the majority.

The upper middle and middle class of
minority groups also lost ground to majority
groups in countries that had diverse ethnic
compositions. The members of the minority
ethnic groups lost their landholdings and
were dismissed from high civil service
positions. Only segments of the middle
class of minority groups made up of independent professionals and businessmen
remained on the level they occupied before
1918. For example, doctors, attorneys, and
merchants in the Slovak half of Czechoslovakia were Hungarians, Germans and Jews until
mid-1930. The public middle class was
divided between Czech and Slovaks. Members
of majority groups in other countries rose

to middle class status in large numbers
because of access to civil service jobs,
and because ethnic quotas were enforced by
the government in the private sector.

A two-way movement took place in the
lower middle class of the minority groups.
People who lost middle class status were
forced into the lower middle class, and
those who lost minor government jobs or
jobs with the railway or the postal service,
descended into the proletariat. The lower
middle class positions were taken over by
members of the majority groups.

Those socioeconomic trends in Eastern
Europe during the interwar period are
exemplified by the occupational composition
of the Hungarian minority in Czechoslovakia.
In Slovakia the percentage of professional
and clerical employees increased from 5.5
to 6.8 percent of the work force while the
percentage of Hungarians in that occupational category declined from 6.4 to 4.0 percent from 1921 to 1930. At the same time,
the percentage of Hungarians in less productive and economically retrograde agricultural jobs increased from 61 to 65 percent
but the percentage of Slovakia's population
in the same category declined from 63.3 to
57.6 percent. The social descendency of
Hungarians in Slovakia was also reflected in
their growing share of the poorest paid
category of agricultural labor. Between
1921 and 1930, the share of the Slovak
population in agriculture declined from 22
to 18 percent, while the share of Hungarians
increased from 24.5 to 25.0 percent.[32]

The social class structure of minority
ethnic groups in Eastern Europe clearly
moved downward while that of majority ethnic
groups persistently moved upward.

The Post-World War II Period

The political settlements following World
War II resulted in territorial and population changes of historical proportions
and exerted a profound impact on ethnic
groups in Eastern Europe. After 1945, the
boundaries of states in Eastern Europe were
radically revised thus altering the political and cultural geography of the area.
Parts of Czechoslovakia, Poland and Romania
were ceded to the Soviet Union and Poland
expanded to the west into formerly German
territory. These territorial changes moved
what was known as Eastern Europe slightly
westward.
        Greater changes occurred in the ethnic
composition of Eastern Europe after 1945.
The proportion of minority ethnic groups in
the total population of the region has
declined considerably. During the interwar
period minority groups comprised almost 26
percent of the total population. Following
World War II their proportion was reduced
to 8.6 percent as a result of the political

rearrangements and population movements.
The total population of Eastern Europe is
now 102 million but only 8.8 million belong
to the various minority ethnic groups. The
Hungarians represent the largest bloc, 2.7
million divided among Czechoslovakia, Romania and Yugoslavia. The Albanians in Yugoslavia are the only other solid bloc and
they number 1.2 million. The Macedonian
minority in Yugoslavia numbers about 1 million, and the Turkish minority in Bulgaria
and Yugoslavia less than 1 million. A small
number of Germans and Ukrainians that
constituted the two largest minority groups
in Eastern Europe remained in minority
status after 1945. Former Polish, Czech and
Romanian provinces populated by Russians
and Ukrainians were annexed by the Soviet
Union and became part of the majority. The
ethnic Germans were expelled from the East
European countries (with the exception of
Romania) and resettled in West Germany.
Of the six million Germans who lived in
Eastern Europe before 1939 only 700,000 are
left and they are widely dispersed and no
longer form a cohesive group.
      This reduction in the absolute number
and proportionate share of nationalities
in minority status has fundamentally changed
the ethnic composition of East European
states. Hungary, Bulgaria, Czechoslovakia
and Poland are now nationally homogeneous
states with minority ethnic groups constituting less than 10 percent of their
populations. The 1966 Romanian census revealed that minority ethnic groups

represented less than 13 percent of the
population. Yugoslavia alone remains as
a multiethnic state and non-Slavic minorities represent more than 20 percent of its
total population.

It should be emphasized that those
census figures are not accepted unequivo-
cally since semiofficial Hungarian sources
question the accuracy of the Romanian census
figures. According to their estimates,
there are approximately 2.5 million Hungarians living in Romania instead of the 1.6
million reported by the 1966 Romanian
census.[33] A painstaking analysis of that
census data led Satmarescu to the conclusion
that the number of Hungarians "were significantly underestimated in 1966" and "evidence
suggests that the Hungarian population in
Trans ylvania is closer in number to 2 million than to the 1.6 million enumerated at
the 1966 census." He believes that the
number of other minorities are also under-
stated in the Romanian census.[34] Figures
of the Hungarian census of 1960 indicated
that 61,000 Germans and 31,000 Slovaks
lived in Hungary. These figures are questioned by the representatives of these
minority groups, and by the Hungarian
Statistical Office and the Ministry of Culture. Those government bureaus estimated
the number of Germans and Slovaks in Hungary
in 1960 to be 200,000 and 100,000 respectively. Even if the higher figure is
accepted, the number of non-Hungarians
living in the country did not exceed 5 percent of the population.[35]

The decline in the number and proportion of minorities in Eastern Europe after 1945 have adversely affected those groups economically and socially. Minority ethnic groups constituted a large share of the total population in their respective countries during the interwar period and usually formed a unit front vis-a-vis majority groups and sometimes successfully resisted assimilation by them. For example German and Hungarian minorities constituted almost 30 percent of the Czechoslovak population, and their combined political and economic strength was instrumental in preserving their ethnicity. After World War II, only the Hungarian group retained some quantitative importance but it represents a modest 4 to 5 percent of the population. Even under different political conditions that group could not carry much weight in the political affairs of Czechoslovakia.

Economic Differentiation After 1945

After 1945, the economic levels of ethnic groups in Eastern Europe was determined primarily by a transformation of East European economies into a Soviet-type socio-economic system. The Soviet Union gained effective political and military control

over the region after 1945 and all six
states slavishly copied the Soviet socio-
economical model.

The private sectors of the East European economies were brought under the
direct control of the state. Collectivization was accelerated after 1945 and the
socialization of the nonagricultural sectors
was completed in all six states by 1950.
Peasant resistance slowed collectivization
of agriculture and it was never completed in
some East European states.

The transformation of the economic
system and the virtual elimination of the
private sector affected all the ethnic
groups in Eastern Europe but it was a particularly heavy blow for ethnic groups in a
minority status. Before 1945, the quasi-
capitalistic economies of the East European
countries comprised a relatively small
public sector over which the government
exercised direct control, and a large private sector covering about 90 percent of the
economy. Members of minority ethnic groups
were pushed out of the public sector and
the agricultural segment of the private
sector represented an economic haven for the
minorities. After the initial agricultural
reforms, the minorities thus enjoyed relative freedom and continued to maintain their
economic status without succumbing to assimilation by majority groups.

After 1945, however, the adoption of
the Soviet system resulted in the virtual
elimination of the private sector. As a
result, minority ethnic groups lost their

324

independent economic base and except for
those occupying lands that temporarily
escaped the process of collectivization,
all of them became employees of the states.
Thus, the economic existence of minorities
now depends entirely on governments which
act for the state and are controlled by
majority ethnic groups.[36] The Sovietization
of the region thus delivered minority groups
to the political and economic control of the
majorities.

After 1945, the economic level of minority groups has been entirely determined
by the policies pursued by the government
of East European countries. Those policies
played an important role in shaping the
economic destiny of minorities even before
1945, but the full control exercised by the
Communist governments over the economy after
1945 intensified the policies affecting
minority groups. The policies of East
European governments toward minorities from
1945 to 1956 were characterized by the
uniformity achieved through Soviet control
of the region and the principles of Marxist-
Leninist nationality policies. According
to Lenin, "Marxism cannot be reconciled with
nationalism. In place of all forms of
nationalism, Marxism advances internationalism."[37] As King suggested, "Communist
ideology places the party above nationality
... as the representative of the interest of
the working class on a specific territory,
but not for a specific nationality."[38]
Marxist-Leninist policies on minorities stem
from Lenin's belief in the primacy of class

over nationality.[39]

Thus, after 1945, the East European communist governments were confronted with two conflicting principles in forming policies affecting nationalities. The tradition of nationalism was heightened during the interwar period, and later the Marxist-Leninist nationality policy was promoted by the Soviet Union. Proletarian internationalism, the leading principle of Marxism-Leninism, was the antithesis of chauvinist policies during the interwar period and it flourished under the tight control of Moscow during the first decade of Soviet domination.[40] As a result, East European governments uniformly adopted the principles of Marxism-Leninism in dealing with their minorities between 1945 and 1956.

During this first phase the minority policy of the Romanian government generally followed the Moscow line. This was partly due to the ethnic composition of the Party leadership. The Communist Party in Romania was controlled by old line Communists from Moscow until 1952 and their majority was non-Romanian. In 1944 the Romanian Communist Party had less than 900 members and "most of them were not ethnic Rumanians at all, but representatives of the minorities."[41]

In the beginning the leadership was impressed by Soviet demands to grant equal rights to the Hungarian minority and Transylvania was allegedly returned to Romania under the condition of granting equality to the Hungarians.[42] As a result, the 1952

Constitution established a Hungarian Autonomous Area in Szekelyland which included
about one third of the Hungarians in Romania.[43] In the rest of Transylvania the
1945 and 1952 constitutions guaranteed Hungarians the right to use their own language
in public discourse, in education, and in
their relations with government.[44] The
1952 Constitution was a high mark of the
liberal policy of the Romanian government.
The Muscovite leaders of the Party, who
were partly responsible for those liberal
policies had already been purged in 1952
and were replaced by ethnic Romanians.
Their real minority policies were not revealed until the Soviets assumed control
under Stalin. After Stalin's death and the
beginning of the "thaw," the minority policy
of Romania has undergone several changes
and each change has aggravated the political
and economic position of the Hungarian
minority.

The second phase of Romania's minority
policy began shortly after the 1956 Hungarian revolution and Marxist-Leninist
internationalism was replaced with "polycentrism." The Soviet control over East Europe
was loosed by the Polish and Hungarian
revolutions and the door was opened to ideas
and policies other than those of the Soviet
Communist Party. Consequently, various
ideological schools of Communism emerged in
Eastern Europe, and the numerous centers of
ideological authority within the Soviet bloc
became polycentric.[45] Polycentrism permits
East European states with large minority

groups to establish minority policies quite
different from Marxist-Leninist internationalism.

The Communist Party in Romania led by
ethnic Romanians after 1952 combined Stalinist control and Romanian nationalism. This
resulted in a chauvinistic policy directed
against minority groups using the oppressive
methods of Stalinism. The policy distinctly
separated "the Romanian working people" from
the "coinhabiting nationalities" and this
distinction reduced the political and economic status of minorities vis-a-vis the
majority ethnic group particularly that of
the Hungarians in Transylvania.[46] After
1956 government policies further diminished
the rights of the Hungarian minority. The
central organization of Hungarians had already been outlawed in 1952 on the grounds
that it represented nationalistic tendencies. Later, in 1959, the Hungarian
university in Cluj was absorbed by the Romanian university and the use of the Hungarian language was limited. Even more
significantly the Autonomous Hungarian Region was gradually eliminated.

Since 1964 a growing nationalism and
a corresponding antiminority policy has
characterized the attitude of the Romanian
government toward its nationalities. Fischer-Galati observed that "the non-Rumanian
inhabitants have little or no say in the
formulation of Rumania's policies. Thus,
Rumania is alienating her principal minority
groups."[47] The 1965 Constitution further
changed policies toward the minorities.

Article 22 refers to "resident nationalities"--the term 'resident' implies "that
the nationalities have no fundamental
right to be considered full-fledged Romanians but are merely tolerated."[48] Schoepflin
concludes that "there is little doubt that
Bucharest is working for the total fragmentation and assimilation of the Hungarian
minority."[49] Ludanyi, another student of
Romanian minority policies, believes that a
drive toward the more unitary and centralized conception of Romanian statehood
"leaves less opportunity to the nationalities ... to develop their respective cultures unhindered."[50]

The post-1945 minority policy in
Yugoslavia developed differently than that
of Romania. Minority policy in Romania has
become increasingly oppressive, while
Yugoslavia's policy moved toward decentralization and liberalization. The Yugoslav
Constitution of 1946 followed the Stalinist
pattern but after the "thaw," the Yugoslav
government continued its liberalizing trend
without interruption. The Constitution of
1954 actually provided for more self-government for the nationalities. The Hungarians
of Vojvodina and the Albanians of Kosovo
thus had an increased opportunity to participate in the local and provincial governments of their regions. The two largest
minorities were granted further rights when
two autonomous provinces were established
within the Serbian Republic of Yugoslavia.

The position of minorities was pre-
carious in Czechoslovakia between 1945 and

1948. The Germans were totally expelled
and the government also planned to expel
the Hungarians. However, following the
expulsion and exchange of nearly 10,000
Hungarians, under pressure by the Allied
Powers, nearly 600,000 remaining Hungarians
were allowed to stay. The 1948 Constitution
restored their citizenship and extended
them nationality rights. The "thaw" in
Czechoslovakia occurred later than in the
other East European countries and the advance toward polycentrism began with the
1960 Constitution. Article 25 reiterated
the rights of nationalities, provided for
the use of their language in education and
cultural activities. According to some
experts, the 1960 Constitution was a step
backward.[51]

The changed attitude toward minorities
was also evidenced in the administration
reorganization of Slovakia. The numerical
strength and political influence of the
Hungarians were diluted by rearranging the
administrative units (counties) in Slovakia
in 1960. Counties with Hungarian majorities
were consolidated with those having Slovak
majorities. As a result, Hungarians are now
in the majority in only two of the enlarged
counties. The consolidation affected the
use of the Hungarian language in education
and government offices.[52]

The constitutional reform of 1969 established Czechoslovakia as a federation
composed of the Czech Socialist Republic and
the Slovak Socialist Republic and further
reduced the political and economic positions

of the Hungarians. The Slovaks have traditionally been more intolerant toward the
Hungarian minority than the Czechs and the
reform delivered control of the Hungarian
minority entirely to the Slovaks.

Economic Policies of East European Governments

The changing minority policies of the East
European governments have been mirrored in
economic policies affecting their nationalities. The majority of people affiliated
with minority ethnic groups are engaged in
agriculture so the land reforms and farm
collectivization hit them hardest. Land
reform after 1945 was primarily used to
punish ethnic groups whose behavior during
World War II was judged to be disloyal. The
lands of ethnic Germans were confiscated
throughout Eastern Europe, even in Romania
where they were not expelled. The Nosek
land reform in Czechoslovakia expropriated
the lands of ethnic Germans as well as
those of many Hungarians and they were par-
celed out to Czech and Slovak "colonists."[53]
    Romania also carried out a substantial
land reform soon after World War II and it
primarily affected the German minority. The
strong, independent peasantry, the backbone

of the German minority, was consequently
broken. The Hungarians did not suffer economically from land reform but their ethnic
position was adversely affected since land
confiscated from the Germans was given to
ethnic Romanians transplanted from Bessarabia. This move partly diluted the Hungarian
ethnic group and partly isolated it from the
Germans. The subsequent collectivization
was used by the Romanian government to integrate the Hungarian peasants with the
Romanians and the Hungarians were forced to
participate in collective farms controlled
by Romanians. This dispersed the Hungarian
agricultural population and facilitated
their assimilation.[54]

The Communist Party ordered a general
land reform in Yugoslavia after 1945 and
its impact was felt intensively in Vojvodina.
The Law of Agrarian Reform and Colonization
of 1945 expropriated estates exceeding a
certain size, and also confiscated lands
belonging to the "enemies of the people."
The Germans who comprised one third of the
population of Vojvodina before the war were
forced to give up their land holdings. This
reform ruined the Germans and also threatened the economic position of the Hungarians.
Few Hungarian laborers obtained land since
most of it was distributed among South Slavs
who migrated from Bosnia, Hercegovina and
Montenegro. This movement caused a vast
shift in the ethnic composition of Vojvodina.
The Germans were expelled and the mass
settlement of South Slavs reduced the share
and influence of Hungarians in the total

332

population. The South Slavs became dominant
politically and in the collective farms
formed subsequently.[55]
Following the reform, however, the
economic position of the Hungarians and the
few remaining Germans stabilized and, as a
result of the more liberal minority policy
of the Yugoslav government, it has actually
improved. Unlike the government of Romania
Yugoslavia has pursued an economic policy of
decentralization and has granted virtual
autonomy to collective farms and industrial
plants. Those organizations are administered by their own members and the Hungarian
and Albanian workers' councils participate
in the management of economic organizations
located in their respective autonomous
regions. The Yugoslav government permitted
the peasants to leave the collective farms
and return to individual farming during the
1960s thus improving the living standard
of ethnic Hungarians and Albanians who took
advantage of the government's liberalized
agricultural policies.[56] Ludányi has noted
that the agricultural policies of the
Yugoslav government, with the notable exception of the 1945 land reform, have not been
detrimental to minorities and do not threat-
en them with assimilation.[57]
The introduction of central planning
by the East European governments has produced policies increasingly shifted toward
accelerated industrialization which in turn
has affected the economic position of ethnic
groups in Romania and Yugoslavia. Romania
was one of the least developed countries of

Europe before 1945 and almost 77 percent of
the population was engaged in agriculture
and dwelled in rural communities. After
1945 Romania's policy of centrally planned
industrialization produced an increase of
industrial production 2.7 times greater than
in 1938.[58] In the sixties and early seven-
ties, basic industries have grown at an
annual rate of 12 to 20 percent.[59]
    Naturally, industrial growth trans-
formed the economic and occupational structure of Romania and rapidly expanded the
urban centers where most of the new industries are located. But Hungarians, the
largest minority group in Romania, have not
been permitted to participate in the economic growth and its benefits. Most of the
new industrial establishments were constructed in areas heavily populated by ethnic Romanians. Székelyland, where the
largest bloc of ethnic Hungarians live, has
been excluded from the process of economic
development. The exclusion of the Hungarian
minority from participation in industrialization was also caused by a reduction in
the number of technical schools using the
Hungarian language for education which might
have prepared Hungarians for industrial
jobs. In 1951-52, Hungarians had 18 technical schools with 12,200 students and by
1957-58 their number had declined to 8 and
1,400, respectively.[60] Hungarians living in
rural areas were not permitted to move to
cities where industrial jobs became available. Shortly after the War, the Romanian
government promulgated a decree forbidding

rural inhabitants to settle in cities without special permits and this restriction
has been applied only to Hungarians since
1953. Thus, the urban expansion since the
early fifties benefited ethnic Romanians
almost solely.[61]

Hungarians could take industrial jobs
only by commuting from rural areas to the
cities and 70-80 percent of the adult male
population in some Transylvanian villages
commute daily to faraway cities. The commuting often takes 5-6 hours and workers
have little time left for families and cultural activities. Other Hungarians had to
settle in the urban slums to find jobs and
under such conditions they have become
separated from their villages and ethnic
backgrounds and are exposed to assimilation.[62] Industrialization also contributed
to the Romanization of cities where Hungarians had been in the majority for decades. By prohibiting Hungarians to move to
cities and by encouraging Romanians to do
the same, the large Transylvanian cities
that formerly had large Hungarian majorities
are rapidly losing their Hungarian character.[63]

Yugoslavia has not used industrialization against the minorities, nevertheless
it has affected them adversely particularly
in the Vojvodina. Most industrialization
occurred primarily in the mountain regions
rich in raw materials but Vojvodina is a
rich agricultural region void of industrial
raw materials. The resulting lack of industrialization and the mechanization of

agriculture caused a high rate of unemployment in Vojvodina. The unemployed could find jobs only by moving to other parts of Yugoslavia or by seeking employment in West Germany. These alternatives do not favor the retention of Hungarian ethnicity.

Social Differentiation

The political and economic revolution that overtook Eastern Europe after World War II profoundly affected East European societies and the minority ethnic groups. The social and class differences among ethnic groups are best outlined in the model social structure adopted by the six East European societies with only minor variations. A comparison of the social structure of the minority ethnic groups with that model reveals their differences. The new social structure following World War II developed in two phases. The old social order was first effectively destroyed; and the social structure that now prevails in the East European countries was then erected.

The social classes of the old social system developed over a long period and were destroyed in a few years. The upper classes in East European countries that existed before 1945 were physically eliminated, or

had their economic base confiscated. The
upper middle class shared that fate. Members of the upper middle class whose social
status was based on industrial wealth or
agricultural holdings lost their assets
entirely. Members of the upper middle class
who occupied high positions in the government before 1945, either fled to the West
or were held responsible for the acts of
their governments during the War and sometimes punished as war criminals.

Members of the middle class who gained
social recognition as owners of medium sized
industrial or commercial enterprises lost
their property through nationalization, but
those with expertise were retained to help
the new managers to run their former enterprise. Consequently the professional segment of the former middle class survived
the social revolution almost intact because
they were permitted to continue functioning
in their professions and to salvage their
previous status in the new society.

The lower middle class did not suffer
as much physically and economically as the
upper classes. The wealthy peasants
("kulaks" in certain countries) lost their
property to collective farms, but after a
"cooling off" period most were permitted in
the collectives where their expertise was
utilized. Peasants with small or dwarf
holdings were included in collectives or
permitted to retain their farms so their
former status was essentially unchanged.
The social status of the pre-1945 proletariat, landless agricultural laborers and

unskilled industrial workers has not been
adversely affected by postwar developments.
Changes in their status have actually been
for the better.

The disintegration of the old social
system was accomplished differently in the
East European countries. The most violent
measures were taken in Yugoslavia where the
Hungarian upper middle and middle class
(some 40,000 persons) were eliminated by
partisans who reoccupied Vojvodina after the
retreat of the Hungarian troops. As a result, the Hungarian minority was left without a middle class after 1945 and shared the
fate of the middle class Serbs and Croats
who perished in the fratricide during the
war.

Mainly economic measures were used in
Romania and Czechoslovakia to disintegrate
the middle classes of all ethnic groups.
Currency reforms reduced the value of money,
all commercial, industrial and financial
enterprises were nationalized, and discrimination against those of "suspect social
origin" settled the fate of the bourgeoisie
except for professionals employed by the
state with above average incomes and social
status.[64]

The first phase resulted in the destruction of the old social system and an
amorphous society remained. Heltai noted
that,

> By the late 1940s a peculiar social
> formation emerged in Eastern Europe.
> On the one hand, there was an
> immense peasant class, increasingly

opposed to the urban masses ...
and with fading revolutionary zeal,
which was the result of their recent
acquisition of the long desired
land. On the other hand, there was
the amorphous mass of urban white-
collar workers and laborers, forcibly
united by the state nationalization
of the nonagricultural economy.[65]

Following the first phase of social
development, "a new process of social differentiation began almost concurrently."[66]
The result is a society as structured as
the one it destroyed but with a different
pattern. The structure of communist
societies in Eastern Europe now consists of
four basic strata: (1) the ruling elite,
(2) a middle class, (3) industrial workers,
and (4) peasants.

The development and composition of the
ruling elite (the "new class") was analyzed
and described by Milovan Djilas: "The new
class may be said to be made up of those
who have special privileges and economic
preference because of the administrative
monopoly they hold."[67] The new class ob-
tains power, privileges, ideology and
customs "from one special form of ownership - collective ownership - which the
class administers and distributes in the
name of the nation and society."[68] As
Djilas indicates, the ruling elite is a
rather thin layer of Party members who
exercise political control over state
administration and manage economic enterprises and cultural and humanitarian

organizations. The new middle class is
made up of one group composed of government
officials in high and middle positions who
lack political power, but execute the orders
of the new class and another group comprised
of professionals, primarily technocrats.
Some professionals are not members of the
Party, but are accepted because of their
expertise.

The working class is numerically largest in East European societies because of
industrialization. It is slightly different
from that before 1945. The average income
is still the second lowest and the differential between the average income of blue-
collar workers and the managers of
enterprises is almost as great as in the
capitalistic era. However, the working
class and their children now have an opportunity to ascend to the upper classes. As
Djilas observed, the new class is made up
of "professional revolutionaries and former
sons of the working class."[69]

The amorphous mass of peasantry remain
at the bottom of the new society in terms
of income and social status. The peasantry
includes peasants who still own land and
cultivate it on an individual basis; members
of collective farms; and agricultural laborers on state farms. The size of each peasant group varies from country to country
depending on the division of the agriculture
among individual farms, collective farms and
state estates.

In Hungary the size of the four basic classes in the early 1970s exemplifies the structure of the new East European societies. The ruling elite, or new class, is estimated to be 3 percent of the total population, the middle class 15 percent, the working class 40 percent, and the peasantry 34 percent. The remaining 8 percent are pensioneers, institutionalized persons, and people on the fringe of the society.[70]

In general, the structure of minority groups deviates from our model negatively. There are almost no members of minorities in the "new class," they are underrepresented in the middle class, and an overwhelming majority are found in the lower classes. The degree of minority group distribution among social classes varies in the three East European countries which still contain compact minority groups.

In Romania, between 1944 and 1952, ethnic minorities were well represented in the emerging ruling elite. In 1944, the majority of leaders in the Romanian Communist Party were members of minority groups. However, ethnic Romanians took over the Party in the purge of 1952 and members of ethnic minorities are now represented by figureheads in the Party leadership. Hungarians constituted 8.7 percent of the Party membership in 1968 but their share in the upper and middle level of the Party structure is now under that figure and is steadily declining. The masses of Hungarians in Romania have sunk to the bottom of the new society and constitute the

proletariat in Transylvania. On the other
hand, the social status of ethnic Germans
has improved in Romania and since they are
dispersed they no longer threaten the unitary Romanian state and economic discrimination is no longer directed against them.
Most Germans are skilled craftsmen and
generally well educated. As a result, they
are found at the top of the working class
and in the lower middle class.[71] The
mobilization of ethnic Romanians after 1945
brought them up to--and above--the socioeconomic level of Hungarians and Germans.
The socioeconomic status of other minority
ethnic groups however, declined in relation
to the Romanians and in absolute terms.

Since the end of World War II Hungarians in Yugoslavia have gained access to the
Communist Party but that access is limited
mainly to the Party organization in
Vojvodina. On the federal level Hungarians
enjoy only token representation in the
ruling elite. In Vojvodina, where Hungarians comprise about 25 percent of the
population, they constitute only 8.4 percent
of the Party membership[72] and they have
limited representation in the power structure. A few are found in the middle class,
but less than their proportion in the
population. Because of the limited industrialization in Vojvodina Hungarians are
mostly of the lowest class which includes
those working in the agriculture.

Albanians form the least advanced group
in Yugoslavian society economically and
educationally. The per capita income is

lowest in Kosovo where most Albanians
live.[73] Their status is inferior even to
the Hungarians in Vojvodina.

The social structure of these minorities follow the pattern found in the other
multiethnic states. Hungarians the only
large minority group left in Czechoslovakia
after 1945 are not to be found in the ruling
class, but a few are professionals in the
middle class but not proportionately within
the total population. The Hungarian minority in Czechoslovakia thus "enjoys a low
socioeconomic status, and the new federal
structure, a response to Slovakian nationalism, is unlikely to bring about an im-
provement."[74]

Recent (1967) data on the occupational
structure of the three largest ethnic
groups (Czechs, Slovaks, Hungarians) in
Czechoslovakia, show that more Hungarians
(84.3 percent) are employed as industrial
and agricultural workers and that fewer
(12.1 percent) are employed as professional
and clerical workers. The figures for
Czechs were 65.3 and 31.5 percent respectively.[75]

The steady decline in the socioeconomic
status of Hungarians in Czechoslovakia is
also documented by the findings of Pavel
Machonin and Robert Rosko who evaluated
the relative socioeconomic level of seven
ethnic groups in Czechoslovakia. On the
basis of six criteria (quality of employment, education, income, life style, living
standard, share in leadership) they ranked
seven ethnic groups one to four--the seven

groups were ranked as follows: Czechs 2.95,
Poles 2.65, Slovaks, 2.32, Ukrainians 2.32,
Germans 2.31, Hungarians 2.00, Gypsies
1.50.[76]   The Hungarians were at the lowest
socioeconomic level of the Czechoslovak
society except for the Gypsies. Obviously,
that is the price they must pay to avoid
assimilation by the Slovaks. The South
Slovakian counties where Hungarians live in
a cohesive bloc are the least industrialized and their populations are engaged
almost exclusively in agriculture. Hungarians can improve their socioeconomic
status only by migrating to industrialized
areas where the Czechs and Slovaks are in
the majority. That would involve accepting
certain assimilation.
    The new society is still emerging in
Eastern Europe and in the three countries
where large ethnic minorities exist their
social status is found at the lower end
of the social ladder.

    The two world wars profoundly affected
the ethnic composition of East Europe and
the ethnic composition of the individual
states in that area. The changes caused
by the wars and their political settlements
included (1) the elimination of some major
ethnic groups (the Jews) which inhabited the
region for centuries or their expulsion from
the area (Germans). (2) The uniting of
ethnic groups that were in minority status
for several centuries to form majorities in
other countries (Romanians, Serbs) or the
establishment of their own states (Czechs,

Slovaks, Poles). (3) The resolution of many ethnic problems that had plagued the area for centuries, in some cases by force. (4) The limiting of East European ethnic problems to Hungarians and Albanians who now occupy minority status in three countries of the region.

The governments of East European states now determine the social and economic positions of ethnic groups in the multi-ethnic states. This factor is singularly important because those governments are firmly controlled by majority ethnic groups and because they have virtually unlimited power. Their power is used to shape the socioeconomic status of ethnic groups to benefit the majority at the expense of the minority groups. Ironically, the excessive power of the states and their governments was supposed to wither away according to Marxist ideology.

The importance of the ethnic question in Eastern Europe has decreased but the two multiethnic states, Romania and Yugoslavia, are still preoccupied with ethnic problems. The conflict between the Stalinist domestic policy and the independent foreign policy of Romania can be explained only in terms of that government's determination to solve the Hungarian question once and for all. The Stalinist domestic policy provides firm control of the Hungarian minority while an independent foreign policy frees Romania to practice that domestic policy. The Western powers, particularly the United States, normally would be expected to raise their

voices on behalf of a persecuted minority
group but they are silent because they want
to avoid antagonizing Romania--apparently
the only dissenting voice within the Soviet
bloc. Such strange interactions in world
politics has given Romania a free hand to
pursue oppressive policies against the
minorities.

Yugoslavia has chosen to reconcile
an independent foreign policy with liberal
domestic policies affecting her minorities.
Members of minority groups in Yugoslavia
frequently question whether this ethnic
policy will continue after Tito, the
architect of Yugoslavia's minority policy.
The existing trend in Romania and the un-
certainties in Yugoslavia provide little
hope for the future of the minority groups
in Eastern Europe.

CHAPTER VIII

RELIGION AND ETHNICITY

by

Cynthia H. Enloe

Three questions have especially bothered
analysts trying to unravel the meaning and
implications of ethnicity. First, and
most fundamentally, researchers are not
certain that ethnicity is real--it may be a
more basic social phenomenon in disguise
(class, race, or interest group). They also
question whether its reality is objective
or subjective--is ethnicity in the eye of
the beholder or in the mind of the believer?
Second, if ethnic groups are real and dis-
crete, are they subject to cross pressures,
how porous can they be and remain distinguishable? Third, analysts are divided over
how transient ethnicity is; is ethnicity a
form of "traditional" identification bound
to wane with the onslaught of modernity, or
is it resilient enough to persist and thrive
in the era of modernization.[1] Another
question of general concern is particularly
pertinent to an analysis of Eastern Europe.
How can the State shape a sense of a people's ethnic identity? Ethnic pluralism is
conventionally portrayed as an independent
variable (a predictor) affecting the operations of the political system. In many

347

348

instances, however, it is more accurate to designate ethnicity as a dependent variable (a criterion) shaped deliberately by political authorities.[2]

Religion is frequently a critical factor in answering these questions. In cases as disparate as Northern Ireland, Lebanon and India, the events usually labeled as interethnic conflicts might also be labeled as merely or basically religious divisions by analysts skeptical of ethnicity's empirical reality. Likewise, in multiethnic societies such as the United States or France, religious similarities produce so many mixed ethnic identities that ethnic boundaries seem to be so porous that they are practically invisible. Modernization tends to dilute, even obliterate, ethnic communalism and secularization is the most effective modernizing tendency in that regard. As religion loses its potency as a societal bond, ethnic ties perform fewer and fewer functions for modern men and women and ethnicity wanes. State policies influence on ethnicity and religion is a crucial factor because political elites can manipulate religious symbols and organizations to heighten or dilute ethnic divisions.

The underlying question that leads to an examination of the interaction between religion and ethnicity is "What does religion add to ethnic differentiation?"

The relationship of religion and ethnicity (How much of ethnicity is merely religious affiliation?)--has preoccupied social science investigators concerned with

social and political change in the industrial postcolonial period. The relationship
has also concerned politicians interested in
maintaining stability during all periods
because the religious element in ethnic
identity appears to be especially threatening. The religious component of ethnicity
allegedly contributes intensity and irrationality, at least an absence of reason.
Croatian nationalism would be less virulent
if it was divorced from Catholicism. Many
modernist social scientists and policy
makers reason that if the religious quotient
could be reduced ethnic differentiations
would become benign or disappear. The result would add momentum to the presumably
irresistable forces of modernization and
reduce the destabilizing conflicts that
drain scarce state resources. This presump-
tion is admittedly simplistic, but it is
closely related to the assumptions implied
in many current discussions about the connection between ethnicity and religion.
This paper will explore those assumptions
to determine whether religion and ethnicity
are separable, and whether religion actually
threatens modernity and stability in multiethnic societies. The special qualities of
sociopolitical change in Eastern Europe and
the distinctive intimacy of ethnicity and
religion in that region makes this explora-
tion particularly relevant to Eastern European studies.

350

Ethnicity and Religion

There is no consensus on what constitutes
ethnicity but there is growing agreement
that it is both objective and subjective.
Ethnicity involves cultural attributes
that can be observed, but those attributes
must be of conscious value to a collection
of people to amount to ethnicity. There
is a growing agreement among scholars that
ethnicity requires a sense of belonging
and an awareness of boundaries between
members and nonmembers, however vague and
mutable those boundaries may be from
situation to situation or from time to
time.[3]

Ethnicity is difficult to define because it is composed of an intertwining
cluster of attributes and not a singular
cultural characteristic. Language, religion, territory and custom--by them-
selves--are insufficient to identify, or
sustain, an ethnic group. Moreover, the
cluster of attributes assigned a collective
value by a group will vary. A common language is a typical component of the ethnic
cluster, but it is neither necessary nor
sufficient to distinguish ethnicity. The
linguistic component in the ethnic cluster
is verified by Austria's Slovene population and a government language census used
as a basis for general Slovene mobilization.
Yet clear ethnic boundaries among Africans
and East Indians survived in Guyana long
after the British successfully made English-
speakers out of both groups.

This essay will explore the effect of
religious differences on intergroup boundary
visibility and maintenance between two ethnic groups to determine whether there is
something peculiarly intense or profound
about religion when it is a part of ethnic
differentiations and the gap between communities is especially wide. Eastern European
societies have experienced an historically
high level of interethnic contact. Ethnic
boundaries in that region are rarely maintained by the sheer physical remoteness
often found in Asia or Africa. Thus an
investigation of how ethnic boundaries and
group integrity are maintained and the role
played by religion in that process is especially rewarding in analyzing Romania,
Yugoslavia and Czechoslovakia.

Religion appeals to a suprahuman or
supraempirical authority to formulate
explanations, judgments and goals. But in
practice religions are markedly diverse.
For instance, the extent to which supraempirical authorities are explicitly and
coherently defined differs widely. This
is the basis of conventional distinctions
between the "Great" religions (Hinduism,
Islam, etc.) and the presumably "lesser"
religions (animism, eclectic folk versions
of the Great religions, etc.). The explicit
organizational structures used to implement
clerical authority and the extent of hierarchy and integration in those organizations
also differ among religions. Thus Roman
Catholic Christianity stands out because of
its explicit, elaborate and hierarchical

organization and animist religion is distinguished by its low degree of explicit
organization and clerical professionalism.
Religions can also be categorized according
to the extent of their taboos determining
dress, diet and other behaviors. Finally,
religions differ in their approach to
evangelical proselytizing. Islam and
Christianity have ardently pursued converts
and thus have absorbed a diverse range of
cultural groups, Judaism has been remarkably
nonevangelical.

The kind of religion--along these
lines of distinction--as part of an ethnic
group's communal package will determine
how porous the ethnic boundaries are, how
capable a group is of withstanding outside
pressures to assimilate, and how prone the
group will be to absorb outsiders through
intermarriage or conversion. The type of
religion confessed by group actors is also
a significant factor in interethnic dynamics. The most tense interethnic relationship occurs when two ethnic groups confess
different religions, each religion is
theologically and organizationally elaborate
and explicit, and when those religions have
generated taboos operative in the routine
aspects of life, for instance diet. The
intensity is increased when each religion
has a tradition of evangelism. This situation approximates the situation in comtem-
porary Lebanon but it is not applicable to
the situation between Malays and Chinese in
Malaysia, between Walloons and Flemings in
Belgium, or between Great Russians and

Ukrainians in the Soviet Union.

Therefore, when assessing what religion
adds to ethnic identification and interethnic relations, it is essential to note
that there are critical differences among
religions which bear directly on how ethnicity is expressed and maintained collectively. It is not simply a matter of "religion"
being a part of the boundary setting package, but which religion.[4] To add another
complexity the boundaries may often be
affected by a sect of a major religion.
Some ethnic boundaries persist when persons
are all Muslims, all Hindus or all Christians but the distinction between Sunni and
Shiite Muslims is a salient factor in Iraqi
ethnic politics; and there are divisions between Lebanese Christians--Maronite, Orthodox and Catholic.

Ethnic communalism does not appear to
be lessened when groups are distinguished
by sectarian differences rather than by
major religious confessional orientations.
Interethnic hostility however, may be particularly acute when each ethnic group is
convinced that its own interpretation of
the basic theology is correct while the
other's is corrupted. Moreover, when the
religious beliefs of two ethnic groups are
relatively close the other differences
may become especially important since they
are necessary for boundary maintenance.
Richard Gambino observes that Italian-
Americans traditionally felt more antagonism
toward Irish-Americans than against Jews or
Protestants because of what they perceived

354

to be the deviations of Irish Catholicism.[5]
This suggests that when ethnic boundaries
are firmly established on extrareligious
grounds, group members who appear to be
religiously identical will have a stake in
denying religious homogeneity.

The most common way of rendering the
extent to which religion sustains ethnic
boundaries operative in the study of ethnicity has been to focus on rates of intermarriage which is, in a sense, the "bottom
line" of ethnicity. The rate of intermarriage is not determined by religious
rules exclusively since class and racial
factors are also important in reducing or
promoting intermarriage. Marriage is a
sacred act in most cultures and religious
divisions are significant even when they
operate in company with class and racial
factors. The rising rate of intermarriage
between gentiles and Jews in the United
States has alarmed many Jewish leaders who
believe it indicates a lowering of the
religious quotient in the American Jewish
ethnic package and a weakening trend. In
contrast secularization has been deliberately promoted in the Soviet Union and the
State has encouraged cross-ethnic and cross-
confessional marriages. Nonetheless Muslims
(who themselves are ethnically diverse) are
less likely to marry non-Muslims than they
are to marry Muslims.[6]

It may be futile and unrealistic to
separate religion and ethnic identity.
Many individuals behave as if their ethnic
affiliation and professed religion are one

and the same: to be born Croatian is to be
born Catholic. But there have been attempts
in the United States to pry religion and
ethnicity apart analytically. American
political analysts have questioned (as
have the elected politicians they advise)
the existence of a "Catholic vote" and
wondered, on the other hand, if "ethnic
votes" determine polling outcomes. Historically analysts have been interested in the
immigrant experience (or assimilation experience).   That interest has raised questions about the interplay of religion and
foreign nationality in shaping behavior in
the American society. Most such questions
are directed toward Catholic-confessing
ethnic groups because of the American pre-
occupation with Church and State and because Catholic groups have presumably had
the most electoral impact. Actually the
effort to distinguish religion and ethnicity is just as valid for Protestants and
other religious subgroups.
     If ethnicity is merely religion in
disguise, then holding religion constant
should reveal few significant differences
among ethnic groups. A recent study of
American Catholics' political attitudes
and values revealed wide-ranging differences among Catholics and those intra-
Catholic differences fell into distinctly
ethnic patterns. Furthermore, the survey
was most directly related to spiritual
values and not concerned with such differences as US foreign policy vis-a-vis Poland
or Ulster, questions that would normally

elicit group differences. For example, 76
percent of the Irish Catholics opposed mis-
cegenation laws, whereas 58 percent of the
Italian Catholic respondents and 66 percent
of the Polish Catholic respondents agreed
with those laws. Likewise, only 32 percent
of the Irish Catholics favored legalized
abortion when a mother "is married and
doesn't want any more children," while 43
percent of the Italian Catholics favored
legalized abortion. The same study also
found that ethnic attitudinal differences
persist among American Protestants along
ethnic group lines although the differences
were less wide-ranging overall. For
instance, 37 percent of German Protestants
favored legalized abortion whereas 57 percent of the Scottish Protestant respondents
did so.[7] Kathleen Frankovic made an important related attempt to determine
whether religion is simply the class phenomenon in disguise by studying religion's
impact on American political behavior. She
found that in voting behavior and issue
orientations, "No matter what type of class
measures were used - income, education,
occupation, or even residence in urban areas
- religious distinctiveness remained relatively high." Furthermore, Frankovic
found little evidence that interreligious
differences in political behavior were being
diluted over time in the United States.[8]
Thus if religion is a factor which helps to
sustain ethnic boundaries it is not losing
sufficient impact to lend credence to "end
of ethnicity" predictions. Moreover, a

cross-national Gallup Poll survey conducted
in 1976 revealed that 56 percent of American
respondents considered their religious beliefs "very important" to them, while only
5 percent labeled them "not at all important." The same survey found, however, that
only 17 percent of West Germans and 12 percent of Japanese considered their religious
beliefs "very important."[9]
    Many nation-states have been formed on
the assumption that religion and ethnicity
were separable, but that when an overwhelming majority of citizens all confessed an
identical religion--ethnicity would lose
saliency and functional value. This was
the hope underlying the formation of Israel
and the postcolonial establishment of
Pakistan. It is increasingly obvious, however, that even when religion is a constant,
ethnic boundaries remain and sometimes
ethnic group members even hold them in
greater esteem. Being Jewish has not
eliminated the sense of the Russian Jew's
ethnic integrity inside Israel. This is
not as surprising as it first appeared to
observers because, according to a study by
Jeffrey Ross, recent Russian Jewish immigrants in Israel do not think of their
Jewish identification as a religious identity, but rather as a national identification. Only 8.1 percent of Ross' sample of
new Russian Jewish immigrants considered
themselves to be religious.[10] Similarly,
Bengalis in precivil war Pakistan assigned
more and more value to their supra-Islamic
ethnic distinctiveness. There was a growing

interaction between Muslim and Hindi Bengalis across the India-Pakistan border as the rift between East and West Pakistan Muslims widened. The civil war was not just territoriality masquerading as ethnicity; today Western Pakistan is all Muslim yet it is still threatened by interethnic conflict.

Within some multiethnic and multireligious states there is a feeling that religion may cause less system-threatening cleavages than ethnicity. Thus political parties with religious orientations are formed to comprise two or more ethnic groups--at least at election time. Political integration in Belgium typically involved ethnically crosscutting religious and secular parties. When these parties--Socialist and Catholic--collapsed or split into communal wings the existence of the Belgian state appeared to be in serious jeopardy. The Belgian political system, in other words, tolerated political mobilization based on religion but could not withstand political mobilization based on ethnicity without a new constitutional and elitist formula for integration. The Netherlands and West Germany also experienced formalized religious cleavages in social and political affairs which have not caused the profound anxiety occasioned by, past and potential, ethnic changes.

Finally, in order to see how much religion contributes to the intensity and the sustenance of ethnicity it is possible to examine ethnic groups that are internally

divided along religious lines. There are
few multireligious ethnic groups and their
relative scarcity suggests that religion is
the root of ethnic differentiations or that
religious distinctiveness is a key to ethnic
saliency. The overseas Indian ethnic group
is internally divided more often than not
by religion. Indian ethnic communities in
Malaysia, Guyana, Trinidad, Uganda, and
Great Britain are divided between Muslims
and Hindus and, in smaller numbers, by
Christians. A cursory review of those
Indian communities suggests that (1) the
existence of religious heterogeneity has
not made Indian qua Indian ethnicity less
real for its members than ethnicity for
religiously homogenous groups, (2) religious
diversity frequently hinders efforts by
Indians to mobilize communally to pursue
Indian interests. Thus in Guyana common
local political gossip suggests that the
largely African ruling party has deliberately exploited the religious split among the
Guyanese Indians intending to coopt Muslim
Indians. The Indian political party in
Guyana, however, is secular and does not
depend on religious appeals. Despite being
a majority in Guyana, the Indians have
failed to translate their numbers into an
effective political mobilization.[11] The
divisions among the Indian population in
Britain are linguistic, caste, country of
previous residence and religious, and those
divisions have hampered Indian political
development in labor, immigration and hous-
ing policy.[12]

One of the most prominent religiously divided ethnic groups in Eastern Europe is the Czech community. That community is divided between Catholics and Protestants, but the Czechs have sustained a strong sense of ethnic boundaries. Similarly, Albanian ethnic nationalism has flourished in recent generations despite intraethnic divisions.

Religious homogeneity may not be the sine qua non of ethnic boundary maintenance but religious pluralism within a community still has genuine consequences in the operation of the community in society at large.

The Uses of Religion by Ethnic Groups

The religious component of the ethnic boundary maintenance package varies markedly from group to group depending on (1) how sophisticated and organizationally elaborate and evangelical the group's religion is, (2) how similar that religious component is to that of the ethnic groups with which it has most frequent or critical interaction, (3) how uniform religious identification is within the group itself. But religion is a valuable resource for many ethnic groups, so useful that it is often difficult to tell where religious functions end and purely communal functions begin.

Many political historians have noted that religious mobilization is the earliest phase of ethnic group political development. In this scenario, religiously framed demands, religiously legitimized leaders, and religiously oriented organizations are the basis for the first stage of ethnic group self-consciousness and collective activism. The religious character of early ethnic mobilization was visible in American Indian politics during the nineteenth century. Religion was used time and again as a conquered ethnic group's surrogate for politics throughout Eastern European history and the church has provided an alternative political arena when the state structure was closed.

However, in theory as the ethnic group develops, becomes more sophisticated about its real needs, learns organizational skills, and more educated young people fill leadership positions the religious basis of communal mobilization will recede. If it does not recede, it will prove to be a drag on the community. Priests and monks serve an ethnic purpose, but they should know when to back off the communal stage. Ethnic communal development may not be dependent on secularization as such, but it may require sustaining religious bonds while nurturing mobilization vehicles less confined by spiritualism.

There has been an important political controversy in Malaysia over the relevance of religious resources for enhancing the Malay community's development (more than 50

percent of the population is Malay). Only
one political party in postindependence
(1957) Malaysian politics is avowedly
religious, and it is exclusively Malay
(though there are Indian Muslims as well
as Malay Muslims in the society). The
Malay elite's conventional argument commonly
adhered to by foreign analysts, is that the
Parti Islam (formerly the PMIP) is out of
step with the Malays' ethnic needs and religious definitions of national issues and
communal goals is a hindrance to ethnic
progress. Some foreign and Malay observers,
however, recently adopted a more positive,
at least a neutral stance, in analyzing the
PI's function. Clive Kessler contends that
the PMIP was not a reflection of "backward"
elements in the Malay rural community rather
that it was a reflection of serious and
genuine dilemmas facing nonelite Malays in
the 1960s. Islam and the PMIP as its
political articulator were relevant in helping rural Malay peasants make sense of the
intracommunal and intercommunal changes
taking place around them.[13]
During the French Canadian ethnic revolution in Quebec the Catholic Church lost
much of its communal power, but the Catholic
Church remains in the forefront of community
political affairs in Ulster. The role of
religious resources for ethnic mobilization
among Ulster's Protestant community has,
however, remained markedly important. Religion and ethnicity are intimately intertwined in Ulster and that is not surprising
although Ulster Protestants trace their

origins back to Scottish and English settlers transplanted by an English government
eager to pacify the Irish colony. A political scientist who examined the Orange
Order, the leading religious ethnic political organization in the Ulster Protestant
community, concluded that its religious
dimension has not waned despite fundamental
alterations in the socioeconomic conditions
of Ulstermen. The basic code of the Orange
Order declares that, "The Institution is
composed of Protestants, united and resolved
to the utmost of their power to support and
defend their rightful sovereign, the Protestant religion, and the laws of the Realm
..."14
        Even though the Orange Order remained
religious while political conditions
changed and even though its organizational
influence remains undiminished despite
persistently defining ethnicity and issues
in religious terms--the continued dominance
of the Orange Order within the community is
proof of political underdevelopment.
Orangism only serves to blind the lower
class members of the socioeconomic class
to cleavages among Protestants. Thus reli-
giously-defined organizations may either
blur or accentuate intraethnic class cleavages: the Malay Parti-Islam seemed to
sharpen them, whereas the Ulster Orange
Order masks them.
        The leadership and organization pro-
vided by many religions (not all) are not
the only resources that ethnic groups may
tap for the sake of ethnic mobilization.

Symbols are sometimes critically needed for
ethnic cohesion and activism, but many
religious symbols are so confined to special
ritualistic settings that they are of
limited use to ethnic groups in wider social
or political contexts. The dietary and
dress codes dictated by religious doctrine
may be the most useful ethnic symbols, since
they are constant reminders of the conflicts
in values between members of the ethnic
groups and outsiders. The Malays who rioted
against the Chinese in Kuala Lumpur in 1969
claimed they were provoked by Chinese youths
who had ridden motor bikes through their
neighborhoods tossing pieces of pork. The
story may be apocryphal but it reflects the
symbolic importance of dietary rules for
Muslims. In Britain Asians and Blacks
(which comprise only 3 percent of the population) have not been able to exert political influence at the national level and
very little at the local level. A major
exception has been the ability of Sikhs to
mobilize over the question of municipal
labor regulations in several industrial
towns. Local uniform regulations required
Sikh bus conductors--Asians and West Indians
provide a large proportion of the British
transport personnel--to give up their turbans or resign their transport jobs. Since
the wearing of turbans is a spiritual duty
for Sikh males the Sikh community mobilized
over this issue to a degree unmatched by
other British-Asians in other social
spheres.[15]

Ideology is a third communal resource
that is potentially derived from religion
and the most obvious ideological reliance
on religion appears when ethnic groups pro-
pound a theocratic state. But the useful-
ness of religion for building distinctly
ethnic ideology can take a subtle form by
supplying the essential values for an
apparently nontheocratic political ideology.
The British Liberal Party became a vehicle
for Welsh ethnic political expression in
the early twentieth century because it derived normative sustenance from NonConform-
ist Protestantism. American Indians have
been hammering out a political platform in a
less organizationally articulated form that
self-consciously relies on the values of
Indian religious convictions about man and
nature.

Increasingly, however, modernist elites
have assumed leadership roles in ethnic
groups and they have tried to cut the religious dimension out of group ideologies for
two reasons: First, the new leaders want
to assert their autonomy and when they rely
on religiously legitimized ideologies they
have to compete with rival religious elites
for community leadership. Second, modernist
leaders may try to broaden the ethnic
group's support base and gain a serious
hearing in public affairs by purging the
community of seemingly narrow or traditional norms. In that case secularized
ideologies become tactically and strategi-
cally advantageous. For example, the
Palestinian Liberation Front has publicly

sought to secularize its ideology so that its appeal is socialist and not simply Muslim Socialist. The leader of the newly created Lebanese Arab Army, Lieutenant Amed al-Khatib declared during the civil war in 1975, "We are fighting against bigoted Maronites, bigoted Sunnis, bigoted Shiites and bigoted Druses. This is an anti-bigot war. This is a war for secularization."[16] However, the war is also being waged to redistribute Lebanese interethnic power.

In summary, religion is neither necessary nor sufficient for ethnic group maintenance but it does provide valuable resources--organizationally, symbolically and ideologically--for groups in need of collective mobilization. The common assumption is, nevertheless, that these resources are most valuable for ethnic groups only in the earliest stages of communal political development. That thesis suggests that ethnic groups will inevitably outgrow their dependence on religious resources. Or, if they do not then they risk deflation of their political potential and even their capacity to survive as distinct groups. Ironically, when the religiously-derived symbols, values, institutions are critical elements in a group's distinctiveness vis-a-vis other groups, the secularization apparently necessary for continual development may result in a collapse of the ethnic boundaries it was intended to preserve.

State Manipulations of Religious-Ethnic
Connections

State authorities concerned over the stability produced by ethnic pluralism have
sought to use religion to reduce or eliminate that threat. They have either sought
to secularize thoroughly the culture and
the concept of citizenry thus making the
religious differences which exacerbate
ethnic antagonisms politically irrelevant,
or they have sought to bind all groups together and to the central state through a
common legitimizing religion. The problems
that face the Soviet regime suggests that
the secularization strategy is indeed difficult. The dissolution of the Pakistani
state demonstrates how little guarantee
there is in legitimizing religion.[17]
    Ethnicity has too often been portrayed
as a "burden" that struggling central
government officials must "cope with." In
reality, state elites as often as not have
exploited ethnicity to divide and rule, in
party building and in creating state symbols.
Similarly the standard development literature usually portrays religion as a burden
that enlightened policy makers must bear until they can find a way to get their
citizens to adopt more rational modes of
thought. In practice, however, religion
has served state elites as the base for
integrating culturally disparate groups and
for legitimizing state programs. The
colonial powers rarely prohibited religious
missionaries from seeking converts. Mission

churches and schools were effective vehicles
for integrating various ethnic groups into
the colonial state system and some of the
significant interethnic conflicts in Asia
and Africa are fueled partly by differences
in Christian missionary targeting. The
Karens in Burma are distinct from the
dominant Burmans partly because of their
Christianity; ethnic splits were exacerbated
in Nigeria by the Christian missionaries
who focused on the Ibo while leaving the
Hausa in the north relatively unconverted.
David and Audrey Smock note that Ghana
is unique because Christian missionaries
did not carve out ethnic blocs, so that
religious lines crosscut ethnic lines and
dilute disintegrative forces.[18]

Some central state leaders have chosen
to adopt neither religious strategy to cope
with multiethnic pluralism. The religious
convictions of the main groups were sometimes so deep and antagonistic that it
appeared impossible to attempt secularization or to pretend that a common religious
consensus could be found acceptable to all
their communities. When the British annexed
Quebec in the eighteenth century they acknowledged the role of the Catholic Church
in French Canadian affairs. Administrators
in Northern Ireland today, both in Ulster
and Westminster, are afraid to tamper with
the ethnic-religious laissez-faire that
permits Protestant and Catholic churches to
exert critical influence in social and
political affairs.[19]

Another perhaps more common approach permits each ethnic group to hold on to its particular religious distinction, yet it confines the operation of religious institutions so that they become peripheral and eventually wither away. In some states this approach may coincide with the attempt of ethnic group leaders to enhance communal capabilities through secularization. In China, for example, the Muslim ethnic minorities are permitted to maintain their religious practices and institutions, but those functions have been strictly circumscribed. This has been the practice in many Eastern European states as well.

This approach may produce a condition of perpetual unease in state leaders who may fear attenuated religious institutions can be revived to serve a rearound ethnic self-consciousness. This apparently is the case in Yugoslavia in the aftermath of outbreaks of Croatian nationalism now that Tito's integrative presence is about to disappear. This anxiety has prompted central elites in Croatia and Serbia to take strong actions against churches. Religious activism, of course, is contrary to secular Marxist-Leninist ideology, and religious revitalization could intensify interethnic hostilities in the admittedly fragile federalist state.[20]

The central state leaders intent on modernizing development (like their ethnic counterparts) face a dilemma because religion is an immensely valuable means for defining national goals, legitimizing collective norms and mobilizing the energies

370

of otherwise politically disinterested
citizens. How can state elites draw upon
religious strengths without risking interethnic fragmentation? The experiment
launched by General Amin in Uganda warrants
analytical attention despite the contempt in
which he is held. Uganda is ethnically
divided in ways that make religion a generally disintegrative force. General Amin's
military coup in 1971 initially was interpreted as heavily ethnic in its form and
goals. Amin, himself a Muslim, was thought
to be bolstering his regime not only
through ethnic purges but through the
deliberate promotion of Muslims in the army
and through religious conversions. However,
Ali Mazrui, a respected African analyst,
recently argued that Amin is really seeking a religious formula that draws on
Christian missionary traditions in Uganda
as well as on Islamic commitment to provide
the Ugandan society an evangelical basis
for national mobilization.[21] The point is,
nonetheless, that Amin's effort is full of
risks in a multiethnic society and, regardless of his intentions, it could eventually
heighten older communal hostilities.

When discussing relationships between
religion and ethnicity it is easy to slip
into mere "variable juggling." It is true
that religion has various impacts on ethnic
awareness and interethnic contacts under
different conditions but it is not very
helpful analytically. It may be more useful
to ask whether religion is important for

ethnic boundary maintenance and ethnic
mobilization in the course of modern development. The foregoing discussion produced
several tentative conclusions regarding this
problem:
     1.   Ethnicity and religion are analyti-
cally separable phenomena, though intimately
interwoven in the self-perceptions of certain ethnic group members.
     2.   Certain types of religion do, how-
ever, provide resources that greatly assist
ethnic groups in their own communal developmental efforts: church organizational structures; legitimized communal leaders; and
widely accepted symbols.
     3.   Central state officials have sought
to dilute threatening ethnic identities by
accentuating overarching religions and by
trying to purge religion from public affairs.
Where state elites have themselves been
specific ethnic elites they may rely on
particular religious resources even at the
risk of alienating other communities.
     4.   Religion, like ethnicity, may be
more adaptable to the needs of modern men
than previously assumed.
     5.   The recent resurgence of ethnicity
in highly industrial societies may provide
religious value systems and organizations
with newly relevant functions.

CHAPTER IX

RELIGION AND ETHNICITY IN
EASTERN EUROPE

by

Michael B. Petrovich

The Religions of Eastern Europe

Historically there have been five major
religious divisions in Eastern Europe:
Orthodox, Catholic, Protestant, Muslim, and
Jewish. It would not be helpful to confine
our inquiry to these broad categories since
there are diverse religious organizations
and expressions in Eastern Europe--just as
there are several linguistic families and
ethnic groups. Church jurisdictions have
been organized along national lines so that
there is a Romanian Orthodox Church, a
Bulgarian Orthodox Church, a Serbian Orthodox Church, and so on. These "autocepha-
lous" churches differ in administration,
language, customs, historical legacy, and
outlook so the Western term "Greek Orthodox"
to cover them all is a misnomer.
     The national Orthodox churches contrast
with the administratively centralized
organization of the Catholic Church since
there is no equivalent to Rome or to the
Pope of Rome in the Orthodox world. Yet a
closer look at the organization of the

Catholic Church in Eastern Europe shows that
national divisions play a part. The Archbishop of Esztergom is primate of Hungary
and is, or claims to be, the voice of his
church and of his people, even when in exile
as in the case of Cardinal Mindszenty.
Cardinal Wyszinski is the primate in Poland,
Archbishop Seper is primate in Croatia, and
so on. Moreover, the Uniate churches in
the Catholic fold, also known as "Greek
Catholic" or "Byzantine rite" churches are
also important. These were originally
Orthodox churches which often accepted the
supremacy of the Pope of Rome and the dogmatic formulations of the Church of Rome
during the sixteenth to eighteenth centuries. They retained their own ritual, non-
Latin liturgical language, the custom of
the laity receiving the Eucharist, a married
pristhood, and other Orthodox customs.
These churches, sometimes large and sometimes miniscule, are located between the
Catholic West and the Orthodox East from
the Baltic to the Mediterranean. They are
all based on a predominant ethnic element--
Ukrainian and Byelorussian, Romanian, Serb-
turned-Croat, and Greek.
      The Protestants are also divided on
ethnic lines as indicated by such names as
"Czech Brethren." It is not by chance
that Slovak Protestants tend to be Lutherans
while most Hungarian Protestants are Calvinists.
      The Jews have various sects which may
not be divided along national lines because
of the Jewish diaspora, but which nonetheless

reflect regional or subethnic divisions.
The Ashkenazic Jews of central Eastern
Europe historically speak Yiddish (derived
from German) and the Sephardic Jews, especially those of southeastern Europe, speak
Ladino (derived from Spanish). The Ash-
kenazim are historically linked with Germany, Poland, Austria-Hungary and the
Russian Empire while the Sephardim lived
in the Ottoman lands of the Balkan Penin-
sula. Each group maintains certain differences of ritual and outlook. There have
also been Jewish sects in Eastern Europe
that are regional. The Chasidim, or
pietists, of Poland are the best example.
    The Muslims are similarly divided
into regional and sometimes ethnic sects.
Most Muslims in Eastern Europe are Sunnites
rather than Shiites, but the Bektashi, a
sect often considered heretical by other
Muslims, is especially strong and played
a particularly prominent role in the rise
of Albanian nationalism.
    The treatment of religion in Eastern
Europe, especially when it involves ethnicity, must consider those major religious
divisions as well as the subdivisions. For
example, a macroscopic view may lead to the
notion that religion plays a homogenizing
role that blurs ethnic lines since each
major division includes various ethnic
groups. That is not an unwarranted conclusion since there is evidence that
religion has been consciously used to sub-
merge or transform ethnic groups by coopting
them. Thus the Greek Catholic Uniates of

Croatia no longer see themselves as Serbs but as Croats. The Austro-Hungarian Empire encouraged Catholics, regardless of ethnic origin, to have a special loyalty for His Catholic Majesty the Habsburg Emperor-King-- or so it was hoped. Yet in Eastern Europe religious communality has not prevented Catholics, Protestants, or members of the Orthodox faith from making war on other Catholics, Protestants, or Orthodox. In his memoirs Milovan Djilas, the ex-Communist leader of Yugoslavia, recalls an incident that occurred in Sofia in 1945. The Communist organizers of a Panslavic Congress decided to add a traditional note to the proceedings by having the delegates attend a thanksgiving service in the Orthodox cathedral. When, according to custom, the head of the Bulgarian Orthodox Church extended his hand cross to each delegate to kiss, Djilas and his Yugoslav communist delegation declined even though the Soviet, Polish and Czech and Slovak delegates had kissed the cross. Djilas asked a non-communist member of his delegation from Serbia, why he had not kissed the cross since he was an Orthodox believer. The Serb replied, "I cannot kiss a Bulgarian cross."[1] The answer is shocking from the Orthodox Christian perspective even though it is understandable in light of Serbian-Bulgarian rivalries and the role of the Bulgarian army of occupation in Serbia during the Second World War. Thus the problem of religion and ethnicity viewed microscopically produces different patterns.

The starting point of this essay will
be clear to any East European and alien
to most Americans in their modern pluralistic and secular society. The formulation
outlined by Paul R. Brass that in the movement from ethnic group to community, "religion becomes not only a matter of personal
belief and of a relationship between a
person and a deity, but a collective experience that unites believers to each
other"[2] is the concern of this paper. That
subject is too vast so it is hoped that a
few selected examples will illustrate some
basic patterns.

Historic Roots

It is axiomatic that religion played a
significant role in the shaping of ethnic,
national identities in Eastern Europe. Yet
one otherwise useful textbook (The Role of
Religion in Modern European History) omits
any reference to the nation-building role of
religion while it ends with an essay on
"Reflections on Religion and Modern Indivi-
dualism."[3] The table of contents of that
work reveals that "European History" in the
title refers only to Western Europe. Nevertheless, there is much to say about religion
and ethnicity even in West European history.

For example, Robert A. Kann notes in a
study entitled "Protestantism and German
Nationalism" that "it is a fact that integral German nationalism, particularly in
Austria, identified Protestantism largely
with the notion of a German religion and a
Great-German empire comprising all ethnic
Germans. Concepts of this kind preceded
the rule of National Socialism by at least
a generation."[4]
    Westerners who have a scant knowledge
of East European history and its complexities tend to think that most East European
peoples have emerged recently. Supposedly
those peoples achieved a sense of national
consciousness in modern times as they
evolved from ethnic masses submerged under
alien empires into nationalities that
gained statehood during the modern "Age of
Nationalism." This view is partly based on
an ignorance of the earlier history of
Eastern Europe before its people became
submerged by those empires. It is also
based on the presumed relationship between
nationhood and statehood. The modern
American understandably views his "nation"
as a country identical with the United
States for historical reasons. Yet, several
generations of Poles believed that although
the Polish state disappeared with the partitions of the late eighteenth century "not
yet has Poland been destroyed," to use the
proud words of the Polish national anthem.
As long as some Poles were conscious of
their identity as Poles there was a Poland
though the state was temporarily gone as an

independent entity.

Most of the peoples of Eastern Europe
achieved a sense of identity and some political expression of that identity in medieval
times, long before the Age of Nationalism.
This sense of identity and the political expressions naturally differed from those of
modern times, but it was there nevertheless.
Indeed, that sense of identity persisted
even after its political forms were destroyed by alien conquerors. The East European peoples assiduously preserved this
continuity and resurrected it in modern
times as a veritable cult of medievalism
which forms an important part of their
Romantic nationalism.[5]

Given the pervasive role of religion in
medieval Europe, it was altogether normal
that the church played a significant role in
transforming separate ethnic groups into
communities and in preserving their consciousness.

During the late Middle Ages various
rulers of pagan ethnic groups in all of
Eastern Europe sought to bring their peoples
into the Christian fold. Church tradition
turned many of those rulers into saints and
portrays them as pious men and women with
eyes turned heavenward as they knelt in
baptismal fonts. Actually of course Prince
Rastislav of Moravia, Tsar Boris of Bulgaria,
Géza and King Stephen of Hungary, Mieszko of
Poland, and Grand Prince Vladimir of Kievan
Rus' had similar motives which, regardless
of religious sincerity, were quite worldly.
These nation-builders wished to unite

disparate tribes, ethnic groups and regions
into single peoples and states. When the
Moravian Prince Rastislav invited the
Byzantine missionary brothers Saints Cyril
(Constantine) and Methodius to bring Christianity to his realm in the midninth century
as part of a military and cultural alliance
with Byzantium his purpose was to keep the
German Franks from expanding further into
Slavic territory. The missionaries' efforts
were successful because of their regard for
the ethnic identity of their converts; Cyril
and Methodius devised the Glagolitic alphabet and translated the church ritual into
the Slavic tongue. The Glagolitic alphabet
was later replaced by the Cyrillic (named
after St. Cyril) and it is used, with local
variations, by all the Orthodox Slavs--
Russians, Ukrainians, Byelorussians, Bulgars,
Serbs, and Macedonian Slavs--to this day.[6]
The Slavic church of the ancestors of the
Czechs and Slovaks gave way to the Latin
church of the militarily superior Franks but
its memory was never lost. A few years
later Boris, the khagan or prince of the
pagan Bulgars, bargained with Rome and
Constantinople to establish Christianity in
his realm. His paramount aim was to create
a national church beholden to no foreign
authority which would cement the ethnic
unity of his proto-Bulgar, vastly more
numerous, Slavic subjects and break the
power of the Bulgar nobles. Thanks to the
efforts of the disciples of SS. Cyril and
Methodius the result was the first Slavic
church to survive. The ancestors of the

Ukrainians and Russians, the Serbs, and the
non-Slavic Romanians later adopted this
ethnic form of orthodoxy.[7]
     Again, nation building was the underly-
ing factor in the official establishment of
Christianity in Poland. Mieszko accepted
conversion to the Catholic faith voluntarily,
in 966, to forestall a German crusade
against his pagan Polish tribes. However,
he took care to select his priests from his
friendly Slavic neighbors the Czechs and not
from the Germans.[8] "Since Bohemia was bi-
liturgical at that time, we may assume
that, besides Latin priests, there came to
Poland priests who used the Slavonic language in the celebration of the sacred mys-
teries."[9] This act of statesmanship
probably had a permanent effect on the ethnic structure of Eastern Europe for it
presented an obstacle to the German eastward
drive contemplated by Emperor Otto I in 967.
Poland's church was Catholic and Latin, but
it was Polish. The Catholic hierarchy played a prominent role in the national life
throughout Polish history and from the beginning the church assumed hegemony in the
cultural development of the Polish people.
It also played a vital political role and
in times of political chaos the church
organization remained as the center of national cohesion. Moreover, the religion
bound all classes of the society and gave
them a national conscience and a sense of
common ethnic consciousness.[10] After the
Reformation in the West and the rise of a
powerful Muscovy in the East Polish

Catholicism merged with Polish patriotism
in the historic confrontation with both
Protestant Prussia and Orthodox Russia. As
a result, Poland has been described as a
<u>diarchy</u> in which state and church cooperated
in a powerful partnership.[11] The shrine of
Our Lady of Częstochowa, one of the Catholic
world's most celebrated goals of pilgrimage,
is a symbol of this partnership and it
evokes patriotic as well as religious feelings. The icon of Our Lady has been venerated since 1656 as a symbol of national
survival, dating from the expulsion of the
Swedish invaders, when King John Casimir
(Jan Kazimierz) dedicated his throne to
Our Lady of Częstochowa as the "Queen of the
Polish Crown."[12]

Historians generally use superlatives
when discussing Stephen (István), Hungary's
first king and national saint, Magyar ruler
from 977 to 1038. He has been described as
"the best-beloved, most famous and perhaps
the most important figure in Hungarian history,"[13] while his coronation as "Apostolic
King" in the year 1000 with the crown sent
by Pope Sylvester II has been called "probably the most significant single act in
the history of Hungary."[14] As a Christian
ruler under the banner of St. Martin of
Tours, his chosen patron saint, Stephen put
down the pagan warlords of his realm, and
his national Catholic church organization
laid the groundwork for the ethnic and
political amalgamation of a multilingual and
multiracial land into a united and powerful
Magyar state. For centuries the expression

"the crownlands of St. Stephen" denoted the
Hungarian realm proper, and regardless of
the question of its authenticity, the "Holy
Crown" of St. Stephen is still held to be
the most ancient symbol of the Hungarian
nation.[15]

The great religious figure among the
Serbs was also a prince but primarily a
churchman, Rastko, the youngest son of
Nemanja, better known under his ecclesiastical name--Saint Sava (1175-1235). His
father founded the united medieval Serbian
state and national dynasty of kings and
emperors, and St. Sava similarly founded a
Serbian Orthodox Church independent of the
Byzantines and was its first primate. One
of St. Sava's most distinguished Serbian
biographers has stated,[16] "One of the reasons why Sava's church organization was so
excellently carried out, that it had such
success and influence on the whole life and
development of the people, lies without
doubt in the fact that St. Sava established
his church organization on a national basis.
St. Sava created a Christian Orthodox Serbian popular church.... Conceived and
founded on a purely national basis, Sava's
church quickly became identical with the
Serbian people, merged with it into a
single whole, and constantly drew its
strength from their racial traits." On
the feast day of St. Sava (January 14 O.S./
27 N.S.) the sermons of nationalist Serbian
priests (and there are hardly any other
kind) often stress that Sava preserved the
Serbian people for Orthodoxy even though

his brother Stephen Nemanja ("the First-
Crowned") accepted a crown from a Pope of
Rome. The implication is that the Serbs
were spared a fate worse than death.

The Church as a Surrogate National State

Religion in Eastern Europe served a nation
building role and it acted as a surrogate
state for people who had lost political
independence. When the Mongols wrecked
what was left of an already disintegrating
confederacy of Russian principalities in
the thirteenth century and imposed their
rule on the Russians and the ancestors of
the Ukrainians (the name "Ukrainian" had
not yet come into being) the Orthodox
Church remained as the only institution
capable of embodying the unity of the whole
people of Rus'. The Ottoman conquest in
the late fourteenth and fifteenth centuries
was a similar phenomenon. The name of the
Ottoman Empire was derived from a particular
branch of Turks, the Osmanli, but the Ottoman Empire was a multinational amalgam of a
theocracy based on military feudalism. The
Empire was based on the supremacy of the
Muslim religion and the exploitation of non-
Muslim subjects in conquered lands. Thus
the role of the individual in that society

and state was determined by religious
affiliation. Religious differentiation
kept the Christian and Jewish peoples of the
Ottoman Empire separate from their Muslim
rulers and helped to preserve their ethnic
identities.

The Ottoman rulers divided their non-
Muslim subjects into religious communities
known as millets comprising Orthodox Christians, Armenian Christians, and Jews. Each
millet had its own organization under its
religious leaders and bodies. The millet
was defined by religious affiliation but
its autonomous administration was concerned
with secular matters such as the allocation
and collection of taxes, education, and
intracommunal legal matters such as marriage,
divorce, and inheritance. All non-Muslim
subjects of the Sultan related to the imperial government by way of the millet. The
Turkish word millet has no religious conno-
tation, it is simply the word for "people"
or "nation." The Muslim rulers of the
Ottoman Empire took for granted that there
was an identity between a people and their
religion.[17]

That was not the case among the Orthodox. Their millet was regarded as "Greek"
(which the Turks designated Rum or Roman,
referring to the Eastern Roman or Byzantine
Empire). Yet most members of the Orthodox
Church in the Ottoman Empire were not Greek
ethnically or linguistically. They were
Slavs, Albanians, and Romanians. Eventually
this surrogate for the Byzantine state favored the hegemony of the Greeks who

controlled the Patriarchate of Constantinople.

A remarkable change in this system of
great importance in the history of the Serbian people took place in 1557. The Serbian
Orthodox Church, previously subordinated to
the Greek Archdiocese of Ohrid after Serbia's fall, was restored by an Ottoman
decree to the level of an independent entity within the Empire, the Patriarchate
of Peć. This act enabled the Serbian Church
to assume the role of a national center
mandated and even protected by the Ottoman
state. It is not necessary to analyze all
of the reasons for this act, but it is worth
noting that the Ottoman Grand Vizir who
engineered it, Mehmed Sokolli, was a
Bosnian Serb and he made his brother
Macarius Sokolović the patriarch of the restored Serbian Church. There were also
certain reasons of state that had greater
importance. In any case all Serbs within
the Ottoman Empire, and even those outside
of its border, owed allegiance to an organization of their own from 1557 to 1766. The
patriarchs of Peć were not merely spiritual
heads but ethnarchs with a quasi-political
function.[18] They governed their own people,
had the power to levy taxes, and even dared
to conduct foreign relations with the enemies of the Ottoman state. This led to
their undoing in 1766 when Sultan Mustafa II
abolished the Serbian Patriarchate of Peć
and placed it under the Patriarchate of
Constantinople.

The Serbian Church continued, however,
to be the voice of the politically leader-
less Serbian people, particularly in Montenegro and southern Hungary, both centers
outside of Serbia. Though nominally under
Ottoman sovereignty, Montenegro constituted
an independent state whose mountain clans
governed themselves but who recognized the
bishop of Montenegro as their leader after
1516. Political necessity, not popular
religiosity, forced a national political
role upon the Orthodox Church of Montenegro
when the Crnojević princes and feudal lords
died, fled or were converted to Islam. The
Church remained as the single unifying
institution and central authority. A Marxist historian of Montenegro wrote: "In such
conditions the clergy has a very prominent
role which the very course of events imposed on them .... This role during that
time was historically progressive."[19] The
Church of Montenegro (more specifically the
Metropolitanate of Cetinje) was "a political
organization whose interests, both political
and economic, extended over the entire territory of Montenegro."[20] And it was that
church that led the national struggle
against Ottoman domination. There was an
almost complete identification between
church and state, and after 1696 the ruling
bishops of Montenegro all belonged to the
Petrović-Njegoš family. This dynastic
succession from celibate uncle to nephew was
not secularized until 1851 when Prince
Danilo II refused to become a bishop. Some
Western writers have referred to Montenegro

under the bishops as a theocracy but it
was not. It was not the church that controlled the nation but the nation that gave
the church a secular role.

The Serbian Orthodox Church in the
Austrian Empire came to assume a quasi-
political role of its own under quite
different circumstances. The "Great Migration" of Serbs from the Ottoman Empire into
southern Hungary occurred in 1690 under
the leadership of the fleeing Patriarch
Arsenius III of Peć and his clergy. Several
imperial charters by Emperor Leopold recognized the Serbian Patriarch as the leader
of his people and granted the Serbs certain
limited rights of political autonomy within
their church organization, including the
election of their own community elders, an
assembly of clergy and laity, and even a
militia.[21] The imperial charter of August
21, 1691, granted Patriarch Arsenius only
the customary ecclesiastical prerogatives,[22]
but the Serbs broadly interpreted those prerogatives to include their entire identity
as a people within an empire. Patriarch
Arsenius comported himself as an ethnarch,
and the report of an imperial commission
observed in 1699 that the Serbs regarded
Arsenius as though he were their king.[23]
The Orthodox Church of the Serbs in the
Habsburg Empire continued to play a dominant
political and social role even with the rise
of a Serbian middle class precisely because
the laity found public expression and exerted its influence in the governance of
the Church and its assemblies. Thus it was

entirely natural that a Serbian assembly
granted Metropolitan Josif Rajačić the
revived title of "Serbian Patriarch" in May
during the 1848 revolution without any
authorization from above.[24] The prelate
assumed civil powers and eventually, military powers as well.[25] Thanks to his
conservative, pro-Habsburg policies, and
increasing secularization the Serbian Church
in the Austrian Empire gradually lost its
hegemony, but the Serbian subjects of the
Habsburgs continued to cling to their religion as the most distinctive badge of their
nationality. The relatively few Serbs who
became Roman Catholics or Uniates were lost
to the Serbian community and began to think
of themselves as Croats by virtue of their
religious conversion.

The Serbian Church did not lose its
national character and role in Ottoman Serbia after the abolition of the Patriarchate
of Peć in 1766. On the contrary, once it
had nothing more to expect from the Ottoman
state it became more than ever a people's
church.

The monks and priests, now alienated
from their Greek bishops, became
even more closely tied to the life
of the people, whose poverty they
shared. At this popular level the
Church continued its role as a
symbol of national unity and as the
propagator of a national mythology.
From a political standpoint, the
chief contribution of the Serbian
Church to the rise of a modern

Serbian nationalism was that it
nurtured, for over four centuries
of Turkish rule, the idea of the
political unity of the Serbian
people. It kept alive and idealized
the memory of the medieval state of
the Nemanja dynasty. It did this
by all the means at its disposal--
its literature, art, sermons, and
even that highest endorsement of all,
canonization. There are today in
the Serbian church calendar some
fifty-eight Serbian saints, including
eighteen tsars, kings and queens,
princes, and lords, beginning with
St. Sava and his father, Nemanja.
The cult of Serbian royal saints--
"the sacred stock of Nemanja"--
constantly reminded the Serbian
people, with all of the awesome pomp
and artistry of the Byzantine ritual,
that the Serbs had once had an
independent kingdom, indeed, an empire, blessed by God through His
wonder-working saints. The Serbian
Church was never preoccupied with
theology or learning, but it was
eminently successful in giving its
people a sense of Christian cultural
and national identity under a non-
Christian and alien government. It
united a people divided by geography
and political administration. It
represented its people before the
Ottoman [and Austrian] government.
On occasion it even led them in open

rebellion. It maintained contacts
with the outside world of Christian
states. It served as a devoted
caretaker of the idea of Serbian
political unity, a link between
the Serbia of the medieval past and
a reborn Serbia of the ever near
future. It was a repository of the
national culture and tradition.
Finally, it was for centuries the
center of social life for a submerged and increasingly oppressed
people.[26]

The Bulgars of the Ottoman Empire unlike the Serbs were not given a church
administration of their own but were placed
under Greek bishops. This resulted in a
cultural Hellenization which particularly
affected the Bulgarian merchant class and
what few educated men there were. This loss
of Bulgarian cultural identity was protested
by the first great awakener of modern Bulgarian nationalism, Father Paisii of
Hilendar (1722-1798?), in his pioneer work
The Slaveno-Bulgarian History in 1762.[27]
This impassioned Orthodox monk had nothing
but scorn for Bulgars who preferred to speak
Greek and who knew nothing of their people's
glorious past before the Ottoman invasion.
The Bulgarian national identity was re-
pressed by Turkish political overlordship
and by the ecclesiastical domination of the
Greeks. The latter was easier to deal with
so the modern Bulgarian national movement
really began with the effort to obtain
church autonomy during the mid-nineteenth

century. That effort was crowned with partial success in 1872 with the establishment of the Bulgarian Exarchate.[28] This autonomous church body was of vast importance in the Bulgarian national revival and the achievement, in 1878, of a Bulgarian national state.

The Bulgarian Exarchate had a large bearing on the problem of ethnicity in Eastern Europe when it opened another phase of the Macedonian Question. The Macedonian Slavs developed no clear consciousness of themselves as a separate nationality so the Bulgars, Serbs, and Greeks competed in claiming them. This struggle was waged largely on a religious platform, and the churches of each contender exerted their spiritual and cultural influence in an intra-Orthodox Kulturkampf. The Ottoman censuses of Macedonia are an unreliable source for determining nationality because the local population tended to equate nationality with religious affiliation.[29]

Religion played a particularly clear role in the ethnically diverse principality of Transylvania. Three ethnic groups or "nations" banded together politically, in 1437--the Magyars, the related Szeklers, and the German "Saxons"--to suppress the Romanians, who outnumbered them all. It was not nationality but social and economic status that determined membership in a "nation," but peasant serfs were excluded and since the vast majority of Romanians were peasant serfs they were barred from political life. The Romanians of

Transylvania were similarly deprived on
religious grounds. Only four religions
were recognized by the Transylvanian Diet:
the Roman Catholic, Lutheran, Calvinist,
and Unitarian. The Orthodox religion of
the majority of people in Transylvania, was
not recognized. Ethnic differences also
played a role: the Germans or Saxons were
Lutheran; the Calvinists, Unitarians and
Roman Catholics were Magyars or Szeklers;
and the Romanians were Orthodox. The members of the recognized churches enjoyed
legally guaranteed freedom of worship, internal autonomy, and proportional representation in all branches of the central
administration but the Orthodox were merely
tolerated. Indeed, they had to pay tithes
for the upkeep of their own church and
that of their landlords. This system remained intact when Transylvania became part
of the Habsburg Empire at the end of the
seventeenth century.
     Given the depressed level of their
social organization and their lack of other
spokesmen, the Romanians of Transylvania
relied on their church and priests for
organization and leadership. "In the absence of public institutions and a political
base from which to operate, the Orthodox
Church, which had sheltered their language
and preserved their national identity during
the oppressive fifteenth, sixteenth, and
seventeenth centuries, served as a center
around which the movement for national
regeneration might coalesce."[30] Inasmuch as
the priests and their flocks had endured

oppression together, there was a strong
bond between them so that the clergy
exerted "a decisive influence upon the
Rumanian national movement throughout the
eighteenth and nineteenth centuries."[31]
     Many Orthodox clergy and people in
Transylvania united with the Church of Rome
between 1697 and 1700. They were prompted
mostly by a desire for official recognition
of their nationality and a better life and
not by religious feeling. The Uniate
Church allowed them to keep their Byzantine
ritual, the Romanian language of worship,
and their customs intact, and still gave
them hope for legal recognition as a "fourth
nation." Though relegated to second-class
citizenship in the Habsburg state and the
Catholic Church, the Uniate Church played
an even more active role than the Orthodox
in serving as spokesman for the exploited
Romanian people, in lifting the cultural
level of the Roman people of Transylvania,
and in preparing the way for the Romanian
national movement. Significantly all four
of the major figures of the Romanian cultural rebirth in late eighteenth century
and early nineteenth century Transylvania
came from this Uniate milieu: Bishop Samuel
Clain (Klein, Micu), Father Gheorghe Şincai,
Father Petru Maior, and Ion Budai-Deleanu.
Only Budai-Deleanu was not a priest but he
was the seminary-trained son of a Uniate
priest. These men wrote historical and
linguistic works which contributed to the
Romanians' perception of themselves as a
people with a proud, Roman, past and

separate ehtnic identity. In Maior's words,
"true Romans descended from true Romans."[32]
        The Transylvanian Romanians were de-
prived of representation in the central
government and Diet of Transylvania, so the
government of their church, especially the
Orthodox where lay participation was traditional, permitted them to experience a
quasi-civil as well as spiritual identity.
Thus the Orthodox and Uniate clergies played
leading roles in the Romanian national
movement that was powerfully manifested in
the mass meeting on the "Field of Liberty"
at Blaj during the 1848 Revolution. The
popular assembly that proudly proclaimed
the dignity of Romanian nationhood in
Transylvania on that occasion elected Orthodox Bishop Andreiu Saguna and Uniate Bishop
Ioan Lemenyi as its copresidents.[33] However abortive that attempt was, Bishop
Şaguna went on to win many rights for his
people before he died in 1873, "and his
services to the Romanian national cause were
no less signal than those of his great contemporary, Bishop Strossmayer, to the cause
of Yugoslav culture and national unity."[34]
        The Soviet Union is outside the scope
of this survey, but the Ukrainians are a
part of the history of Poland and the Habsburg Empire. The Orthodox and Uniate
churches since the union of 1596 have been
standard-bearers of Ukrainian ethnicity, and
continued that role under the Russians--
despite tsarist and communist persecution.
The weakening and assimilating of the
Ukrainians was the goal when the Polish

Crown and Roman Catholic Church engineered
the Union of Brześć (Brest) in 1596. However, the union revitalized the Orthodox
Church in its struggle and forced the
Uniate Greek Catholic Church to eventually
become "the very fortress of Ukrainian
separatism against Poland" in defense of
Ukrainian rights.[35]

The Jews of Poland were similarly a
religiously defined ethnic group before and
after the Partitions of the eighteenth century. As in the Ottoman Empire, the Jewish
community in Poland was a religious as well
as a civil entity. The unit of self-
government was the kahal or local community.
The charter of King Sigismund Augustus
(1551) the magna charta of Jewish autonomy
in Poland entitled the Jews to elect by
general agreement (unanimi voto et consensu
are the exact words of the document) their
own rabbis and lawful judges to take charge
of their spiritual and social affairs.[36]
When the rabbi of Brześć complained to the
king in 1531 that the Jews did not always
respect his decisions but came with their
suits before royal judges, Sigismund I
warned the Jews to submit to the jurisdiction of their own "doctors" or rabbis, who
dispensed justice according to the "Jewish
law" and who could impose all kinds of
penalties, including excommunication.[37] The
"Jewish law" was based on the Bible and the
Talmud. This firmly knit organization of
communal self-government, theocratic as it
was, involved the "laity" as much as in the
Jewish or Christian Orthodox and Armenian

millets in the Ottoman Empire. The Jewish
historian S.M. Dubnow observed, "It provided
the stateless nation with a substitute for
national and political expression, keeping
public spirit and civic virtue alive in it,
and upholding and unfolding its genuine
culture."[38] It follows that modern Zionism
is largely the creation of Central and East
European Jewry. Their religion was also
nation building in that it preserved the
memory of the lost homeland and the hope
that all would gather "next year in Jerusalem" in a liberated Zion.

Religion as the Ally of Militant Nationalism

The Church has been literally militantly
involved in movements for ethnic survival
and wars for national independence in Eastern Europe from medieval times to the present.
       The Czech wars of religion during the
Reformation cannot be understood without
reference to the social and national self-
assertion of the Czech Slavs against the
Germans. The eminent British historian of
the Reformation, Bishop Mandell Creighton,
put it clearly, "The condemnation of Hus was
not merely a matter of faith; it was a step
towards suppressing the movement of the

398

Czechs against the Germans in Eastern Europe."[39] The Czech historian František Palacký referred to the government of the victorious Protestant Czech crusaders in Prague as a "theocratic Republic."[40] Another Czech historian, Kamil Krofta, observed that the Hussite struggle permanently affected the Czech national character by giving Czechs

> the idea of some special character
> attaching to the Czech nation, of
> its call to great deeds in the
> service of God and the divine
> law. The national consciousness
> of the Czechs thus acquired a
> special mystical tinge and im-
> pressive fervour, and the Czech
> national idea was enriched by
> the thought that the nation,
> apart from its defensive struggle
> against the German menace, had
> had a great positive task laid
> upon it--a fight for the pure truth
> of God.[41]

The Czech religious reformers strengthened national sentiments by raising the Czech language above Latin in their worship. One of the basic motifs in the Czech Protestants' "Holy War" was a national struggle against German overlordship, so they naturally undertook to "Czechisize" the University of Prague and the municipal administration in Bohemia by purging the German element and by replacing Latin with the Czech language in the church, the administration, the courts, and the Diet.[42]

The chorales of these Czech crusaders,
the Taborites and the Czech brethren, were
resurrected in the nineteenth century by
Smetana, Dvorak, and other national musi-
cians to inspire a modern Czech national
upsurge. Their numerous fortress churches
can still be seen in Slovakia.

Churchmen played a prominent role in
the Serbian and Greek wars for independence
against the Turks in the nineteenth century
as supporters and martyrs and as fighting
leaders. There was nothing in the Serbian
national ethos to prevent a Christian priest
such as Luke Lazarevic from leaving his
parish to become a revolutionary fighter,
similarly the Greeks honor the memory of the
fiery and unsaintly priest, Papaphlessas as
a heroic warrior.

Dozens of Orthodox priests played
active roles in the Serbian insurrections
against the Turks. During the First Serbian
Insurrection in 1804-1813 Archpriest Matija
Nenadović served as a diplomat, as a procur-
er of weapons and ammunition, and as a
mounted warrior.[43] The first head of the
newly autonomous Serbian Orthodox Church in
1831, Bishop Meletius Pavlović, earned the
sobriquet "The Drummer" during the Battle
of Ljubić in 1815 when he saved the day by
beating a drum to rally the wavering Serbian
soldiers.[43] His portraits frequently show
him either with a drum[44] or with a cross
in one hand and a drawn sword in the other.[45]
This was entirely appropriate to a people
whose avowed aim was to fight "for the
venerable Cross and golden freedom."

The Greek War of Independence is
traditionally thought to have begun on
March 25, 1825 (O.S.) when the Metropolitan
Bishop of Patras Germanos raised the flag
of revolution at the monastery of Aghia
Lavra in the northern Peloponnesus.[46] The
modern Greek flag is different in color but
it still bears a cross. The conservative
Greek hierarchy was mostly hesitant and
skeptical about the uprising, but the village priests were solidly with the people.
Every Greek child is familiar with
Athanasius the Deacon (Diakos) who fought
for three hours with eighteen comrades
against 18,000 Turks. He was taken prisoner
and told his life would be spared if he
became a Muslim and he replied:

Go you and your faith, you filth,
to hell with you! I was born a
Greek, a Greek will I die.[47]

The Serbs also have a folk hero (recently canonized) in Avakum (Habbakuk), who
went to his execution carrying the stake on
which he was to be impaled singing, "There
is no fairer faith than the Christian."
He also refused to become a Muslim, and the
Turks recognized his courage by stabbing him
to death before impaling him.[48]

Monasteries played a vital role in the
Serbian and Greek insurrections against the
Ottoman Empire. The monasteries were centers of Serbian national life and culture
for centuries, particularly under Ottoman
rule when the culture of the towns of Serbia
was Turkish and Levantine. The monasteries
were often situated in remote areas, away

from the Turks, and thus provided the rebel
Serbs ideal meeting places, havens of refuge, rallying points for troops, head-
quarters for commanders, and even munition
dumps and storehouses. Serbian monasteries
served as the seat of government for the
rebel Serbs on several occasions. The
monastery of Arkadi in Crete was the scene
of a celebrated event in the Second War of
Greek Independence in 1866. The Greek
defenders blew up their powder magazines
killing 450 Turks along with almost as many
Greeks.[49]

During the wars for independence from
the Russians in 1830-1831 and again in 1863,
the Roman Catholic Poles used their churches
and monasteries for protection, and fighting
priests were not unknown according to the
account of a Russian Panslavist in 1863:

From the thickness of the woods ...
a band of insurgents is making its
way to the village. At the head
of the column rides a Catholic
priest. Merely an hour ago he
might have celebrated the holy mass.
In one hand he still holds the
cross, in the other ... what would
you think? Perhaps the swords of
Peter, that symbol of secular
power? No, this sword which had
once threatened the universe had
long dropped from the senile hand.
It had been relegated to the
arsenal and in its stead the servant
of the Roman Church holds a six-
barrel gun. Where words are powerless

a bullet will do the job....[50]
The closing of a number of Catholic
monasteries in 1864 was one of the chief
features of the cruel Russian pacification
of the insurrection. The Catholic Church
paid the price for the clergy's part in the
uprising.[51]

The Situation Since World War II

Despite the subjective and objective difficulties involved it is important to study
the role played by East European ethnicity
today. That role is interesting since almost all of Eastern Europe, except for
Greece, is Communist and the Marxist leaders in the East European countries continue
to expect that religion "the opium of the
people" will wither away. It is, however,
impossible to obtain adequate data since
the Communist states neither collect nor
report religious statistics in their
censuses on the specious grounds that religion is a private matter.
Certainly many East Europeans, not
just Communists, regard themselves as nonbelievers in any religion. In 1962, for
example, the Bulgarian Academy of Sciences
announced the result of a survey that revealed only 35.5 percent of the population

was religious.[52]   A questionnaire in Yugoslavia similarly purported to show that 10
to 15 percent of the population of the six
Yugoslav republics is "non-believing" except
for Montenegro, where nonbelievers reportedly comprised 25 percent.[53]   It is also
possible that religious affiliations in
Eastern Europe may have very little to do
with personal beliefs or church attendance.
In 1968 another poll purported to find that
only 51 percent of all Yugoslavs believed
in God, or were willing to say so; however,
the reporter wrote, "many more Yugoslavs
cross themselves and observe holy days than
believe in God."[54]   In that milieu people
may practice no religion at all and yet
identify themselves with a particular religion in ethnic or cultural terms.   That
viewpoint is accepted by the Yugoslav
government which introduced the categories
of "Muslims in the sense of ethnic affiliation" (1961) and "Muslims in the sense of
nationality" (1971) in its postwar censuses.
These designations did not comprise all the
Muslims in Yugoslavia, the Albanian and
Turkish minorities were excluded for example.   They did, however, apply to the million and a half South Slavs of Bosnia-
Hercegovina with Muslim cultural backgrounds
though they were originally of Serbian or
Croatian stock.   The Yugoslav censuses under
the Communist regime deliberately avoid
statistics on religion so the use of the
term "Muslim" has nothing to do with religious affiliation.[55]   One of those Muslims
from Bosnia-Hercegovina, sociologist Esad

Čimić, observed in a scholarly study that "in the final analysis, religion is an <u>integral part of national culture</u>" whereas "atheism has no very significant influence in the <u>cultural</u> legacy."[56] [italics his]

There is evidence that religion, like nationalism, lingers tenaciously in Communist Eastern Europe and occasionally shows signs of vigorous life. It is difficult to gauge the factors that may account for this, particularly those subjective factors that may involve individual beliefs and relationships to a deity. Where religion is a badge of ethnicity, however, it survives and takes on renewed vigor. Two examples lend credence to this assertion.

Two minorities at opposite ends of Eastern Europe, the Albanians and the Lithuanians, are both under Communism. It appears that organized religion in Communist Albania is virtually dead. The government closed 2,169 mosques and churches in 1967 and proudly proclaimed Albania to be the first atheist state in the world.[57] This action followed two decades of state interference and harassment in the affairs of three major faiths--Muslims, Bektashi and non-Bektashi and the Orthodox (especially the Catholic).[58] The Communist regime simply banned religion from public life, but the true feelings of the people may be another matter. Nevertheless, the success of the regime should not be attributed simply to its own harsh measures because religion never played the same role in the rise of Albanian nationalism that it did in

adjacent states. The Albanians were divided
into Muslims and Christians, and each group
was divided within itself, so Albanian ethnic unity was not based on religion. Modern
Albanian nationalism flourished despite
those religious divisions and religion did
not play a divisive role politically or even
educationally. Albania never had an official state religion either as a republic or
as a kingdom after its founding in 1912.[59]
Religious tolerance in Albania was not an
expression of enlightenment rather it was
born of national expediency and a general
lack of strong religious convictions.[60]
     The Lithuanian experience was quite
different. The Lithuanian nation has been
committed to Roman Catholicism ever since
the fourteenth century when the rulers
chose a pro-Polish rather than a pro-
Moscovite policy. Lithuanians are almost
by definition Roman Catholics. Roman
Catholicism is as much a badge of Lithuanian
ethnic identity as it is with the Irish.
In both cases religion has been used to preserve the ethnic community from the en-
croachments of an alien imperialism.
Language, folk culture, and Catholicism
defined the Lithuanian people in the old
Russian Empire. The persistence of the
religious factor helps explain why the Soviet regime has been particularly hard on the
Roman Catholic Church in the Soviet Socialist Republic of Lithuania. Yet persecution
has promoted an upsurge of national revulsion and protest among Lithuanians. This

sentiment was dramatically expressed in December 1971 when 17,059 Lithuanians defied the Soviet regime by signing a "Memorandum of the Roman Catholics of Lithuania."[61] That public protest decried the antireligious measures of the government as an abuse of the Soviet Constitution itself. Without impugning the religious motives of the Lithuanian protesters, it must be noted that the religious question in the Soviet Union is the most effective issue on which Lithuanians can express their national sentiments and solidarity against Russian Soviet control.

It has become commonplace to note that Yugoslavia contains six republics, five nationalities, four languages, three religions, two alphabets, and one political party. The tensions caused by these differences render the relationship between ethnicity and religion in Yugoslavia acute. Various competing economic and political rivalries repeatedly result in outbursts of cultural nationalism and religion played a significant role in those tensions because nationality and religion have been traditionally linked. The fateful Serbian-Croatian Question is a dominant, but not the only, factor in this problem. The ineradicable memory of the Croatian Ustasha massacre of from 300,000 to 600,000 Serbs of Croatia during the Second World War colors the whole issue. The Serbs feel, and the feeling is buttressed by official Yugoslav publications, that the Roman Catholic Church was implicated in the

massacre.[62] There is no doubt that the
Roman Catholic Church converted thousands
of Orthodox Serbs who were thus saved by
adopting the national religion of the
Croats. The degree to which the Croatian
Catholic authorities acted as accomplices
of terrorism or from compassion is not easy
to answer.

During the last decade religion has
exhibited various manifestations of a
particularist nationalist role in Yugoslavia
and the Orthodox religion has been most
assiduous in that respect.

The Serbian Orthodox Church has traditionally assumed the role of guardian of the
Serbian nation and its cultural heritage.
The Serbian Patriarchate went beyond religious impulses when it buried the remains
of Tsar Dusan the Mighty (1308-1366) in an
ornate sarcophagus in St. Mark's Church
in Belgrade as tens of thousands looked on
in 1968.[63] The political leaders were
conspicuously absent and judging by certain
pronouncements in the press, they felt that
it was inappropriate for the Serbian Church
to be concerned with a secular political
matter since Tsar Dusan was neither an
ecclesiastic nor a saint. Indeed, he mur-
dered his own father. Nevertheless, the
Serbian Church leaders found it normal to
honor Dusan's memory in a splendid public
ceremony that seemed to be a mass demonstra-
tion of Serbian national feeling more than a
religious fete.

The role of the Serbian Church is particularly significant since the Serbs are

politically divided among the various republics of Yugoslavia, yet they are nationally united by the church. Unlike the
Yugoslav state, the Serbian Church is not
federalistic but centralistic and sees the
Serbian nation as an integral whole. Thus
when Patriarch German declares that the
Montenegrins are Serbs, though the state
regards the Montenegrins as a separate
nationality it is a direct affront to official policy.[64] The Orthodox Archbishop
of Montenegro Danilo II has no doubts about
his Serbian ethnicity.

One of the most important ecclesiastical developments in Southeastern Europe
was the establishment of a separate Macedonian Orthodox Church in Yugoslav Macedonia in 1967.[65] This act, plainly abetted
by the Yugoslav League of Communists since
1945, was a major step in affirming a
separate Slavic Macedonian nationality.
The move hurt the Serbian Orthodox Church,
which had jurisdiction over the Orthodox
dioceses of Yugoslavia the most but it also
pained the political and church leaders of
Bulgaria and Greece. They shared the Serbian Church's reluctance to recognize the
Macedonian Slavs as a nationality. The
official Yugoslav press chastised Serbian
church leaders for referring to the Macedonians as an "ethnic group" rather than
as a nationality as proclaimed by the constitution.[66]

Since achieving autonomy the Macedonian
Orthodox Church has asserted its role as the
symbol of the national unity of Macedonian

Slavs wherever they reside, presumably including Bulgaria and Greece. The Bulgars,
who have traditionally regarded Cyril and
Methodius as "their" saints, were vexed
when the Macedonian Church appropriated the
"Apostles of the Slavs" as its own symbols.
The same may be said of the apostles' Bulgarian disciple, St. Clement of Ohrid; a
visit to the tomb of St. Cyril in the Church
of San Clemente in Rome will reveal that
wreaths and plaques are left there by separate Macedonian and Bulgarian delegations.[67]
In 1969 during the Macedonian delegation's
visit, Archbishop Dositheus (himself a
Serb!) addressed St. Cyril directly in the
name of "the children of the people from
whose loins thou too hast sprung."[68]
        Such symbols are, of course, important
to the Orthodox and to the Roman Catholic
Croats in recent years. The Roman Catholic
Church in Croatia has undergone a steady
process of "Croatization" especially in the
last decade. The substitution of Croatian
for Latin in the Mass was in line with the
worldwide introduction of the vernacular in
the Roman Mass. In Croatia, however, it had
special significance as a vindication of the
centuries old use of the Glagolitic Slavonic
Mass in some Croatian regions. This Croatian version of Church Slavonic held out
against Romanizing influences particularly
in northern Dalmatia under Venetian and
Austrian rule and became a badge of Croatian
ethnicity. In addition, a new Croatian
translation of the Bible appeared in 1968,
a traditional landmark of cultural

nationalism in European history.[69]

The Roman Catholic dioceses of Rijeka and Split were elevated to the rank of Metropolitan Provinces in 1969. The elevation of Split evoked particularly strong national feelings because Split was an important national ecclesiastical center during the medieval period. The leading Croatian Catholic newspaper Glas Koncila (Voice of the Council) observed "The restoration of this archbishopric and metropolitanate evokes the ancient glory of the Croatian kingdom."[70]

The national pride of Croatian Catholics was further enhanced by the beatification of a Croat, St. Nikola Tavelić, in Rome on June 21, 1970. The ceremony brought over 15,000 Croats to Rome from Yugoslavia and elsewhere to honor the memory of an obscure fourteenth century martyr who had spent most of his life outside of Croatia and died in Jerusalem. That did not matter since Tavelić was the only Croat sainted in the 1300 years since Croats were converted to Christianity. The ethnic significance of his beatification was vividly recorded by the correspondent of Glas Koncila who reported "One must experience this in Italy, in a world arena where not to have a saint of one's own is to be an incomplete, immature nation."[71] The newspaper reported that every time Pope Paul mentioned the words Croat and Croatia the Croatian pilgrims applauded mightily. They also sang their national songs and danced their circle dances in St. Peter's

vast square. Some visited the Croatian
Institute of St. Jerome in Rome and prayed
at the grave of Katarina Kotromanić, who
died in 1478 as the last Croatian queen.
Tito and other Communist leaders had chided
the Roman Catholic Church of Croatia for
not being more national, more tied to the
people as an ethnic entity, it was feared
that the Croatian Roman Catholic Church was
too much a propagator of Croatian nationalism.
     There are other illustrations of the
continuing bond between ethnicity and religion in Eastern Europe today. Indeed,
the lack of such bonds would be unnatural
since the roots of both have been intertwined for a millenium. It is particularly
interesting to note the different patterns
of this linkage in Eastern Europe.
     Religion and nationality are inextri-
cably bound among the non-Communist Greeks.
The Orthodox Church is the established
church in Greece, and it maintains the
prerogatives of a state church, including
direct influence on the young through its
participation in the system of public education. The dictatorial regime of the
colonels was overthrown in 1974, but it is
well to remember that the most visible
slogan, emblazoned on walls and specially
built arches everywhere, was "Greece of the
Christian Greeks" that slogan cultivated an
official Orthodox piety to dramatize anti-
Communism and to gain acceptance by the
Greek people at large.

412

Strife between Greeks and Turks has
marred the history of Cyprus almost from its
inception as a republic in 1960. Religious
beliefs are not necessarily the cause of
that strife, but there is no doubt that
religion plays a major role. It provides
a badge of distinction between the two
ethnic communities on Cyprus (Greek Orthodox and Muslim), and it symbolizes an inherited set of attitudes toward each other.
Like the Montenegrin archbishops of past
centuries, Archbishop Makarios III, ruled
in Cyprus from 1960 until his death in 1977,
not just as president of the republic but
as the ethnarch of the Greek Cypriotes.
All religions in Communist Eastern
Europe have felt the heavy hand of authoritarian and atheist regimes whose ideologies
anticipate the eventual disappearance of
religion. Yet the treatment of religion
varies widely from country to country and
from religion to religion. The treatment
ranges from the seemingly complete obliteria-
tion of organized religion in Albania, to
the official patronage of religion in
Yugoslav Macedonia next door. In any case,
ethnicity plays a decided role in this
variation. No one religion in Albania is
associated with the folk ethos or with the
rise of modern nationalism, and hence none
has the strength that comes with such a
role. The Communist government in Yugoslav
Macedonia eagerly promotes acceptance of a
distinct Macedonian Slavic nationality and
homeland, and the establishment of an autonomous Orthodox church as a time-honored way

to signal a nation's coming of age. That
signal has been heeded by thousands of
Macedonian Slavs in neighboring countries
and even in the New World and Australia.
    Something similar occurred in Bulgaria
in 1935 under the auspices of the Communist
state, when the Bulgarian Exarchate was
raised to the higher rank of a national
Patriarchate. Bulgaria again had a patriarch of its own after 560 years.[72] The
step was reminiscent of Stalin's decision
during the Second World War to allow the
Russian Orthodox Church to elect its first
patriarch in over a quarter century. The
state desired the support of a national
church in both cases. From the standpoint
of ethnic rivalries it is interesting to
note that representatives of the other
Orthodox churches of the socialist states
were present at the ceremony in Sofia,
while representatives of the Greek Churches
were conspicuously absent. The Patriarch
of Constantinople took several years to recognize the Bulgarian Patriarchate.[73] The
new Bulgarian Patriarch, Cyril, was an
accommodating ally of the Communist state
and appeared often at special state functions. The feast day of SS. Cyril and
Methodius remains a national holiday in
Communist Bulgaria as the Day of Bulgarian
Literacy. It is observed annually by a
mammoth parade in Sofia, as grand as that
on May Day. The University of Sofia is
named after St. Clement of Ohrid (in
Yugoslav Macedonia!), and an icon of the
saint occupies a place of honor on the wall

behind the Rector's chair. Father Paisii
of Hilendar (the Serbian monastery in Greek
Mount Athos!) is as much a national hero
under the Communists as he was under the
"monarcho-fascists" of former days. A
modern statue of him graces the square in
front of St. Sophia's Church near the Par-
liament. "The Oath," a painting by S. Rusev
done in 1966 is displayed in the National
Gallery of Art and it depicts a group of
Bulgarian nineteenth century freedom fight-
ers crossing themselves as they take an
oath before an altar on which there is a
pistol, a knife, a Gospel, and a cross.

After a forceful purge of the Orthodox
hierarchy and clergy in Romania by the new
Communist regime after the Second World War,
the Communist state found a cooperative ally
in the newly elected head of the Romanian
Orthodox Church Patriarch Justinian (Marina).
Yet even as that Church collaborated with
the Communist state, it continued its role
as a symbol of Romanian national unity.
The canonization of seven Romanian saints in
1955 was symbolically important in that
respect.[74] More substantially, the Romanian
Orthodox Church increased its numbers by
taking the Uniates into its fold. As in
Communist Czechoslovakia and the Ukraine,
the Stalinesque regime in Romania used the
national Orthodox Church to terminate the
Uniate Greek Catholic Church. The Communists abhorred the Uniates for ideological
reasons and because the latter had ties with
Rome and the Catholic West. The Uniates
were branded less patriotic because of those

ties. That was the message conveyed by
Patriarch Justinian when he was enthroned
on June 6, 1948. He addressed the Uniates
as follows: "What separates us at this
time? Nothing but the faithful submission
you still give to Rome. Give back this
loyalty to the Church of our nation, the
Church of our forefathers and of yours...."[75]
In that same year the Uniates were forced
by state decree to be "reintegrated" into
the Orthodox Church. At a solemn ceremony
of reintegration held in the Orthodox
Cathedral of Alba Iulia, a joint declaration
proclaimed, "Starting from today, all Romanians are united in faith, united in the
constant service of our people, in the
faithful obedience to the precepts of the
new life of our beloved R[omanian] P[eo-
ple's R[epublic]."[76] Thus Romanian ethnicity, the Orthodox religion, and the
Communist regime joined forces in a new
nationalism despite the opposition of many
martyred Uniate dissidents who preferred
persecution to submission. With the inclusion of the Uniates, who comprised about 8
percent of the population, the Romanian
Orthodox Church now included over 80 percent
of the population and all but a handful of
ethnic Romanians.

The Uniates was not the only religious
group to be persecuted in Romania after the
Second World War. All were, including the
Orthodox. However, most of the other groups
are notably associated with particular ethnic minorities. The vast majority of Roman

Catholics, Calvinists, Lutherans, Unitarians, and Baptists in Romania are either Hungarians or Germans. Another 4 percent of the population is Jewish, and 1 percent is Muslim. They share common religious and cultural ties with coreligionists outside of Romania and in the non-Communist world and they are all suspect. The statutes of 1949 which govern religious bodies stipulate that they be independent of foreign religious authorities; the only exception are the Armenians, because their religious leader resides in the Soviet Union.[77]

Religious loyalties and ethnic tensions in Yugoslavia continue to reinforce each other under the watchful eye of a wary government. In Poland the Roman Catholic Church maintains a surprisingly strong position in the modus vivendi between church and state that has survived a succession of Communist governments. This is less so in Czechoslovakia, where the Czechs have long been lukewarm in their Catholicism, and in Hungary, where almost a third of the population is non-Catholic and largely Protestant (Calvinist and Lutheran).

Whatever the ultimate fate of ethnicity, religion and Communism in Eastern Europe, Communism as a newcomer on the scene has had to come to terms with both ethnicity and religion. These terms differ according to the degree of identification between a given religion and an ethnic group, especially since Communism has taken

on national forms, the strength of that
identification is not likely to dissolve
easily where it has had a long tradition.

CHAPTER X

ETHNICITY IN EASTERN EUROPE

by

Peter F. Sugar

The last chapter of any study written by
several scholars can take several forms.
It might briefly recapitulate the major
points and original contributions of the
authors; it might contribute a conclusion;
or it might add to the treatment of the
topic. Each of these alternatives is
appealing yet this volume will be ended
differently. The approach taken grew out
of the discussions held during the three
day conference. When theoretical issues
were debated during that meeting, some
area specialists prefaced their remarks
by saying, "but in Eastern Europe ..." and
others who were not East European specialists asked, "why in Eastern Europe...?"
The participants tried to bring together
theory, worldwide observation, and the
East European experience, yet were repeatedly faced with East European peculiarities
that made this attempt very difficult. One
participant even suggested that the theoretical introduction, Chapter I, should be
paralleled by a short historical introduction explaining the peculiarities of Eastern

419

Europe. These remarks and suggestions gave impetus to this attempt to present the "Case of Eastern Europe," for those interested in the problem of ethnicity.

Rereading the original and the reworked chapters several times confirmed the need to devote the last chapter to the "peculiar" features of ethnicity in Eastern Europe. These "peculiarities" are in no way "abnormal, atypical, sui generis," or so unique they cannot be found elsewhere, too; there is no need to present a picture of East European ethnicity as something special. The goal is to focus on several historical features and developments--all of which have also been observed outside of Eastern Europe--that created a matrix for the birth, growth, and persistence of ethnicity in Eastern Europe giving it characteristics that led to this inquiry.

Several authors have noted that states are not nations, nations are not ethnic groups, and that ethnicity is different from nationalism. They have paid more attention to the process that transforms an ethnic group into a nation than to any other topic. This chapter will focus on ethnicity.

There is no universally accepted definition of ethnicity. Yet, the concept is clear judging by the general agreement reached by the contributors to this volume. Professor Enloe stated that "... there is growing agreement that [ethnicity] is both objective and subjective. It involves cultural attributes that can be observed, but those attributes must be assigned conscious

value by a collection of people in order to
amount to ethnicity.... Ethnicity is a
social phenomenon, requiring a sense of belonging and an awareness of boundaries
between members and nonmembers however
vague...." This definition takes into
consideration the "objective attributes,
subjective feelings, and behavioral patterns," often manifested by the use of
numerous symbols, that result in a sense of
ethnic identity by "a group of people ...
in order to differentiate themselves from
other groups," to quote Professor Brass.
Professor Fishman stressed the same thing,
in different terms, when he insisted on the
importance of "experiencing ethnicity from
the inside,"--the subjective feeling--before
it can be understood. Dr. Hofer's approach
to the problem is that of a scholar looking
at ethnicity from the inside. This same
approach reappears in Dr. Connor's analysis
when, following Max Weber, he writes about
the myth without which no ethnic feeling of
solidarity can develop.
    The problem, then, is not to define
what ethnicity is, but what forces bring
it into being and make it the common belief
of an "ethnic category" or an "etnnic
group." This crucial question presents a
difficulty.
    There seems to be agreement when this
problem is approached "chronologically."
According to Professor Fishman ethnicity
developed in the premodern, preindustrial
period produces "pre-mobilizational ethnicity ... the untutored and largely

unconscious ethnicity of everyday life."
Professors Gellner and Brass address "ethnicity in industrial, or industrializing"
societies during and after the eighteenth
century. Their version of ethnogenesis
suggests that it is important to recognize
problems of economic competition, class
distinction, and the numerous cultural and
social boundaries that Professor Gellner
schematizes with such remarkable skill.
But by dealing with national and not ethnic
conflict situations, he provides a good,
first indication of where to look for important boundaries separating ethnicity
from nationalism. He notes:

> Nationalism is, essentially, the
> transfer of the focus of man's
> identity to a culture which is
> mediated by literacy and an ex-
> tensive, formal educational
> system. It is not the mother
> tongue that matters, but the lan-
> guage of the école maternele.

Each chapter in this book touched on the
problem of schools and Professor Rezler
provides some important statistical details.
The use of scholars as a major propaganda
weapon available to the state to teach and
enforce conformity is nothing new. Those
who fight for private schools that teach in
a multiplicity of languages strive to maintain their "nationality" or national minority rights because the state dominated,
modern school system belongs to a modern,
industrialized world. The Poles made the
organization and maintenance of a private

school system a fundamental goal of "organic work" in the mid-1820s to defend their
nationality, not simply to preserve their
language or ethnicity. By then the Poles
had acquired the "activated consciousness
of ethnicity" that transformed it into nationalism. This transformation had occurred
more slowly among the other people of Eastern Europe by 1820. The Poles were ahead
of everybody else and their advanced status
was due to the early attempts at modernization and industrialization following the
partitions of Poland in 1772 and later in
1793 and 1795.

The Poles retained, with their nationalism, features of their ethnic identification, "those socio-cultural behaviors and
values that derive from and define membership in communities of putative common
ancestry." (See Fishman, p.   ) Those features are perceived in Professor Petrovich's
discussion of the Poles.

The Poles of the 1820s were ethnically
and nationally conscious. The relevant
literature on that subject has never seriously considered the existence of that dual
consciousness since nationalism is traditionally considered to be a "modernized,"
politicized form of ethnicity. Economic
modernization and political nation building
in Eastern Europe and several other regions
occurred simultaneously under difficult
circumstances amidst linguistically, religiously, and culturally heterogenous people.
That does not involve the "orderly" development of ethnicity first and a transformation

into nationalism, rather it is an emergence
of the phenomenon that Dr. Connor calls
"ethnonationalism." "Ethnonationalism"
differs from premodern ethnicity and post-
modern nationalism. It develops under
circumstances with the same characteristics
under which ethnicity develops "organically"
in the pre-modern setting, and those of nationalism developed "artificially" and
rapidly by government pressure, modern
communications, and schools in a "modern"
surrounding. "Ethnonationalism" did not
mature over centuries and then change like
the ethnic, later national, values of the
organically developing value systems, and
it was not subjected to the pressure exercised by all-powerful modern governments.
In other words, it is a kind of ethnicity
to which all our theories and experiences
apply either partially or with reservations
because it did not emerge in a liberal or
command society in the premodern or modern
period. "Ethnonationalism" developed in
modernizing societies that remained basically agricultural and politically medieval
under theoretically powerful, but extremely
inefficient, imperial governments. Those
governments were replaced and the economic
transformation accelerated in Eastern Europe
beginning in 1945--by then ethnonationalism
was a well-established "experience of rooted, intimate, and eternal belonging" (Fishman) that had to be protected against
"foreigners" who proposed to change it
overnight from the "outside." Ethnonationalism is still alive, but it is impossible

to predict whether it will live or be replaced by a form of nationalism that will
fit preconceived models of western scholar-
ship.
     The next few pages deal with "ethno-
nationalism" as a social phenomenon "in
limbo" between the modern and premodern
worlds. The philosophies which governed
those worlds were not laissez faire;
"modernization" never managed to eradicate
agrarianism; urbanization often meant the
creation of large "villages"; competition
between "haves" and "have nots" speaking
different languages and belonging to
different churches was the reality. Under
these circumstances development differed
from the usual model. Ethnonationalism was
an East European phenomenon that appeared
elsewhere but not in emigre communities that
left this region. That phenomenon will
serve future scholars by helping them to
understand societies that are neither "modern" nor "premodern," but almost eternally
"semimodern."
     Before the features of East European
ethnonationalism can be analyzed the "semimodern" society, polity, or state needs to
be defined as a community consciously embarked on changing a traditional way of
life. Such communities may move away from
tradition, even alter it drastically, but
they never succeed in fully emulating, let
alone in "catching up" with the model that
they propose to substitute for the system
they wish to abandon. Thus a "semimodern"
society resembles an acrobat suspended by

his toes and finger tips between two chairs
continually being pulled further and further
apart. When that circus act is performed
by an unwilling star, and most people in
any society undergoing change are unwilling
acrobats, they naturally tend to recall the
prestress situation with longing; they see
it as a peaceful ideal, and hope to land in
its midst again, not between two, but on the
older chair when the stress becomes un-
bearable.

Yet, even though modernization might
not succeed, states might fail or disappear,
the community continues to exist. The act
never fails! Furthermore, in spite of its
innate conservatism, surviving communities
adjust to pressures and change. This often
imperceptible change makes landing on the
old chair as impossible as taking refuge on
a new one never fully built. The community
suspended between two chairs or unable to
accept either a premodern ethic or modern-
national role, comprises the ethnonationalism of semimodernity.

Eastern Europe was in a state of semi-
modernity beginning with the first movements
to change its social-political-economic
structure in the second half of the eighteenth century until 1948. The development
since then is inconclusive and impossible
to evaluate. Yet, during the last thirty
years the changes introduced were dictated
by forces located outside the ethnic-na-
tional-state boundaries. Those changes
were resisted by local forces which relied
upon self-identifying values developed

during the preceding two hundred years--
those of East European ethnonationalism.
Those years encompass the crucial developments.

First, the modernizing forces need to
be examined to explain why they did not
achieve their goals; then it is easier to
explain how ethnonationalism developed in
reaction to modernization. The major
modernizing forces in Eastern Europe were
the Romanov, Habsburg and Ottoman Empires.
The need for change became apparent when
the power of the western states became
evident in comparison. Any attempt to
"westernize" and "modernize" those Empires
had to fail because the rulers were reluc-
tant or incapable of giving up old values,
they lacked the power and skills to affect
thorough change, and the people lacked
primary loyalty to the monarchy or state
directed government.

The reluctance or inability to break
with the past was most apparent in the
Ottoman Empire. Its major reform movement
was called <u>Tanzimat</u> (meaning purification)
and its aim was to purify the state, get
rid of corruption and forces that perverted
the old, perfect system that was to be reestablished. In Russia, modernization
began with either Alexander I or Nicholas I,
and the twin pillars of the old order,
orthodoxy and autocracy, were to be the
foundations on which the new was to be
built. Maria Theresa, the originator of
reform in the Habsburg Empire, considered
loyalty to the dynasty (later called

428

Kaisertreue) and Roman Catholicism to be
the unchangeable rocks on which her realm
stood. Her son, Joseph II, rejected her
approach, but subsequent Habsburgs returned to it in one form or another.
Russians never foresook their pillars of
wisdom and the government attempted to return to them even after 1905. Modernization
based on those premodern principles resulted, at best, in semimodernity.

The lack of power and political and
technological skills in the three empires
hardly requires explanation. All three
states lacked financial strength and were
frequently bankrupt for all practical purposes. Individuals were often forced into
playing the roles of modernizers and
industrial enterpreneurs against their
will, and financial problems precluded the
development of military forces commensurate
with the power position coveted by the three
empires. All three however developed large
political units in the course of the nineteenth century, "modern" bureaucracies in
which the members never became true civil
or state servants in a western sense. Those
bureaucrats played the self-serving game
played by Djilas's New Class in the communist
states by advancing the aims of the state
only when they coincided with their own
advantages. They successfully avoided
performing their duties by barricading themselves behind mountains of red tape or
through delaying tactics that became known
as Schlamperei in the Habsburg Empire and
as "Balkan conditions" in Southeastern Europe.

The bureaucrats failed because they
did not acquire the mentality of their
colleagues in the West, and because of an
appalling absence of technical skills. All
sectors of the economy--finances, banking,
industry, agriculture and services--in the
three empires were unable to educate and
recruit experts. Consequently, they remained more often than not fully dependent
on the western states for investments,
expertise and economic aid.
    The three modernizing empires ruled
over multiethnic, multireligious, multi-
lingual populations without commanding
sufficient loyalty to ensure support of
their governments' efforts. The Ottoman
Empire failed to recognize ethnic differences when it embarked on modernization and
the concept of nationhood was unknown in
that state. Ottomanism, Turanism and Turk-
ism appeared at the end of the nineteenth
century too late to support the creation
of a state-supporting nation. The Habsburg
state was a conglomeration of political
entities with traditional, mainly medieval,
rights and a degree of self-government.
When these rights fell into disuse they were
reestablished by the Pragmatic Sanction of
Emperor Charles VI that assured the right
of inheritance of the throne through Maria
Theresa and the female line of the Habsburg
family. Since only a small minority, the
"natio" or political nation, profited from
these rights the government was faced with
ruling in cooperation with these political
nations or governing "unconstitutionally."

The first alternative hamstrung the government either through the "natio's" conservatism or its egotism and when it tried to
rule without having the cooperation of local
authorities its efforts were faced with
practically universal resistance. The
Habsburg situation does not fit neatly in
any of Professor Gellner's categories because there is no clear division between
those who had power and those who did not.
The masses, who clearly had no power, and
the government, which theoretically had it
all, were separated by the "natio" that
could make common cause with either. When
the "natio" allied with the government the
government's power was diluted and could not
be fully utilized; when it identified with
the masses the "natio" became the main
force creating ethnonationalism.

Russia experienced neither the Ottoman
nor the Habsburg problem. The tsar-autocrat
and his government possessed power and the
rest of the nation, including the nobility,
its wealth notwithstanding, had none. Yet,
the Russian nobility that manned the military and civil offices was, in a sense, an
equivalent of the Habsburg "natios." Within the limits of their military, civil, and
legal jurisdictions and on their estates
they enjoyed the same alternative as those
who possessed local privileges in the Habsburg lands. The masses viewed the nobility
as "the authority" who had a relative
latitude in exercising it. The Russian
peasant in Kazan was as far removed from the
direct jurisdiction of the Tsar as the

Romanian farmer in Transylvania was from the
Emperor-Kings. The Tsar and the Emperor
were quasi-mythical personalities who ranked
just below God and, though good by definition, were unapproachable by the common
people. In everyday life the local power
holder was the reality.

These circumstances and the lack of
effective communications created a chasm
between the "modernizers" and those who had
to accept change and under those conditions
the western model of nation building was
inoperative. Yet, despite these handicaps,
governments reached even the lowest levels.
Taxes were increased and collected, military service and the quartering of troops
was enforced, land was expropriated to
build roads, railroads and government build-
ings, and the law courts functioned. The
authorities increasingly interfered in the
everyday life of practically everybody in
proportion to the governments' desire to
modernize. Demands for change and additional sacrifice were made in the name of
the state and nation; yet both were alien
concepts. The need to sharpen and heighten
existing feelings of self-identification
developed in reaction to those demands
and out of this need grew ethnonationalism
to distinguish the community lacking a
state orientation from other groups within
the boundaries of semimodernity.

Ethnonationalism developed almost
unconsciously and it was based on religion,
ethnic collectivity, and language based on a
"putative common ancestry." Religion played

an interesting role, but not religion defined as a belief in the dogmas and myster-
ies of an organized church. That kind of
belief is unknown among illiterate people
who have lived for centuries in practical
isolation. Religion for those people involved a localized and superstitious folk-
religion--a major symbol of self, identity
to differentiate "us" from "them." "Our
belief" in God made "us" what "we" were;
and "we" are the "chosen people." In this
sense Professor Fishman is correct,
"ethnicity ... was God-given." The
"chosen-people" had common ancestors and
a common past making the group an entity
on its own without a state. Yet belief
was not enough since belonging needs spiritual as well as palpable symbols. The
symbols are supplied by the physical artifacts found in any house of worship: the
Ka'aba in Mecca, the Wailing Wall in Jerusalem, and include the icons and statues of
the Christian denominations. Those kinds
of symbols, venerated as they are, are remote and insufficiently identified with the
local self--"they do nothing for us." The
people need living symbols that will act
for the good of the self--the ethnic hier-
arch discussed by Professor Petrovich.

Every group had an ethnarch. The sul-
tan was Khalif; Hungary had an Apostolic
King and a Bishop-primate; Poland a Bishop-
Primate; the Greeks had the Patriarch in
Istanbul and later the Archbishop of
Athens; the Montenegrins had the Prince-
bishop; the Serbs looked to the apostolic

authority of Ipek and Sremski Karlovci; the
Bulgarians to Ohrid; the Regateni Romanians
to Bucharest; the Orthodox Transylvanian
Romanians had an ethnarch in Sibiu and the
Uniates had the Bishop in Cluj. It really
did not matter if the sees were occupied
or empty or if the incumbents were interested in the ethnic welfare of their
flock; however the symbol of these religious
offices to the various communities was important. The ill-timed radio address
delivered by Cardinal József Mindszenty
of Hungary on November 3, 1956, can only be
explained by his belief that he was still
Hungary's ethnarch and her only true representative.   In this sense religion is
one of three boundary settlers between
ethnic categories in Eastern Europe, part
of the triad on which the region's ethnonationalism rests.

In any ethnic collectivity, ethnicity
is "God-given" and it parallels religiosity.
A "chosen people" must first have a feeling
of being a people and the various groups of
Eastern Europe that desired to establish an
ethnic identity turned as far into their
past as they possibly could in their search
for roots. The belief systems of people are
strikingly similar and the legends include
such ancient characters reminiscent of
Romulus and Remus, magic animals, fanciful
raids and stories that cannot be verified
but which survive in folklore. These subjective and fanciful stories establish a
common origin and those who claim such
common origin become "brothers" and "sisters" in the way that contemporary American

434

blacks use those expressions. The South
Slavic villager community (zadruga) and the
Russian mirs are narrowly delimited surviv-
als of such "brotherhood" feelings. The
monotheistic religions and cultural
orientation of these collectivities influenced the old stories to some extent. The
cross of St. Hubertus appeared over the
heads of mythical animals important in the
stories of ancestors, but "sanctification"
did not change the role played by these
beasts. Their role was that of friends or
enemies of forefathers whose descendants
made up a specific in-group. Monotheism
added the quality of "God-giveness" as
understood by those whose faith was expressed by folk-religion, thus God became
a partner or friend of the mythical
ancestors.

The third aspect of ethnicity, language, is in a narrow sense a basic, indispensable means of communication. In the
broad sense it is the major element of
communications required to tie a group
together. In the broadest sense language
includes gestures, feelings expressed by
dress, rituals, dietary habits and taboos,
and other social manifestations that differ
from one ethnic region to another. Numerous
signals and symbols of that kind survive in
Eastern Europe.

The basic importance of language is
apparent. None of the ideas and beliefs
mentioned here could carry feelings of
identity without a language to express them,
and Professor Fishman and Dr. Hofer have

verified the importance of language in that
context. It is equally important to note
that language is used to unify and to differentiate ethnic groups. Obviously the
creation of the Serbo-Croatian language did
not result in the birth of a Yugoslav nation. Yet, it is reasonable to suggest that
language unifies the Croats and that dialectical differences, representing various past
historical experiences, still reflect primary loyalties among them. The Macedonians
had to wait until their idiom was officially
recognized as a language before they could
insist on nationhood. Dialectology is
therefore of interest to philologists, lin-
guists, anthropologists, and ethnographers,
and it is of primary importance to students
of ethnicity interested in creating or
advancing ethnic awareness among a given
group of people. This was true during the
"national movements" that emerged in Europe
during the eighteenth and nineteenth centuries and is true today in the third World
and in the Celtic revival movement.

      Yet, the emphasis on language assumed a
special form in Eastern Europe and Chapter
III deals with that problem almost exclusively. Ethnic consciousness and language reform are directly related to an
interest in the East European peasant, the
unspoiled carrier of ethnic characteristics
and the basic features of ethnic identity
have often been applied to all processes of
its formation. The peasant orientation involved in the study of language as a factor
in developing ethnonationalism introduces

yet another difficulty. Since any phenomenon comprised of several components becomes
different from all similar ones when one
component is altered, we must assume that
the linguistic component provides an explanation of ethnonationalism.

Feelings of ethnic belonging and nationalism developed naturally during the
premodern, preindustrial period. In modern
times, irrespective of the political system
and the state of the economy at the time of
a given state's "take-off" moment, the locus
of such development is the urban, industrial
society with no use for peasants. Modern
attempts to pull populations together and
create state-supporting communities will
skip the ethnic identity phase and try to
create a nationalist awareness coincidental
with political borders. They will often try
to eradicate existing ethnic loyalties to
achieve their goals. Professor Gellner
treated the alternatives that determine
governmental success or failure under these
circumstances. If his analysis is correct
then those nations that emerged in the premodern period and those formulated in the
modern period felt the need to find within
a broad group of people a specific core with
characteristics that could be expanded to
cover an entire "nation" and legitimize its
existence. That need arises under "semimodern" circumstances when the institutions
that dominate everyday life and those interested in creating "nations" lack both
the means to enforce their policies and an
understanding of "modernity." Those

"nation-builders" rely on remnants of the
past--the unspoiled segment of their would-
be "nation" (the peasantry in Eastern
Europe)--to create a future that has no
relationship with the values and life styles
of those who represent the basis for the new
identity. Without a past, a common heritage, no future is possible--it is impossible
to make a silk purse from a sow's ear. What
will eventually emerge from this effort will
not be ethnicity or nationalism, it will be
ethnonationalism.

Nobody in the three empires, from the
rulers down to the lowliest subject, really
knew the goals of the reforms contemplated
when the attempt at change began. Those who
believed that the future should reflect the
interests and will of the "people," had to
find, and sometimes create, a people first.
Advocates of the people's interest could not
model their reforms on the people who made
up the state apparatus since that apparatus
was comprised of "foreigners" who advocated
an alien future. Yet, those advocates were
part of the apparatus because their level of
education and sophistication made it easier
to communicate with the "oppressors" than it
was to identify with the people. Before
they could create a power base, they needed
an identity that differed from that of
the establishment. Members of the "political nation" and the clergy legally had such
a base, but it was too narrow, and most
importantly, it was not ideologically and
emotionally appealing. These would-be
leaders turned to the teachings of the West

to find a broader political ideology and
found it mostly incomprehensible or, worse,
irrelevant. The only western thinker
applicable to their need was Herder. Professor Fishman's words are relevant in that
context:

> Herder's words constituted a return
> to and an intensification of the
> ancient Hebraic and Greek vision
> of ethno-linguistic sanctity. God's
> glory was recognizable in the ethnic
> diversity which He had created and
> each ethnicity was quintessentially
> represented by its language, its
> folklore, its glorious past, its
> ancestral traditions, its vision of
> greatness and its unique destiny
> mission.... These beauties de-
> served protection, preservation,
> and cultivation, and whatever
> political and economic realities
> tended to weaken or disregard them
> deserved to be altered.

These words clearly indicated what had
to be saved, cultivated, and developed, and
what had to be weakened and opposed. The
beautiful things were with the people who
had to be made aware; reformers had to become part and parcel of the basic ethnic
community. Unfortunately the absence of a
domestic middle class, an aristocracy or an
"alienated" upper class left only the peasantry as such a basic community. This
realization turned the ethnic awakening of
East Europeans into its specific direction.

Ethnonationalism begins with the peasant fixation of East European reformers and
the survival of this specific form of self-
identification needs to be explained, and
"semi-modernity" becomes a crucial factor
in rationalizing the persistence of ethnonationalism in Eastern Europe. Ethnonationalism does not fit neatly into the
existing models or concepts of ethnicity
and nationalism. Furthermore, it was a
static experience in that area for two
hundred years. In most other cases, ethnicity was transformed into a nationalistic
ideology which had its own history, varieties and transformational patterns. The
history of Eastern Europe was not static
and the tremendous changes which occurred
there, even disregarding the last thirty
years, suggest that the modification of
ethnonationalism paralleled them. Yet
ethnonationalism was a constant phenomenon
in spite of its different manifestations.
     This apparent paradox can be explained
since no nation or state exists in a vacuum.
They are all influenced by their relative
economic and political positions on the
international scene and their internal
affairs, those that influence the development of local movements, reflect their
international position. The position of
East Europe measured in terms of economic
and political-military power never changed.
Eastern Europe was "ahead" of the non-
European world at the end of the eighteenth
century but "behind" those states that were
considered "modern" at that time. Today's

situation is similar since Eastern Europe
has always been in the middle between "backward" and "modern." This position entailed
certain disadvantages such as a dependence
on foreign capital and "know-how," but it
did not prevent "progress."

The empires first had to concede more
"rights" to the population, they then became constitutional states, and finally
disappeared. Their successor states were
constitutional monarchies or republics and
several even introduced universal male
suffrage. Political parties, some of them
ideological, appeared and by 1900 they began acting like the western parties. More
and more cities became self-governing and
the political structure changed drastically.

Similar economic changes occurred.
Capital starved, local banks appeared and a
larger proportion of gross national income
was generated by industry. The city populations grew, at least in the capitals, and
so did the rate of literacy. A native
middle class developed, and, under its
influence, cultural manifestations--theater,
opera, concerts, exhibitions--supported by
this segment of society materialized and
flourished. Western European tourists who
visited the major cities of Eastern Europe
around 1900 felt at home. Yet the conditions that prevailed in Eastern Europe were
markedly different than in earlier times.

Hugh Seton-Watson, a westerner with a
deep understanding of Eastern Europe, wrote
that the late 1930s witnessed numerous
manifestations of the "peasant cult" in the

cities:

> ... if the foreign visitor stays
> a little longer in the country, if
> he leaves the capital ... and keeps
> his eyes open ... he will see mud
> hovels, adorned by no rugs or
> pottery, housing families of seven
> or eight.... He will notice how
> the young peasant labourers ···
> look at the officials who examine
> their labour permits.[1]

Quite clearly, "modernization" had not
reached the countryside and the authorities
were still all powerful, intimidating the
population. The population resented the
authorities who demanded a lot from them
but gave them very little. Obviously, the
state had failed to legitimize the nation
and the actions of its representatives.
By the late 1930s all the governments of
Eastern Europe except that of Czechoslovakia
were dictatorships with access to developed
tools of power greater than those wielded
by the three empires. All the governments
were stricter than those of the previous
regimes. Yet, the occupants of these mud
huts knew who they were and who were their
"brothers" and "sisters." The peasants
could identify those who endangered their
existence. Ethnonationalism was very much
alive.

The conditions observed by Seton-Watson
the result of much more than an urban-
rural, industrial-agrarian cleavage. They
were the result of "semi-modernity." All
the East European states from the moment

they gained their independence to when
dictatorships were introduced, experienced
a similar history. They all had legislative
assemblies which represented only those in
power. Governments lost elections as a
result of foreign influence or when Prime
Ministers decided that it was in their interest to lose. They all had self-serving
bureaucracies recruited from a narrow
segment of the population out of touch with
the rest of the "nation." They were all
intolerant and persecuted minorities. They
all had negative trade balances and most of
their national incomes were produced by
agriculture. They shared a faulty understanding of of economic realities, or denied
reality by hiding behind noneconomic ex-
cuses. The old "political nations" expanded, but the states were run solely in the
interests of those who belonged to them.
They uniformly lacked power in international politics and when they united (e.g.,
the Little Entente and Balkan League) they
misused those alliances and failed to
utilize them to maximize their common power.
The East European states were unable to
compete on the world market and remained
economically "backward." The major cities
were inhabited by people mostly unfamiliar
with the countryside who nonetheless in-
dulged in peasant cults in an imaginary
world. The states thus had "modern," and
"pre-modern" components. They were houses
divided and most of the rooms were still
single unit mud huts.

As the ruling segments of the population became more modern, educated, and
ambitious they understood most of their
countrymen even less and became convinced
that drastic measures were needed to remedy
the situation. The drastic measures they
took furthered their own narrow advantages
or those perceived to be in the "national"
interest. Unfortunately, their view of the
common good did not coincide with that of
the majority. As a result, the gap between
those in power and the rest of the people
grew. Draconic police measures soon followed. Governments became authoritarian, self-
centered, and self-contained and under those
conditions distrust became general so that
the masses rejected even those ideologies
proclaimed to work in their interests. The
rejection of Austromarxism prior to the
first World War illustrates the response of
the people to anything that did not originate in their midst. They listened to
priests and popes rather than to political
agitators because religious figures had a
place in their ethnonationalism and politicians did not. In short, Eastern Europe
never became "modern." It copied the
institutions but not the spirit that made
modernization work elsewhere; it built cities but failed to integrate them into the
country as a whole; it became industrialized, but relied on agriculture for most of
its income; its educational systems were
modernized in the cities yet there were
never enough technocrats to embark on real
economic reform; it claimed sovereignty and

remained dependent; its leaders spoke for
the people, but the people and their leaders
were further apart than their grandfathers
used to be. In other words, the states of
Eastern Europe moved away from their traditional societies without moving the bulk of
their people away from their traditions.
Events moved too fast and started from a
base too high to permit the development of
ethnicity first and a transformation into
nationalism. The resulting halfway house
of "semi-modernity" was something between
ethnicity and nationalism, ethnonationalism
and the politicians lacked the power to
transform it into a true nationalism.

Professor Gellner explained nationalism
stating that "class conflict is a national
one which failed to take off, for lack of
deep cultural and symbolic differentiae."
That conclusion is valid and so is his underlying assumption that all conflicts
result from differences between various
groups of people. Without differences there
would be no class, no ethnic consciousness,
no nationalism and since Eastern Europe
certainly had more differences than any
other region of comparable size those
differences resulted in ethnonationalism.
Ethnonationalism is nationalism that has
failed to take off because it lacked sufficient growth to take it beyond the stage of
semimodernity.

NOTES

CHAPTER I

I am grateful to my colleague, David Paul,
for providing me with some unpublished
work of his that was helpful to me in
revising this chapter and for some detailed
suggestions that have been incorporated
at several places in the text.

1. Even where it is possible to do so,
argues Barth, the use of cultural attributes
to identify ethnic boundaries may be superficial, confusing form with content; Fredrik
Barth, "Introduction," and "Pathan Identity
and its Maintenance," in Fredrik Barth (ed.),
Ethnic Groups and Boundaries: The Social
Organization of Cultural Difference (Boston:
Little, Brown, 1969), pp. 15, 131-32.
2. Barth, "Introduction," and Harald
Eidheim, "When Ethnic Identity is a Social
Stigma," in Barth, Ethnic Groups and Boundaries, pp. 15 and 39-57.
3. George de Vos, "Ethnic Pluralism,"
in George de Vos and Lola Romanucci-Ross
(eds.), Ethnic Identity: Cultural Continui-
ties and Change (Palo Alto, Calif.: Mayfield
Publishing Co., 1975), p. 16.
4. I owe this analogy to my colleague,
Michael Hechter.
5. Cf. Joan Vincent, "The Structuring
of Ethnicity," Human Organization, XXXIII,
No. 4 (Winter, 1974), 376-377. The same
remarks apply to the concept of nationality
or nation as used here; cf. Benjamin Akzin,

State and Nation (London: Hutchinson Univer-
sity Library, 1964), p. 36 and Karl M.
Deutsch, Nationalism and Social Communication: An Inquiry into the Foundations of
Nationality, 2d ed. (Cambridge, Mass.:
M.I.T. Press, 1966), p. 23.
    6. This point has been made by Nathan
Glazer and Daniel P. Moynihan, "Introduction," in Nathan Glazer and Daniel P.
Moynihan (eds.), Ethnicity: Theory and
Experience (Cambridge, Mass.: Harvard
University Press, 1975), pp. 7-10, but they
overgeneralize their argument to other
societies where ethnicity is more than
merely interest, and may be a stage on the
way to a claim to national status.
    7. Cf. Akzin, State and Nation, pp.
10, 12, 29, 31-34, 46, 81, 133, 143.
    8. Since the nation is defined here
as a type of ethnic group and ethnic groups
have been defined without reference to any
specific attributes or set of attributes,
it follows that the nation (or nationality)
also is not to be defined by any particular
attributes such as language, religion,
territory, or any others. Cf. Anthony D.
Smith, Theories of Nationalism (New York:
Harper & Row, 1971), pp. 18, 147-150, 181-
185; Dankwart A. Rustow, A World of Nations:
Problems of Political Modernization (Washington, D.C.: The Brookings Institution,
1967), pp. 47-48; Rupert Emerson, From Empire to Nation: The Rise to Self-Assertion
of Asian and African Peoples (Boston: Beacon
Press, 1960), pp. 102-187. For contrary
views that see a close connection between
language and nation or nationality, see H.

Munro Chadwick, The Nationalities of Europe
and the Growth of National Ideologies (New
York: Cooper Square Publishers, 1973; re-
print of 1945 edition); Carl J. Friedrich,
"Corporate Federalism and Linguistic Politics," unpublished paper presented at the
International Political Science Association
Congress, Montreal, 1973, pp. 3-5; and
Ernest Gellner, Thought and Change (Chicago:
University of Chicago Press, 1964), pp. 163-
165. The predominant European tradition
has been to distinguish the terms "nationality" and "nation," using the former term
for language groups and the latter to define the attachment of people of one or more
language groups to a single state. Cf.
Peter F. Sugar, "External and Domestic Roots
of Eastern European Nationalism," in Peter
F. Sugar and Ivo J. Lederer (eds.), Nationalism in Eastern Europe (Seattle: University
of Washington Press, 1969), pp. 3-6.
Emerson, who considers most other objective
criteria unhelpful in defining the nation,
insists, however, upon an inseparable relation between a nation and a "national
territory," however loosely defined; From
Empire to Nation, pp. 105-109.

9. This definition follows Akzin (fn.
7 above) in not including independence,
statehood, or sovereignty in the definition
of the nation. Many definitions do insist
on this latter criterion; for example, see
Friedrich, "Corporate Federalism," p. 4;
another statement of Friedrich's definition
in Karl W. Deutsch and William J. Foltz
(eds.), Nation-Building (New York: Atherton

Press, 1966), pp. 11-12; and Oscar Jaszi,
The Dissolution of the Habsburg Monarchy
(Chicago: University of Chicago Press, 1961),
p. 26. However, such definitions prepare
the way for the confusion of the concept of
the nation with that of the state from
which much of the existing literature on
nationalism suffers. Some leading scholars
of nationalism have, however, avoided this
confusion; for example, Emerson, From Empire to Nation, pp. 95-102 and Deutsch,
Nationalism and Social Communication, pp.
104-105, who reserves the term nation-state
for nations that have acquired sovereignty.
    The most troublesome issues arise when
the nation is defined in terms of group
solidarity without reference to the state,
but nationalism is defined as the striving
for statehood. Then, any demands made by
nations short of that for statehood cannot
be analyzed in a study of nationalism! See
Rustow, A World of Nations, p. 21.
    10. However, the creation of relative-
ly homogeneous national cultures out of
diverse ethnic groups by the state usually
takes centuries and even then leaves ethnically distinct enclaves, as in modern
France and Spain. Tabouret-Keller has
pointed out, for example, that it required
four hundred years for French to become in
fact the national language of France after
its adoption as the official language of
the country in 1539; A. Tabouret-Keller,
"Sociological Factors of Language Maintenance and Language Shift: A Methodological
Approach Based on European and African

Examples," in Joshua P. Fishman <u>etal</u>. (eds.),
<u>Language Problems of Developing Nations</u>
(New York: John Wiley & Sons, 1968), p. 109.
And, even today, language and dialect
differences remain important in the country
in such regions as Breton and Languedoc.
Moreover, it has been argued that the process of nation-building through the agency
of the state was historically less effective in Eastern than in Western Europe because whereas political centralization
preceded the development of nationalism in
Western Europe, the two processes occurred
simultaneously in Eastern Europe in the
nineteenth century. Oscar J. Janowsky,
<u>Nationalities and National Minorities</u>
<u>(With Special Reference to East-Central</u>
<u>Europe)</u> (New York: Macmillan, 1945), pp.
19-20, cited in Sugar, "Roots of Eastern
European Nationalism," p. 11.

 11. It is preferable to treat ethnic
nationalism and state-centered nationalism
as subtypes rather than either insisting
that only one type of nationalism is the
true type or making the analytically hope-
less error that Smith makes in attempting
to define the nation in ethnic terms and
nationalism in statist terms, rendering it
impossible to discuss analytically the
nationalism of ethnic groups until a claim
for statehood is made explicitly. Actually,
Smith's definition of the nation itself is
not as "ethnicist" as he claims since it
contains the notion of "common citizenship
rights" which rarely exist outside the
framework of the state; Smith, <u>Theories of</u>

Nationalism, pp. 171, 175-176. Fishman
makes an analytically more sensible (but
typographically impossible) attempt to use
different terms to describe the two processes of nationality-formation and state-
formation, reserving the term "nationalism"
for the former and "nationism" for the
latter; Joshua A. Fishman, "Nationality-
Nationalism and Nation-Nationism," in Fishman, Language Problems, pp. 39-51. See
also Walker Connor, "Nation-Building or
Nation-Destroying?" World Politics, XXIV,
No. 3 (April, 1972), 332-336, who argues
rather dramatically that, because "ethnic
identity" is the only "true nationalism"
and because the process of building state
loyalties often involves overcoming ethnic
identities, the appropriate term for the
development of state loyalties is "nation-
destroying."

    12. Deutsch, Nationalism and Social
Communication, pp. 41-44.
    13. Cf. Fishman, "Nationality-Nation-
alism and Nation-Nationism," pp. 40-41.
    14. Karl W. Deutsch, "The Trend of
European Nationalism--The Language Aspect,"
in Joshua A. Fishman (ed.), Readings in the
Sociology of Language (The Hague: Mouton,
1968), p. 599.
    15. Ibid., p. 606.
    16. E.g., compare T. Zavalani, "Alba-
nian Nationalism," in Sugar and Lederer,
Nationalism in Eastern Europe, p. 68 and
Paul Shoup, Communism and the Yugoslav National Question (New York: Columbia University Press, 1968), pp. 107-109. Of course,

the distinctiveness of Islam itself varies
in different contexts, but this does not
seem to be a significant factor as between
Albanian and Yugoslav Muslims.

17. See, for example, Robert H. Bates,
"Ethnic Competition and Modernization in
Contemporary Africa," Comparative Political
Studies, VI, No. 4 (January, 1974), 457-484;
Gellner, Thought and Change, esp. pp. 166
and 171-172; Chong-do Hah and Jeffrey Mar-
tin, "Toward a Synthesis of Conflict and
Integration Theories of Nationalism," World
Politics, XXVII, No. 3 (April, 1975), 373-
379; Michael Hechter, "Towards a Theory of
Ethnic Change," Politics and Society, II,
No. 1 (Fall, 1971), esp. pp. 42-43 and "The
Persistence of Regionalism in the British
Isles, 1885-1966," The American Journal of
Sociology, LXXIX, No. 2 (September, 1973),
319-342; Robert Melson and Howard Wolpe,
"Modernization and the Politics of Commu-
nalism: A Theoretical Perspective," American
Political Science Review, LXIV, No. 4
(December, 1970), pp. 1112-1118; and Smith,
Theories of Nationalism, esp. pp. 116-118,
132.

18. Consider, for example, the case
of rural Slovaks even as late as the turn
of the twentieth century who, upon emigrat-
ing to the United States "were unaware of
their specific national identity, knowing
"only that they were from a certain village
in what was called Hungary, they were
sternly ruled by people who spoke a different tongue, and they were very poor." David
W. Paul, The Cultural Limits of Revolutionary

454

_Politics: Change and Continuity in Socialist
Czechoslovakia_ (Boulder, Colo.: East European Quarterly, 1979), p. 195.

19. Peter Sugar, "The Nature of the
Non-Germanic Societies Under Habsburg Rule,"
Slavic Review, XXII, No. 1 (March, 1963),
2-3.

20. George Barany, "Hungary: From
Aristocratic to Proletarian Nationalism,"
in Sugar and Lederer, _Nationalism in Eastern Europe_, pp. 259 ff.

21. Stephen Fischer-Galati, "Romanian
Nationalism," in _ibid._, pp. 375 ff.

22. Peter Brock, "Polish Nationalism,"
in _ibid._, pp. 325-328.

23. Sugar, Roots of Eastern European
Nationalism," p. 53.

24. Keith Hitchins, _The Rumanian
National Movement in Transylvania, 1780-1849_
(Cambridge, Mass.: Harvard University Press,
1969), ch. i.

25. _Ibid._, pp. 31-32.

26. Stavro Skendi, "Language as a
Factor of National Identity in the Balkans
of the Nineteenth Century," _Proceedings of
the American Philosophical Society_ CXIX,
No. 2 (April, 1975), 188.

27. _Ibid._, pp. 186-187; see also Marin
V. Pundeff, "Bulgarian Nationalism," in
Sugar and Lederer, _Nationalism in Eastern
Europe_, pp. 93-115.

28. Brock, "Polish Nationalism," pp.
315-316.

29. Sugar, "Roots of Eastern European
Nationalism," emphasizes the inseparability
of Catholicism and Polish nationality, p. 34.

30. Skendi, "Language as a Factor in National Identity in the Balkans," p. 188; T. Zavalani, "Albanian Nationalism," pp. 56, 66-68; and Chadwick, The Nationalities of Europe, pp. 32-33.

31. Paul, Continuity and Change in Socialist Czechoslovakia, ch. vii.

32. This account of Greek nationalism is derived from Stephen G. Xydis, "Modern Greek Nationalism," in Sugar and Lederer, Nationalism in Eastern Europe, pp. 207-258.

33. Sugar, "Non-Germanic Societies Under Habsburg Rule," p. 12.

34. In Madras, during British rule, non-Brahman caste leaders who resented Brahman dominance in the public service and in other aspects of life developed a myth that the Brahmans were alien intruders from north India, "descendants of Aryan invaders who had conquered the indigenous Dravidian people;" Marguerite R. Barnett, The Politics of Cultural Nationalism in South India (Princeton, N.J.: Princeton University Press, 1976). See also Eugene Irschick, Politics and Social Conflict in South India: The Non-Brahman Movement and Tamil Separatism, 1916-1929 (Berkeley: University of California Press, 1969).

35. George Barany, "'Magyar Jew or: Jewish Magyar'? (To the Question of Jewish Assimilation in Hungary)," Canadian-American Slavic Studies, VIII, No. 1 (Spring, 1974), 39.

36. Ibid., p. 36.

37. Andrew Janos, "Ethnicity, Communism, and Political Change in Eastern

456

Europe," World Politics, XXIII, No. 3
(April, 1971), 501-508.

38. Hah and Martin, "Toward a Synthesis," pp. 372-374.
39. Ibid., p. 380.
40. Gary K. Bertsch, "Relative Deprivation and Yugoslav Nationalisms: The Rationalization of Frustrations," paper presented at the 1973 meeting of the American Political Science Association, p. 18.
41. Hah and Martin, "Toward a Synthesis," p. 381.
42. Glazer and Moynihan, "Introduction," pp. 12-14.
43. The formulation of my argument here has been influenced in part by comments made by Ernest Gellner on the first draft of this paper.
44. See especially Deutsch's use of the example of Swedes and Finns in Finland in Nationalism and Social Communication, pp. 196-208.
45. Hitchins, The Rumanian National Movement, pp. 46-48.
46. Leon Dominian, The Frontiers of Language and Nationality in Europe (New York: Henry Holt, 1917), pp. 127, 129.
47. Nicholas R. Lang, "The Dialectics of Decentralization: Economic Reform and Regional Inequality in Yugoslavia," World Politics, XXVII, No. 3 (April, 1975), 309-335.
48. Frits W. Hondius, The Yugoslav Community of Nations (The Hague: Mouton, 1968), pp. 326-328.

49. George Klein, "The Role of Ethnic Politics in the Czechoslovak Crisis of 1968 and the Yugoslav Crisis of 1971," Studies in Comparative Communism, VIII, No. 4 (Winter, 1975), 350-351.

50. For an interesting analysis of the rise of "nativist" movements in different parts of India, explained precisely in this way, see Myron Weiner, Sons of the Soil: Migration, Ethnicity, and Nativism in India (Cambridge, Mass.: Center for International Studies, 1975).

51. James S. Coleman, Nigeria: Background to Nationalism (Berkeley: University of California Press, 1963), p. 347 and passim.

52. Paul R. Brass, Language, Religion, and Politics in North India (New York: Cambridge University Press, 1974), pp. 311-318.

53. Ibid., pp. 352-355.

54. Ibid., p. 408.

55. Paul, Continuity and Change in Socialist Czechoslovakia, ch. vii.

56. See especially Akzin, State and Nation, chaps. vi and vii for a comprehensive survey of pluralist state policies.

57. See, for example, the account of the deportation of Romanian Germans to the Soviet Union in Georges Castellan, "The Germans of Rumania," in Journal of Contemporary History, VI, No. 1 (1971), 67 ff.

58. Pundeff, "Bulgarian Nationalism," in Sugar and Lederer, Nationalism in Eastern Europe, p. 142.

458

59. Dominian, Frontiers of Language and Nationality, p. 124.

60. Ibid., pp. 127-128.

61. Chadwick, The Nationalities of Europe, pp. 39-42, 37.

62. See, for example, on this point, Bates, "Ethnic Competition," p. 465.

63. See, for example, Hans Kohn, "The Viability of the Habsburg Monarchy," and the "Reply" by Peter F. Sugar in Slavic Review, XXII, No. 1 (March, 1963), 37-46.

64. For some discussions of federalism in Yugoslavia and Czechoslovakia, see Shoup, Communism and the Yugoslav National Question, pp. 113-119, Paul, Cultural Limits, ch. vii, and Stanislav J. Kirschbaum, "Nationalisme et Fédéralisme en Théorie Communiste: Le Cas de la Tchécoslovaquie," Etudes Internationales, VI, No. 1 (Mars, 1975), 3-29.

65. Jaszi, The Dissolution of the Habsburg Monarchy, p. 346.

66. Ela Ulrik-Atena, "National Linguistic Minorities: Bilingual Basic Education in Slovenia," Prospects, VI, No. 3 (1976), 430-438.

67. Klein, "The Role of Ethnic Politics," pp. 343 and 350.

68. Joseph F. Zacek, "Nationalism in Czechoslovakia," in Sugar and Lederer, Nationalism in Eastern Europe, pp. 194 and 202 and Klein, "The Role of Ethnic Politics," pp. 341, 368.

69. Zacek, "Nationalism in Czechoslovakia," pp. 195 and 198; see also Paul, Continuity and Change in Socialist Czechoslovakia, ch. vi.

70. Klein, "The Role of Ethnic Politics," pp. 353-354.

71. Richard V. Burks, The Dynamics of Communism in Eastern Europe, 2nd ed. (Princeton, N.J.: Princeton University Press, 1965).

72. Shoup, Communism and the Yugoslav National Question, ch. ii.

73. Ibid., p. 115.

74. Ibid., pp. 115-119.

75. Ibid., pp. 120 ff.

76. Jack C. Fisher, Yugoslavia--A Multinational State: Regional Difference and Administrative Response (San Francisco: Chandler, 1966), p. 25.

77. Kirschbaum, "Nationalisme et Fédéralisme."

78. See, for example, Gary K. Bertsch, "Currents in Yugoslavia: The Revival of Nationalisms," Problems of Communism, XXII (November-December, 1973), 1-15 and Teresa Rakowska-Harmstone, "The Dialectics of Nationalism in the USSR," Problems of Communism, XXIII (May-June, 1974), 1-22.

79. Rakowska-Harmstone, "The Dialectics of Nationalism," p. 12.

80. Burks, Dynamics of Communism, pp. xxii-xxv.

81. For a recent and different perspective on Romanian nationality policy, see Marilyn McArthur, "The Saxon Germans: Political Fate of an Ethnic Identity," Dialectical Anthropology, I (1976), 349-364.

82. See the contribution by Trond Gilberg in this volume.

83. Hitchins, The Rumanian National Movement, esp. ch. iv.

84. For example, compare the demands of the leaders of the Romanian and Albanian nationalist movements in the nineteenth century and those of the Croats and Slovaks in the interwar period in the twentieth century. Cf. Hitchins, The Rumanian National Movement, p. x; Zavalani, "Albanian Nationalism," p. 65; Shoup, Communism and the Yugoslav National Question, pp. 10-11; and Paul, Cultural Limits, ch. vii.

85. Deutsch, Nationalism and Social Communication, pp. 126 ff.

CHAPTER II

1. See among others: Deutsch, Karl
W., Nationalism and Social Communication:
An Inquery into the Foundation of Nation-
ality (Cambridge, Mass.: M.I.T. Press, 1953,
2nd 3d. 1966); Gellner, Ernest, Thought and
Change (Chicago: University of Chicago
Press, 1964); Kedourie, Elie, Nationalism
(New York: Praeger, 1960, rev. ed. 1961);
Smith, Anthony D., Theories on Nationalism
(London: Duckworth, 1971).
  2. Fishman, Joshua A., Language and
Nationalism: Two Integrative Essays (Rowley,
Mass.: Newbury House, 1972).
  3. Fishman, Joshua A., "Ethnicity and
Language," in Howard Giles (ed.), Language
and Ethnicity in Intergroup Relations (New
York: Academic Press, 1975); "The Role of
Ethnicity in Language Maintenance and Lan-
guage Shift," Harvard Encyclopedia of
American Ethnic Groups; and the manuscript
written jointly with Vladimir C. Nahirny,
"The Role of Ethnicity in Social Theory,"
(in manuscript).
  4. Jakobson, Roman, "The Beginning of
National Self-determination in Europe,"
Review of Politics, VII (1945), pp. 29-42.
  5. Talmon, Jacob L., The Unique and
The Universal (London: Secker and Warburg,
1965).
  6. Patterson, Orlando, The Tribal Mind
(in press).
  7. Fishman, Joshua A., "Language,
Ethnicity and Racism," Georgetown Roundtable

461

462

on Languages and Linguistics (Washington,
D.C.: School of Languages and Linguistics,
Georgetown University, 1977).
 8. Fishman, Joshua A., and Bernard
Spolsky, "The Whorfian Hypothesis in 1975:
a Socio-Linguistic Re-Evaluation," in Hay-
wood Fisher and Rogelio Diaz-Gucrreso
(eds.) Language and Logic in Personality
and Society (New York: Academic Press, 1977).
 9. Gellner, Ernest, Thought and
Change (Chicago: Chicago University Press,
1964).
 10. Fishman, Joshua A., "The Role of
Ethnicity ...."
 11. Talmon, Jacob L., The Rise of
Totalitarian Democracy (Boston: Beacon,
1952).
 12. Patterson, The Tribal Mind.

CHAPTER III

1. The concept of ethnic patrimony
used by me corresponds to the definition
used in this column by Joshua A. Fishman.
2. József Burszta, "Human culture –
national culture. Outline of the problema-
tics,"*in Problems of Human and National
Cultures (Warszaw-Poznah; Panstowe Wyd.
Naukowe, 1976), pp. 13-22.
3. J.V. Bromley, Ethnic Character
and Ethnography*(Budapest; Gondolat 1976),
pp. 77-79 (Russian original: Yu. V. Bromlei:
Ethnos i etnografiia (Moskva, Nauka, 1972.))
4. István Fenyö, For the commonwealth
of literature. The evolution of our literary critical thinking 1917-1930,*(Budapest;
Akademiai Kiadó 1976), pp. 134-145.
5. The sense in which Ghita Ionescu
and Ernest Gellner (eds.) used the expression refers to a later time period and has
different political connotations, Populism.
Its Meaning and National Characteristics,
(London; Weidenfels and Nicholson, 1969.)
pp. 1-5.
6. The expression covers cultural
phenomena other than literature, also János
Horváth, Hungarian literary populism from
Faludi to Petőfi,*(2nd edition. Budapest;
Akadémiai Kiadó, 1978.), pp. 11-15.
7.Book length works and many detailed
studies exist already dealing with the history of the ethnography of most E. European
*available in Hungarian only
463

people. The most important are S.A. Tokarev,
The History of Russian Ethnography,# (Moscow;
Institut Etnografii, 1966); Viera Urbancová,
Of Slovak Ethnography* (Bratislava; Slovenska
Akademia Vied (Slovak Academy of Sciences)
1970); Małgorzata Terlecka (ed.), The Histor-
ry of Polish Ethnography,+ (Wroclaw-Warszaw-
Kraków Gdańsk; Wyd. Polskiej Akad. Nauk,
1973); Ovidiu Bîrlea, History of Rumanian
Folkloristics## (Bucharest; Ed. Enciclopecă
Romînă, 1974); Michael Sozan, The History
of Hungarian Ethnography** (Washington; Uni-
versity Press of America, 1977); Hristo Va-
karelski, Ethnography in Bulgaria ++ (Sofia;
Izd. Nauka i Izkustvo 1977), pp. 25-90.

    8. Emil Niederhauser, Movements of
National Renewal in Eastern Europe;* (Budapest; Akadémiai Kiadó, 1977), pp. 148-163.

    9. Peter F. Sugar, "External and Do-
mestic Roots of Eastern European Nationalism," in Peter F. Sugar and Ivo J. Lederer,
(eds.) Nationalism in Eastern Europe,
(Seattle and London, University of Washington Press, 1969), pp. 45-54.

    10. János Horváth, op.cit., pp. 142-149.

    11. István Fenyő, op.cit., pp. 173-174.

    12. Peter F. Sugar, op.cit., pp. 173-
174.

    13. István Fenyő, op.cit., pp. 143-144.
Cf. Andrej Walicki, "Russia," in Ghita
Ionescu-Ernest Gellner (eds.), op.cit.,62-90.

#avail. in Russian only ##avail. in Romanian
*avail. in Slovak only **avail. in Hungarian
+avail. in Polish only ++avail. in Bulgarian

14. János Horváth, op. cit., pp. 49-54.

15. István Fenyő, Nation, People's Literature, (Budapest; Magvetö, 1973), pp. 116-178.**

16. Gyula Ortutay, Hungarian Folklore. Essays, (Budapest; Akadémiai Kiadó, 1972), pp. 299-300.**

17. Ibid., pp. 349-356.

18. János Csaplovics, An Ethnographic Essay on Hungary. Tudományos Gyüjtemény (Scientific Digest) (Pest) 1822, Nos. 3,4, 6,8.**Cf. István Tálasi, The Emergence of Our Ethnographic Life, (Budapest, Kelet-európai Tudományos Intézet, 1948) and Michael Sozan, op. cit., pp. 59-66.**

19. See n. 7 and Leopold Schmidt, The History of Austrian Ethnography[x](Vienna, Österreicherischer Bundesverlag, 1951); Ingeborg Weber-Kellermann, German Ethnography Between Germanistics and Social Sciences, (Stuttgart; J. B. Metzler, 1969).[x]

20. Mária Kresz, "The Discovery of Hungarian Folk-Art," Ethnographia (Budapest), Vol. 79 (1968), pp. 1-31.**

21. Zoltán Kodály, In Retrospect. Collected Writings, Speeches and Statements, (Budapest; Zeneműkiadó, 1974), Vol. 2, p. 483.**

22. For the origins of the presentation of national peasant cultures in museums see Schmidt, Leopold, Das östereichische Museum für Volkskunde (The Austrian Ethnographic Museum), (Wien; Bergland, 1960) and

**available in Hungarian only
x available in German only

466

Brückner, Wolfgand and Bernward Deneke
(eds.), Volkskunde im Museum (Ethnography
in the Museum), Special volume of the Bay-
rische Blätter für Volkskunde, (Würzburg,
1976). The Ethnographic Museum of Prague
began with the acquisition of the materials
of the Czech-Slovak ethnographic exposition.
The museum in Vienna was, at that time, only
in the planning stages. Vienna regretted
that in Prague and Budapest ethnographic
museums had been established earlier because the Austrian Ethnographic Society lost
the chance to establish a museum in that
city that would have covered the people in
the entire empire. After the Austro-Hungarian compromise and in accordance with it,
the museum in Vienna did not collect material in Hungary, but did so in Bosnia, Hercegovina, Galicia and Bukovina. The Hungarian
press, including the scientific journal Ethnographia, acknowledged that the Czech-Slovak exposition in Prague was scientifically
important, but ignored its obvious national
and political significance.
    23. Peter F. Sugar, op. cit., pp. 35-
42; Emil Niederhauser, "Problems of Historical Conscience in the National Renewal Movements in Eastern Europe," Acta Historica
Academiae Scientiarum Hungaricae,18 (1972),
pp. 39-73.
    24. Robert Redfield, Peasant Society
and Culture, (Chicago; The University of
Chicago Press, 1956), pp. 40-59.
    25. The development of the concept of

creative "populist culture" was stimulated,
in Germany and Central Europe, by the views
on society held in the 18th and 19th centuries. Elias Norbert explained how the difficulties that prevented a bourgois and
national transformation of Germany induced
the intelligentsia to concentrate on the
study of "culture" which it considered to be
a domestic and valuable asset, while in
France and England where modernization pro-
gressed on a more unified nation-wide plane
the crucial concepts were "civilization" and
"society." Über den Prozess der Ziviliza-
tion (Relating to the Process of Civilization), Vol. I, pp. 44-50. Concerning the
use of "culture" and "people" in German ethnography see Freudenthal, Herbert, Die Wis-
senschaftstheorie der Deutschen Volkskunde
(The Scientific Theory of German Ethnography), (Hannover, Niedersäsischer Heimatbund,
1955) and Lutz, Gerhard, Volkskunde. Ein
Handbuch zur Geschichte ihrer Probleme (Ethnography. A Handbook to the History of its
Problems), (Berlin; Erich Schmidt, 1958).
German examples influenced the development
of professional ethnography and the development of folklore studies to the same degree
to which Herder and the Grimm Brothers influenced earlier all of Eastern Europe. A
reevaluation in the ideological and critical
sense of the history of the older ethnographic works began in the German Federal Republic in the 1960s. For this development
see, Bausinger, Hermann, Volkskunde (Ethnography) (Darmstadt, n.p., 1971), esp. 12-140.

26. More details below.

27. See for example: Fredrick Barth, Ethnic Groups and Boundaries. The Social Organization of Culture Difference. (London; George Allen and Unwin, 1969), pp. 11-13.

28. The Slavs had a predilection for the study of their common, ancestral Slav features and assumed that peasant culture because it was ancestral and old was identical, by definition, with the old Slav culture. For example, František Čelakovský published his collection of Czech folk songs as Slavic Folk Songs.ˣˣThe first Polish ethnographic journal's title was Lud Słowianski.⁺

29. Antal Herrmann, "On the foundation of the National Ethnographic Museum," Ethnographia (Budapest) 1 (1890), pp. 21-26.**

30. On the reception of Austrian folk songs in Hungary, see Fenyö, op. cit., pp. 148-51. On the development of the Austrian and Hungarian ethnographies which, while watching each other, moved in different directions, see Hofer, Tamás, "Stilperioden der ungarischen Volkskunst. Über einige Möglichkeiten des Vergleichs der Volkskunstˣ in Ungarn und Österreich," (Periodisation of Styles in Hungarian Folkart. Concerning some Possibilities to compare Hungarian and Austrian Folkart), Österreichische Zeitschrift für Volkskunde, Neue Folge, No. 29 (1975) pp. 325-38.

31. Gyula Ortutay, op. cit., pp. 348-349; Michael Sozan, op. cit., p. 145.

xx avail. in Czech only ** avail. in Hungarian
+ avail. in Polish only x avail. in German

32. Tamás Hofer, "Anniversary session of the hundred-year-old Ethnographic Museum. Scientific and museological relations of the Ethnographic Museum of Budapest," Néprajzi Értesítő (Budapest) 55 (1973), pp. 83-84.**

33. "...The various people, who for centuries lived side by side in a homeland under the aegis of the Crown of St. Stephen, became intertwined geographically, historically, and in an intimate mutuality partly even ethnographically until their branches created a mighty, green, interrelated tree-top that became a species in the forest of peoples."

34. Małgorzata Terlecha (ed.), op. cit. See also Peter Brock, "Polish Nationalism," in Peter F. Sugar and Ivo J. Lederer (eds.), Nationalism in Eastern Europe, (Seattle and London; University of Washington Press 1969), pp. 353-356.

35. See also Joseph Obreski, The Changing Peasantry of Eastern Europe, (edited by Barbara and Joel Halpern) (Cambridge, Mass.; Schenkman, 1976).

36. This was also typical of Polish populism. Cf. István Fenyő op. cit., p. 140.

37. Cf. Zoltán Horváth, The turn of the century in Hungary, (2nd ed. Budapest; Gondolat, 1974), pp. 479-500.**

38. Dezső Malonyay (ed.), The art of the Hungarian people I. Kalotaszeg, (Budapest, Franklin Társulat, 1907), p. 3.**

39. Peter Brock, op. cit., 352-353.

**available in Hungarian only

40. Joel M. Halpern and Eugene Hammel, "Observations on the Intellectual History of Ethnology and Other Social Sciences in Yugoslavia," Comparative Studies in Society and History, Vol. 11 (1969), pp. 17-26.

41. Gábor Zsigmond, "The debate between Gergely Berzeviczy and Ferenc Kazinczy on the state of the peasants in Hungary," Valóság (Budapest) 18/4 (1975), pp. 77-91.**

42. Bence Szabolcsi, "A stylistic turn in Hungarian music in the 18th century. Contributions to the history of the 'new Hungarian folksong'," in Bence Szabolcsi, The centuries of Hungarian music, (Budapest; Zeneműkiadó, 1961), pp. 121-148.**

43. Péter Hanák (ed.), The history of Hungary 1849-1918. The period of absolutism and dualism, (Budapest; Tankönyvkiadó, 1972), pp. 366-369.**

44. György Litván, "Hungarian thinking - free thinking"; Nationalism and progression in the beginning of the century in Hungary, (Budapest; Magvető, 1978);**István Sötér, Nation and progress. Our literature after Világos, (Budapest; Akadémiai Kiadó, 1963).**

45. Ilona Sármány, "The interpretation of folk art in the public opinion on art at the turn of the century," Ethnographia, (Budapest) 88. (1977), pp. 102-119.**

46. Klaus Beitl, "Folk Wear Associations in big cities in the 19th and 20th centuries", in Gunter Wiegelmann (ed.), ˣ Cultural change in the 19th century

**avail. in Hungarian only; x avail. in German

(Göttingen; Vandenoeck and Ruprecht 1973),
pp. 174-183.

47. Zoltán Horváth, op. cit.
48. Vilmos Voigt, "The theory of folk
poetry in today's Soviet folkloric science,"
Helikon, (Budapest)Vol 13. (1967),75-76.**
49. Mária Kresz, "Evolutionary paths
of our popular decorative art," Ethnographia
(Budapest) 63 (1952), pp. 10-43.**
50. József Burszta, "Folklorism in Poland," Zeitschrift für Volkskunde Vol 65.x
(1969), pp. 15-16; Mária Sági, "The dance-
house," Valóság, (Budapest) 1978, No. 5,
pp. 68-76.
51. József Burszta, op. cit.
52. These debates lead to continuous
empirical research and exchanges concerning
cultural politics in the socialist countries. In several places permanent institutions were established for this purpose.
The Slovak Academy of Sciences published in
1977 and volumes of relevant studies, Pre-
meny ľudových tradícií v súčasnosti.* The
1974 Poznań meeting where the academic delegations of the socialist countries discussed
the present-day significance of peasant culture was already mentioned. In 1978 a folk-
lorist meeting took place in Kecskemét in
Hungary. The systematic organization of
these meetings is planned.
53. Tamás Hofer and Edit Fél, Hungarian folk art,** (Budapest; Corvina, 1975) and
Tamás Hofer, "Phases of change in eastern
Central Europe in the light of theories of

**avail. in Hungarian only
x available in German only
* available in Slovak only

472

cultural anthropology," in Günter Wiegelmann (ed.), Cultural change in the 19th
century, (Göttingen; Vandengoech and Ruprecht 1973), pp. 257-264.^x

54. György Martin, "The traits and
development of the new Hungarian dancing
style," Ethnographia, (Budapest) 88 (1977),
pp. 31-48.**

55. Gyula Ortutay, op. cit., pp. 159-
160.

56. Bertalan Andrásfalvy, "The con-
flict of opposite value systems and bour-
geois development," Tiszatáj (Szeged) 1973,
No. 8, pp. 105-110.**"Contrasting Value
Orientations in Modernizing Peasant Communi-
ties" submitted to the IXth International
Congress of Anthropological and Ethnological
Sciences in Chicago, 1973.

57. McKim Marriott, "Cultural Policy
in the New States," in Clifford Geertz (ed.),
Old Societies and New States, (New York; The
Free Press of Glencoe, 1963), pp. 27-56.

58. Tamás Hofer, "Anthropologists and
Native Enthnographers in Central European
Villages: Comparative Notes on the Profes-
sional Personality of Two Disciplines,"
Current Anthropology, Vol. 9. (1968), pp.
311-315.

**available in Hungarian only
x available in German only

CHAPTER IV

1. The analysis of nationalism suffers
from dogmatic or imprecise use of expres-
sions. For the former see the opening
sentences in Royal Institute of Internation-
al Affairs, Nationalism: A Report by a Study
Group of Members of the Royal Institute of
World Affairs (London: Oxford University
Press, 1939), pp. XVI-XX. For comments on
the imprecise usage of such terms as Nation,
State, Nation-state, and Nationalism see
Walker Conner, "Nation Building or Nation
Destroying?" World Politics, XXIV (April,
1972), particularly pp. 332-36 and The
Study of Nationalism: A Bibliographic Essay
on the Literature Published in the English
Language (Washington, D.C.: External Research Contract, U. S. Department of State,
1975), particularly, pp. 2-8.
        To remedy the resulting confusion some-
what, this writer has found it useful to
differentiate between state-nationalism and
ethnonationalism. Unfortunately the latter
term suffers from the diverse uses of the
expression ethnic. For the numerous definition of the expression see, among
others, George Theodorson, and Achilles
Theodorson, A Modern Dictionary of Sociology
(New York: Thomas Crowell, 1969), p. 135;
Max Weber, Economy and Society (Gunther Roth
and Claus Wittich, eds.) (New York: Bed-
minster Press, 1968), Vol. I, pp. 389, 395;
Tomotsu Shibutani and Kian Kwan, Ethnic
Stratification: A Comparative Approach (New
York: Macmillan and Co., 1965), p. 47; Karl

473

Deutsch, Nationalism and Its Alternatives (New York: Alfred Knopf, 1969), p. 3. Finally, to get a detailed explanation of the meaning of the terms, including ethnonationalism, as used in this chapter, see this author's, "An Overview of the Ethnic Composition and Problems of Non-Arab Asia," in Tai Kang (ed.), Ethnicity in Asia (Buffalo: Council on International Studies, State University of New York Press, 1976).

2. For details, see Walker Connor, "The Politics of Ethnonationalism," Journal of International Affairs, 27 (No. 1, 1973), pp. 1-2.

3. The three exceptions were Portugal, Spain, and Switzerland. Portugal is ethnically homogeneous, while Spain and Switzerland have experienced increasing ethnically inspired dissonance.

4. Lenin linked the national and colonial questions in Lenin on the National and Colonial Questions: Three Articles (Peking: Foreign Language Press, 1967).

5. For a listing of the troubled states as of 1973, see Connor, "The Politics of Ethnonationalism."

6. For details on the ethnonational problems of Western Europe, see Connor, "Ethnic Nationalism in Western Europe" in Abdul Said and Luiz Simmons (eds.), Ethnicity in an International Context (Edison, N.J.: Transaction Books, 1976).

7. Some possible later exceptions to Lincoln's statement, namely the Republic of South Africa and the Soviet Union are noted below.

8. From his "Second Speech on Foote's Resolution" (January 26, 1830).

9. Texas v. White (1869).

10. The Common Program of the Chinese People's Political Consultative Conference (September 29, 1949). The full text is reprinted in Theodore Chen (ed.), The Chinese Communist Regime: Documents and Commentary (New York: Frederick Praeger, 1967), pp. 34-45.

11. Constitution of the PRC adopted September 20, 1954 by the First National People's Congress of the PRC. Text can be found in John Lewis, Major Doctrines of Communist China (New York: W. W. Norton and Company, Inc., 1964), pp. 197-211.

12. Constitution of the PRC adopted January 17, 1975 by the fourth National People's Congress of the PRC. Text can be found in Keesing's Contemporary Archives (1975), pp. 26966-26968.

13. The 1960 Constitution can be found in Albert Blaustein and Gisbert Flanz (eds.) Constitutions of the Countries of the World (Dobbs Ferry, N.Y.: Oceana Publications, Inc.)

14. Cited in Elisabeth Barker, Macedonia: Its Place in Balkan Power Politics (London: Royal Institute of International Affairs, 1950), p. 94.

15. The text of the 1946 Constitution of the Federal Republic of Yugoslavia is reprinted in Robert Kerner (ed.), Yugoslavia (Berkeley: University of California Press, 1949), pp. 487-512. The 1963 Constitution is reprinted in Blaustein and Flanz, op.cit.

16. Chapter III, Article 4 of the 1924 Constitution notes that "each one of the member Republics retains the right to freely withdraw from the Union." Article 17 of the 1936 Constitution states that "the right freely to secede from the U.S.S.R. is reserved to every Union Republic."

17. The relationship between union republic and ethnicity is not as close as the names of the republics would indicate, however. In two of the republics (Kazakhstan and Kirgizia) the titular national group does not represent a majority, and in nine of the fifteen, the titular nation represents less than 70 percent of the total population.

18. For detailed accounts on the manner in which the various groups were reabsorbed, see Robert Conquest, Soviet Nationalities Policy in Practice (New York: Frederick Praeger, 1967), pp. 21-35, and Donald Farmer, The Theory and Practice of Soviet Nationality Policy (Unpublished Doctoral Dissertation submitted to the University of Michigan, 1954), pp. 197-281.

19. Problems of Communism, 17 (July-August 1968), pp. 85-86.

20. For a reference to this reportedly often made challenge, see the New York Times, April 23, 1976.

21. Connor, "The Politics of Ethnonationalism," p. 12.

22. The overwhelming number of non-Arab African states have adamantly insisted upon a hands-off policy toward secessionist

movements anywhere on the continent. Thus
Biafra and Somalia found little support for
their secessionist movements in, respectively, Nigeria and in Ethiopia and Kenya.

23. The text of the Charter can be
found in Louis Sohn (ed.), Basic Documents
of African Regional Organization, Vol. I
(Dobbs Ferry, N.Y.: Oceana Publications,
Inc., 1963), pp. 62-68.

24. For the full text, see Keesing's
Contemporary Archives (1975), pp. 27301-
27309.

25. Extracts from the Resolution of
the Fifth Comintern Congress on the Report
of the Executive Committee of the Communist
International (June 26, 1924) in Jane
Degras (ed.), The Communist International
1919-1943; Documents, Vol. II (London:
Oxford University Press, 1960), p. 106.

26. See Robert King, Minorities under
Communism: Nationalities as a Source of
Tension among Balkan Communist States
(Cambridge: Harvard University Press, 1973).

27. See June Dreyer, Chinese Communist
Policy toward Indigenous Minority Nationali-
ties: A Study in National Integration
(Doctoral Dissertation submitted to Harvard
University, June 1972) and Rasma Karklins,
Interrelationship of Soviet Foreign and
Nationality Policies: The Case of the
Foreign Minorities of the USSR (Doctoral
Dissertation submitted to the University of
Chicago, 1975).

28. See Walker Connor, "Ethnology and
the Peace of South Asia," World Politics,
XXII (October 1969), pp. 51-86.

29. The period terminated with the
overthrow of Sihanouk who later acknowledged an arrangement with Hanoi by which
Cambodians trucked supplies from the coast
to the insurgents who were located near the
border in minority (non-Khmer) territory.

30. Israel's borders with Jordan,
Lebanon, and Syria are excluded for a
number of reasons. The principal factor
is that Israel's persistent policy of
taking major reprisal actions against these
states (not just against guerrilla encamp-
ments) has caused the Arab governments to
frown upon the hosting of guerrillas. Indeed, some of the bloodiest fighting in
the region has occurred between the guerrillas and the armed forces of these Arab
states.

31. For details, see Connor, "Ethnology and the Peace of South Asia."

32. For an interesting article indi-
cating that Sinhalese attitudes towards
Tamils are such that genocide within Sri
Lanka (Ceylon) is a possibility, see the
Christian Science Monitor, January 8, 1974.
One group, presently outlawed, is reported
to have developed a detailed plan to "liqui-
date" all Tamils.

33. Arrangements to transfer people
may also be made at the instigation of the
recipient government. Thus, West Germany
was the driving force behind the arrangement made with Poland during 1975 to permit
remnants of the German community within
Poland to emigrate to the Federal Republic.

34. "Nationality," Home and Foreign Review (July 1862). Reprinted in John Emerich Edward Dalberg-Acton, The History of Freedom and Other Essays (London: Macmillan and Company, Ltd., 1907), pp. 270-300. The citation is from page 292.
35. National Character and the Factors in Its Formation (London: Methuen and Company, Ltd., 1927), p. 125. In the interim between Acton and Barker, Karl Renner, an Austrian Socialist, had noted that "Nations existed before states and will continue to exist after the state has disappeared." Cited in Horace Davis, Nationalism and Socialism: Marxist and Labor Theories of Nationalism in 1917 (New York: Monthly Review Press, 1969), p. 162.
36. National Self-Determination (London: Oxford University Press, 1944), p. 51.
37. Keesing's Contemporary Archives (1976), p. 27503.
38. (Cambridge: MIT Press, 1953 and 1965).
39. "Nation'Building and National Development" in Karl Deutsch and William Foltz (eds.), Nation-Building (New York: Alfred Knopf, 1969). See particularly Chapter I, entitled "The Experience of Western Europe," during the course of which the peoples of Italy, Spain, and Switzerland (as well as of Canada and the United States) are each described as possessed of a single national consciousness.
40. "Nation-Building and National Development," pp. 4-5. Between 1966 and 1969, Deutsch tempered his optimism

concerning the likelihood of assimilation
in the Third World, but he did not change
his view concerning what had occurred within Western Europe. For details, see Connor,
"Nation-Building or Nation-Destroying?"
particularly pp. 321-327.

    41. (London: Hutchinson University
Library, 1964).

    42. Ibid., pp. 63, 83, 84.

    43. See E. N. Mittelman, The Nation-
ality Problem in Yugoslavia (Unpublished
doctoral dissertation submitted to New
York University, 1954), pp. 12-15, and
Walter Connor The National Question in Marxist Theory and Strategy, Chapter 6, "The
Joining of the Yugoslav Nations."

CHAPTER V

A great many sources have been utilized in
preparing this paper. Below, I have only
listed the books and articles utilized most
frequently.

1. Hugh Seton-Watson, Eastern Europe
Between the Wars, 1918-1941 (Cambridge:
The University Press, 1945). See also
Reszler (on economic development) and
Petrovich (on religion) in this volume.
2. A great deal has been written
about the national minorities in Romania
and the regime's nationality policy, both
before World War II and subsequently, e.g.
Gertrude Neuman, "Les minoritées en Tran-
sylvania," Revue de Centre d'Étude des Pays
de L'Est, Brussels, 1971, vol. 1/2; Gyula
Zathureczky, "Die magyarische Volksgruppe
in Rumänien," Handbuch der eurpäischen
Volksgruppen, Vol. 8, (Vienna, 1970), pp.
619-628; Max D. Peyfuss, "Die Deutschen in
Rumanien, " ibid., pp. 420-429; Ferenc A.
Váli, "Transylvania and the Hungarian
Minority," Journal of International Affairs,
vol. 1, 1966, pp. 32-44; Nicolas Spulber,
The State and Economic Development in East-
ern Europe (New York: Random House, 1966).
On Yugoslavia, some of the works utilized
include: Viktor Meier, "Mazedonien;
Geschichte und Politik," Europäische
Rundschau (Vienna, 1974), pp. 127-132;
Stevan K. Pavlovic, Yugoslavia (London:
Benn, 1971); M. George Zaninovich, The

481

Development of Socialist Yugoslavia (Baltimore, Md.: The Johns Hopkins Press, 1968);
H. C. Darby et.al., A Short History of
Yugoslavia (London: Cambridge University
Press, 1968); Phyllis Auty, Yugoslavia
(London: Thames and Hudson, 1972).
 3. For a discussion of the position
of ethnic minorities in one of the socialist states of Eastern Europe, see my
"Ethnic Minorities in Romania under Socialism," East European Quarterly, January
1974, pp. 435-458.
 4. A thorough analysis of the German
minority (and others) in the Soviet Union
can be found in Eric Goldhagen (ed.),
Ethnic Minorities in the Soviet Union
(New York, N.Y.: Praeger Publishers, 1968).
 5. Richard V. Burks, The Dynamics of
Communism in Eastern Europe (Princeton,
N.J.: Princeton University Press, 1961).
 6. Much literature has been summarized in this paragraph; one of the most
significant books on the subject is Peter
F. Sugar and Ivo J. Lederer (eds.),
Nationalism in Eastern Europe (Seattle,
Wash.: University of Washington Press,
1969).
 7. Ibid.
 8. For Poland, see, for example,
Alfred Bohmann, "Die Slowaken in Polen,"
pp. 503-506; Bohmann, "Die Weissrussen in
Polen," pp. 529-534; Bohmann, "Die Ukrainer
in Polen," pp. 536-543; Bohmann, "Die
Litauer in Polen," pp. 558-562, all in
Handbuch der europaischen Volksgruppen,
vol. 8, (Vienna, 1970).

9. See Auty, _Yugoslavia_, for a general discussion of Yugoslav policy in this and other fields.

10. E.g. my _Modernization in Romania Since World War II_ (New York, N.Y.: Praeger Publishers, 1975), esp. ch. 8.

11. Zbigniew K. Brzezinski, _The Soviet Bloc_ (Cambridge, Mass.: Harvard University Press, 1971), esp. pp. 67-155.

12. _Ibid._

13. Gilberg, _Modernization in Romania,_ esp. ch. 3.

14. Zaninovich, _The Development of Socialist Yugoslavia;_ for Romania, see Ghita Ionescu, _Politics in Rumania, 1944-1962_ (London: Oxford University Press, 1964).

15. Brzezinski, _The Soviet Bloc_, pp. 65-155.

16. Summarized in Brzezinski, _The Soviet Bloc_, on the basis of a great deal of literature.

17. Gilberg, _Modernization in Romania,_ ch. 8.

18. _Ibid._

19. For a general discussion see, for example, Andrew Gyorgy (ed.), _Eastern European Government and Politics_ (New York, N.Y.: Harper & Row, 1966).

20. Stephen Fischer-Galati, _The New Rumania_, (Cambridge, Mass.: M.I.T. Press, 1967).

21. I have discussed this area in _Problems of Communism_, July-August 1974, pp. 29-44.

22. Ibid.
23. See, for example, Nicholae
Ceausescu at the 1972 National Conference
of the Romanian Communist Party, as reported in Scinteia, July 20, 1972.
24. Much of the discussion of the
draft theses of the eleventh congress of
the RCP, as well as the major speeches
at the congress reflected this view (see
Scinteia and other Romanian party papers
throughout the month of November, 1974).
25. Gilberg, Modernization in Romania, ch. 8.
26. Trond Gilberg, "Political Leadership at the Regional Level in Romania:
The Case of the Judet Party, 1968-1973,"
East European Quarterly, January 1975, pp.
97-111.
27. Ibid.
28. This fact is clearly illustrated
by a close reading of the organ of the
German-speaking minority Neuer Weg; in this
paper, the policies of the RCP center are
unquestioningly approved and applauded, and
the paper has in fact become the spokesman
for the most prominent ethnic Germans in
the party leadership, especially Richard
Winter.
29. Based on Recensamintul Populației,
1956 (especially pp. 556-558) and
Recensamintul Populației si Locuintelor,
1966 (esp. pp. 159-162). Both these sets
of census figures were published by the
central statistical office (Centrala de
Statistica) in Bucharest, in 1957-59, and
1967-69, respectively.

30. The new leadership cadres after the eleventh congress were properly discussed, evaluated, and accepted into office at the November 1974 congress (see Bucharest: Editura politica, Congresul al XI-lea al Partidului Comunist Român, 1975).

31. See ibid., esp. speeches by Nicolae Ceausescu and Gheorghe Cioara, (pp. 15-88 and 300-305, respectively).

32. A recent and very valuable discussion of Ceausescu's policies in the cultural field can be found in Anneli Ute Gabanyi, "Ceausescus nationaldogmatische Kulturpolitik, ein 'dritter Weg'?" in Osteuropa, March 1976, pp. 194-202.

33. Trond Gilberg, "Ceausescus kleine Kulturrevolution in Romanien," ibid., October 1972, pp. 723-732.

34. This figure is admittedly controversial; I have attempted to verify it in Bonn, but there is little willingness to discuss such a sensitive subject.

35. See, for example, the discussion of nationality problems in Ceausescu's report to the 1972 RCP national conference, in Scinteia, July 20, 1972.

36. A thorough discussion of this problem can be found in Robert R. King, "Rumania's National Minorities: Isolation or Assimilation?" (Paper given at the fifth national convention of the American Association for the Advancement of Slavic Studies, Dallas, Texas, March 15-16, 1972).

37. I have traveled extensively in Romania and can testify to the accuracy of this observation.

486

38. Based on Directia Centrala de
Statistica, Recensamintul Populației 1956,
and Recensamintul, 1966, pp. 556, and
159-162, respectively.
39. Recensamintul 1966, p. 153; Recensamintul, 1956, p. 556.
40. Ibid.
41. Ibid.
42. Recensamintul 1956, pp. 576-577;
Recensamintul 1966, p. 115.
43. Republica Socialista Romania,
Anuarul Demografic al Republicii Socialiste
Romania, 1974, pp. 400-402.
44. E.g. the following articles from
Revista de Statistica (Bucharest): E.
Mesaroş, "Situatia demografica actuala a
Romaniei," January 1974, pp. 60-66; I.
Marinescu, "Probleme ale mobilitatii
spatiale a populatiei, "February 1974, pp.
63-71; I. Dumitrescu, I. Grigorian,
"Tendente si influente ale fenomenelor
demografice in R. S. Romania comparativ cu
alte țari," April 1974, pp. 50-49; I.
Marinescu, "Cresterea populatiei si
dinamismul fortelor productive ale
societatii," July 1974; V. Ghetau, "O
perspectiva conditionala a populatiei
Romaniei in urmatoarele doua decenii.
Metoda. Rezultate," March 1973, pp. 43-
52; E. Pecian, "Probleme ale migratiei
interjudetene," May 1973, pp. 60-66; I.
Hristache, I. Measnicov, VI. Trebici,
"Demografia oraselor Romaniei si unele
probleme statistice," July 1973, pp. 41-
49; I. Mesaros "Cu privire la revolutia
demografica in Romania," August 1973, pp.

487

41-47; R. Halus, "Opinii privind cerintele
viitorolui recensamini ale populatiei si
locunitelor," December 1973, pp. 36-42.

CHAPTER VI

1.   Hechter, Michael, "Towards a Theory of Ethnic Change," Politics and Society, II, No. 1 (Fall, 1971).

2.   Fishman, Joshua A., Chapter II in this volume.

3.   "Nationalism was associated with mass mobilization of precommercial, pre-industrial peasant peoples.... The fact of inequality was perhaps not decisive, but its extent, and its tendency to shrink so slowly, or sometimes even to increase was decisive." Deutsch, Karl W., Nationalism and Social Communication: An Inquery into the Foundations of Nationality (Cambridge, Mass.: M.I.T. Press, 2nd ed., 1966), pp. 190-1.

4.   Kedourie, Elie, Nationalism (New York: Praeger, 1960; rev. ed. 1961).

5.   Ginsberg, Morris, On the Diversity of Morals (London: Royal Anthropological Institute of Great Britain and Finland, 1965).

6.   Marx, Karl, and Friedrick Engels, The German Ideology (Moscow: Progress Publishers, 1969).

7.   Bernstien, Basil, Class, Codes & Control (London: London University Institute of Education, 1971-73).

8.   A Marxist who is sensitive to this problem is Tom Nairn. See, among others, his "Scotland: Anomaly in Europe," New Left Review, No. 83 (1973), pp. 57-82,

489

490

and "Marxism and the Modern Janus," _New Left Review_, No. 94 (1975), pp. 3-29.

9. Kedourie, p. 127.

10. Quoted in Brown, L. Carl, _The Tunisia of Ahmed Bey, 1837-1855_ (Princeton: Princeton University Press, 1974), p. 59.

11. For an interesting example of a national irredentism by an economically privileged, but politically peripheral, group, one which is <u>not</u> dispersed, but, on the contrary, compact -- See: Heiberg, Marianne, "Insiders/Outsiders: Basque Nationalism," _European Journal of Sociology_, XV/2 (1975), pp. 169-193.

12. Plamenatz, John, "Two Types of Nationalism in E. Kamenka (ed.), _Nationalism: The Nature and Evolution of an Idea_ (Australian National University Press, 1973).

13. Kedurie, Elie (ed.) _Nationalism in Asia and Africa_ (New York: World Publishing Co., 1970), p. 20.

CHAPTER VII

1. Kohn, Hans, The Idea of Nationalism (New York: Macmillan, 1951), pp. 10-11.
2. King, R.R., Minorities under
Communism (Cambridge, Mass.: Harvard University Press, 1973), p. 6.
3. Rezler, Gyula, Bevezetés a
Szociologiába (Budapest; 1948), p. 176.
4. Kann, Robert A., The History of
the Habsburg Empire (Berkeley: University
of California Press, 1974), pp. 607-8.
5. Fischer-Galati, Stephen, The
Socialist Republic of Rumania (Baltimore:
Johns Hopkins University Press, 1969), p.
7.
6. Dolmányos, István, "A kelet-
europai föld reformok néhány problémája
(Some Problems of Eastern Europe Land Reforms)," Agrártörténelmi Szemle (1962),
No. 1-2, p. 139.
7. Macartney, C.A., Hungary and
Her Successor States (London: Oxford
University Press, 1937), pp. 79-80.
8. Ibid., p. 82.
9. Ibid., p. 409.
10. Seton-Watson, Hugh, The East
European Revolution (London: Methuen,
1950), p. 20.
11. Morrison, J. F., The Polish
People's Republic (Baltimore: Johns
Hopkins University Press, 1968), p. 6.

12. Kovrig, Bennett, Hungarian People's Republic (Baltimore: Johns Hopkins University Press, 1969), p. 18.

13. Deak, Francis, The Hungarian-Rumanian Land Dispute (New York: Columbia University Press, 1928).

14. Macartney, p. 318.

15. Ibid., p. 399.

16. Ibid., p. 402.

17. Ibid., p. 174.

18. Roos, Hans, A History of Modern Poland (London: Eyre & Spottiswoode, 1966), p. 107.

19. Janics, Kálmán, "A szlovakiai magyar társadalom ötven éve (The Hungarian Society in Slovakia during the past Fifty Years)," Valóság (1971), No. 6.

20. Ibid., p. 21

21. Macartney, p. 330.

22. Ibid., p. 322.

23. Ibid., p. 153.

24. Ibid., p. 292.

25. Bohman, A., Menschen ohne Grenzen (Köln; Verlag Wissenschaft und Politik, 1969).

26. Macartney, p. 410.

27. Ibid., p. 42.

28. Roos., pp. 102 and 110.

29. Kovrig, pp. 28 and 62.

30. Ibid., p. 27.

31. Heltai, George G., "Changes in the Social Structure of the East-Central European Countries," Journal of International Affairs (1966), Vol. 20, No. 1, pp. 165-166.

32. Janics, p. 21.
33. The New Hungarian Quarterly (1976) Vol. 17, No. 6.
34. Satmarescu, G. D., "The Changing Demographic Structure of the Population of Transylvania," East European Quarterly (Winter, 1977).
35. Kővágó, László, Nemzetiségi kérdés - Nemzetiségi politika (Nationality Problems and Politics) (Budapest: Kossuth Kiadó, 2nd ed., 1968).
36. Fischer-Galati, p. 48; Morrison p. 75; Suda, Zdenek, The Czechoslovak Socialist Republic (Baltimore: Johns Hopkins University Press, 1969), p. 40.
37. Lenin, Vladimir I., "Critical Remarks on the National Question," Questions of National Policy and Proletarian Internationalism (Moscow: Progress Publishers, n.d.), p. 30.
38. King, p. 1.
39. Schöpflin, G. A., "National Minorities under Communism in Eastern Europe," in Eastern Europe in Transition (Kurt London, ed.), (Baltimore: Johns Hopkins University Press, 1965), p. 117.
40. King, p. 23.
41. Burks, Richard V., "The Rumanian National Deviation," in London (ed.), p. 95.
42. King, p. 73.
43. Schöpflin, p. 131.
44. Ludányi, Andrew, Hungarians in Rumania and Yugoslavia: A Comparative Study of Communist Nationality Policy (Doctoral Dissertation), The Louisiana State University and Mechanical College, 1971, p. 76.

494

45. Ibid., p. 72.
46. Ibid., p. 80.
47. Fischer-Galati, p. 101.
48. Schöpflin, p. 131.
49. Ibid., p. 133.
50. Ibid., p. 112.
51. Ibid., p. 125.
52. Janics, p. 23.
53. Szulc, Tad., The Czechoslovak Socialist Republic (Baltimore: Johns Hopkins University Press, 1969), p. 28.
54. Ludányi, p. 210.
55. Ibid., p. 234.
56. Ibid., p. 236.
57. Ibid., p. 237.
58. Fischer-Galati, p. 46.
59. Ibid., p. 109.
60. Ludányi, p. 266.
61. Ibid., P. 211.
62. Illyés, Elemér, Erdély változása: Mitosz és Valóság (The Changing Transylvania; Myth and Reality) (Munich: Aurora Verlag, 1975), pp. 143-144.
63. Ludányi, p. 217.
64. Fischer-Galati, pp. 38-39; 48.
65. Heltai, p. 168.
66. Ibid., p. 169.
67. Djilas, Milovan, The New Class (New York: Praeger, 1957), p. 39.
68. Ibid., p. 45.
69. Ibid., p. 42.
70. Keefe, E. K. et al., Area Handbook for Hungary (Washington: U. S. Government Printing Office, 1973).
71. Schopflin, p. 136.
72. Ludányi, p. 172.

73. King, p. 137.

74. Kovrig, p. 179.

75. Janics, p. 26.

76. Ibid, p. 29.

Other works of importance but not cited in the footnotes include:

Acsádi, György, Magyarország népesedése a két világháború között (Population of Hungary between the two World Wars), (Budapest: Közgazdasági Publ., 1965)

Andrew, Gyorgy, "The Role of Nationalism in Eastern Europe," in Eastern Europe in Transition Kurt London (ed.), (Baltimore; John Hopkins Press, 1965)

Asztalos, Miklós, A nemzetiségek története Magyarországon (The History of Nationalities in Hungary), (Budapest; Lantos Publ., 1934)

Gyönyör, József, "Nemzetiség és anyanyelv (Nationality and language)," Irodalmi Szemle (Literary Review), (Bratislava, March 1976)

Helmreich, E.C. (ed.). Hungary, (New York; F.A. Praeger, 1957)

Kulischer, E.M. Europe on the Move: War and Population Changes, 1917-1947 (New York York: Columbia University Press, 1948)

Shoup, Paul, "Yugoslavia's National Minorities under Communism," Slavic Review, (Vol. 22, No. 1, 1963)

Zaninovich, M.G., The Development of Socialist Yugoslavia, (Baltimore; John Hopkins Press, 1968)

CHAPTER VIII

1. This thesis is elaborated in Enloe, Cynthia H., Ethnic Conflict and Political Development (Boston: Little, Brown & Co., 1973).

2. Examinations of State uses of ethnicity for forming and deploying militaries are included in: Enloe, Cynthia H., "The Military Uses of Ethnicity," Millenium: Journal of International Studies (London School of Economics), Vol. 4., No. 3, Winter 1975-76, pp. 220-234, and in Enloe, Cynthia H., "Civilian Control of the Military: Implications in The Plural Societies in Guyana and Malaysia," in Claude E. Welch (ed.), Civilian Control of the Military (Albany: State University of New York Press, 1976).

3. Barth, Fredrick, Ethnic Groups and Boundaries (Boston: Little, Brown & Co., 1969). The situational character of ethnic identity is persuasively described in Nagata, Judith, "What is Malay?" American Ethnologist, Vol. 1, No. 2, 1974, pp. 331-350.

4. Smith, Donald E., Religion and Political Development (Boston: Little, Brown & Co., 1970), pp. 33-56.

5. Gambino, Richard, Blood of My Blood: The Dilemma of The Italian Americans (New York: Anchor Books, 1975), pp. 235-237.

497

498

6.   Dunn, Ethel, and Stephen P.
Dunn, "Ethnic Intermarriage as an Indicator
of Cultural Convergence in Soviet Central
Asia," in Edward Allworth (ed.), The Nationality Question in Soviet Central Asia, (New
York: Praeger Publishers, 1973), p. 46.
7.   Spreitzer, Elmer, and Eldon E.
Snyder, "Patterns of Variation Within and
Between Ethno-religious Groupings,"
Ethnicity, Vol. 2, No. 2, June, 1975, pp.
124-133.
8.   Frankovic, Kathleen A., The Effect
of Religion on Religious Attitudes (unpublished Ph.D. dissertation, Rutgers University, 1974), pp. 1, 214-223.
9.   Gallup Opinion Index, "Religion
in America, 1976," Report No. 130, 1976, p.
8.
10.   Ross, Jeffrey A., "Political
Mobilization of Jews in U.S.S.R.," Comparative Interdisciplinary Studies Section of
The International Studies Association,
Working Paper #13, 1974, p. 13.
11.   Ralph Premdas notes, however,
that The Official Guyanese Indian association in the past was officially close to
the Indian political party: Premdas, Ralph,
Voluntary Associations and Political
Parties in a Racially Fragmented State: The
Case of Guyana.   Occasional Papers No. 2
(Georgetown, Guyana: Department of Political
Science, University of Guyana, 1972), pp.
34-35.   In Trinidad, Muslims in the East
Indian Community are thought to be closer
to the politically dominant Afro-Trinidadi-
ans than are either Hindu or Christian East

Indians: Malik, Yogendra K., East Indians
in Trinidad (London: Oxford University
Press, 1971), pp. 36-37.

12. Of the Indians in Britain (not
including Pakistanis) 85 percent are Hindus,
according to Krausz, Ernest, Ethnic Minorities in Britain (London: Paladin, 1972),
p. 19. An insightful profile of an Indian
Muslim Kutchi refugee family in Britain in
Kramer, Jane, "The Ugandan Asians," New
Yorker, April 8, 1974, pp. 47-93.

13. Kessler, Clive S., "Muslim
Identity and Political Behavior in Kelantan,"
in William R. Roff (ed.), Kelantan: Religion; Society and Politics in a Malay
State (London: Oxford University Press,
1974), pp. 212-314.

14. Roberts, David A., "The Orange
Order in Ireland: A Religious Instiution,"
The British Journal of Sociology, Vol. 22,
No. 3, Sept. 1971, p. 271.

15. Beetham, David, Transport and
Turbans (London: Oxford University Press,
1970). Also see John, DeWitt, Indian
Workers' Association in Britain (London:
Oxford University Press, 1969).

16. Quoted in The New York Times,
April 9, 1975. See also Tessler, Mark A.,
"Secularism in the Middle East? Reflec-
tions on Recent Palestinian Proposals,"
Ethnicity, Vol. 2, No. 2, June, 1975, pp.
178-203.

17. Regarding the slowness of secularization in the Soviet Union, it is
interesting to note that even the most
secular of institutions, the Soviet

500

Military, still is disturbed by Muslim and
Christian religious sentiments of enlistees.
Goldhammer, Herbert, The Soviet Soldier
(New York: Crane, Russak & Co., Inc., 1975),
p. 332.
　18.　Smock, David R., and Audrey C.
Smock, The Politics of Pluralism: A Compar-
ative Study of Lebanon and Ghana (New York:
Elsevier), p. 214.
　19.　Schmitt, David E., Violence in
Northern Ireland (Morristown, N.J.: General
Learning Press, 1974), p. 13.
　20.　New York Times, December 22, 1975.
　21.　Mazrui, Ali A., Soldiers and
Kinesmen in Uganda (Beverly Hills: Sage
Publications, 1975), pp. 250-276.

CHAPTER IX

1.   Milovan Djilas, Wartime (trans-
lated by Michael B. Petrovich) (New York:
Harcourt, Brace, Jovanovich, Inc., 1977).
2.   Paul R. Bass, "Ethnic Groups and
Nationalities: The Formation, Persistence,
and Transformation of Ethnic Identities
over Time," prepared for the Conference on
Ethnicity in Eastern Europe held at the
University of Washington, Seattle, in
June, 1976, p. 10 of manuscript.
3.   Sidney A. Burrell (ed.), The Role
of Religion in Modern European History
(New York: Macmillan, 1965), in the series
Main Themes in European History, edited by
Bruce Mazlish.
4.   Robert A. Kann, "Protestantism
and German Nationalism in the Austro-German
Alpine Lands," in Tolerance and Movements
of Religious Dissent in Eastern Europe,
edited by Béla K. Király (East European
Quarterly, Boulder: Distributed by Columbia
University Press, 1975), p. 21.
5.   See, for example, Hans Kohn, The
Idea of Nationalism: A Study in Its Origin
and Background (New York, 1944). Kohn finds
evidence of nationalism in the medieval
communities; see his article "The Dawn of
Nationalism in Europe," American Historical
Review, LII (January 1947), 265-280.
6.   Francis Dvornik, The Making of
Central and Eastern Europe, 2nd ed. (Academic International Press, 1974), p. 17.

7.   Francis Dvornik, The Slavs: Their
Early History and Civilization (Boston:
American Academy of Arts and Sciences,
2nd printing, 1959), p. 122.
8.   Dvornik, The Making of Central
and Eastern Europe, p. 70.
9.   Ibid., p. 71.
10.   Clifford R. Barnett et al.,
Poland: Its People, Its Society, Its Culture (New York: Grove Press, 1958), p. 64.
11.   Waclaw Lednicki, Life and Culture
of Poland (New York: Roy Publishers, 1944),
p. 83.
12.   W. J. Rose, Poland Old and New
(London: G. Bell and Sons, 1948), p. 183.
13.   C. A. Macartney, Hungary: A Short
History (Edinburgh University Press, 1962),
p. 12.
14.   Denis Sinor, History of Hungary
(New York: Praeger, 1959), p. 36.
15.   As the Rt. Rev. Zoltán Beky,
Bishop emeritus and National President of
the American Hungarian Federation wrote to
the editor of the Christian Science Monitor
on November 22, 1976, "2.   The Crown is not
regarded only as a royal emblem, but as the
symbol of legitimacy and sovereignty of
Hungary regardless of the form of government.   3.   The American Hungarian community
in general and the American Hungarian Federation in particular, are intimately concerned with the disposition of the Crown and
opposed to its return as long as Soviet
troops are stationed in Hungary.   For we do
not recognize that Hungary possesses true
sovereignty unless foreign troops leave the

country." The Crown has been in the possession of the United States government since
the end of World War II. Like previous
American presidents, Mr. Carter must now
decide whether or not to return the Crown
to Hungary. The author is indebted to Mr.
Charles Szabó, Memorial Library, University
of Wisconsin, for a copy of this letter.
    16. Stanoje Stanojević, <u>Sveti Sava</u>
(Belgrade, 1935), pp. 118-119.
    17. On the <u>millet</u> system see, for
example, Norman <u>Itzkowitz</u>, <u>Ottoman Empire</u>
<u>and Islamic Tradition</u> (New York: Alfred A.
Knopf, 1972), p. 59; Ezel Kural Shaw, "The
Ottoman Aspects of <u>Pax Ottomanica</u>," in
<u>Tolerance and Movements of Religious Dis-</u>
<u>sent in Eastern Europe</u>, edited by Béla K.
Király, pp. 169-173; and Stanford J. Shaw,
"The Ottoman Millet System: An Evaluation,"
<u>ibid</u>., pp. 183-184.
    18. In addition to the standard survey
of the history of the Serbian Orthodox
Church by Djoko Slijepčević, <u>Istorija</u>
<u>Srpske pravoslavne crkve</u> (Munich, 1962),
especially Vol. I, there is a special
study on the position of the Serbian Church
under the Turks by Mirko Mirković, <u>Pravni</u>
<u>položaj</u> i karakter Srpske <u>crkve</u> <u>pod turskom</u>
<u>vlascu 1459-1766</u> (Belgrade, 1965). See
also László Hadrovics, <u>Le peuple serbe et</u>
<u>son église sous la domination turque</u> (Paris,
1947).
    19. Jagoš Jovanović, <u>Stvaranje</u>
<u>crnogorske države i razvoj crnogorske</u>
<u>nacionalnosti</u> (Cetinje, 1947), p. 68.

504

20. Branko Pavičević, Stvaranje
crnogorske države (Belgrade, 1955), p. 27.

21. Jovan Radonić and Mita Kostić,
Srpske privilegije od 1690 do 1792 (Belgrade: Srpska Akademija Nauka, Posebna
izdanja CCXXV, 1954) contains all the
various Austrian charters granted to the
Serbs of southern Hungary by Emperor
Leopold and his successors between 1690 and
1792. On Patriarch Arsenius III see the
study by Rajko L. Veselinović, Arsenije III
Crnojević u istoriji i književnesti (Belgrade: Srpska Akademija Nauka, Posebna
izdanja CLI, 1949).

22. The Latin original of Leopold's
charter of August 21, 1691, is given in
Radonić and Kostić, op. cit., pp. 23-25.

23. Dušan Popović, Srbi u Vojvodini
(Novi Sad: Matica Srpska, 1959), Vol. II,
p. 340.

24. The proclamation is contained in
Gradja za istoriju srpskog pokreta u
Vojvodini 1848-1849, Series I, Book I (Bel-
grade: Srpska Akademija Nauka, 1952),
Document No. 183, pp. 259-260.

25. Jovan Savković, "Patrijarh Josif
Rajačić u Srpskom pokretu 1848-1849,"
Prilozi za Političku, Kulturnu i Privrednu
Istoriju Vojvodine; Zbornik Državnih Arhiva
Vojvodine, V (1954), p. 14.

26. Michael Boro Petrovich, A History
of Modern Serbia (New York and London: Harcourt Brace Jovanovich, 1967), Vol. I, pp.
13-14.

27. Among the various editions of
Paisii's Slaveno-Bulgarian History the most
scholarly is that prepared by Boniu St.
Angelov, Paisii Khilendarskii, Istoriia
slavenobolgarskaia (Sofia: Bŭlgarska
Akademiia nu naukite, 1961). The most
complete collection of scholarly studies
on Paisii in Paisii Khilendarskii i negovata
epokha (1762-1962); Sbornik ot izsledvanija
po sluchai 200-godishninata ot Istoriia
slavianobŭlgarska (Sofia: Bŭlgarska Akademiia na naukite, 1962).

28. For works in English that deal
with the establishment and role of the Bulgarian Exarchate, see D. Mishew, The Bulgarians in the Past; Pages from the Bulgarian
Cultural History (Lausanne, 1919) and Thomas
A. Meininger, Ignatiev and the Establishment
of the Bulgarian Exarchate 1864-1872 (Madi-
son, Wisconsin: The State Historical Society
of Wisconsin, 1970). More detailed Bulgarian treatment of the question is to be found
in Petŭr Nikov, Vŭzrazhdane na bŭlgarskiia
parod: Tsurkovno-natsionalni borbi i post-
izheniia (Sofia, 1929).

29. For a brief but good survey in
English, see Elisabeth Barker's Macedonia:
Its Place in Balkan Power Politics (London
and New York: Royal Institute of International Affairs, 1950). For an inside Macedonian view, see Dragan Taškovski, Radjanje
Makedonske naciie (Belgrade, 1969), especially Chapter VIII, "Stanje u Makedoniji
posle stvaranja egzarhije," pp. 150-166, and
Chapter IX, "Makedonija posle Berlinskog
kongresa i afirmacija makedonske nacije,"

506

pp. 167-206. Those who read Russian can
consult Klime Dzambazovski, "Vliianie
serbskikh i bolgarskikh shkol v Makedonii
na formirovanie natsional'nogo soznaniia u
makedonskikh uchashchikhsia v techenie XIX
veka," in La Macédoine et les Macédoniens
dans le passe (Skopje: Institut de l'His-
toire Nationale, 1970), pp. 197-229.

30. Keith Hitchins, The Rumanian
National Movement in Transylvania 1780-1849
(Cambridge, Mass.: Harvard University Press,
1969), p. 2.

31. Ibid., p. 14.

32. Ibid., p. 89, citing Petru Maior,
Istoria pentru începutul Românilor în Dacia,
3rd ed. (Budapest and Gherla, 1883), p. 11.

33. Hitchins, op. cit., p. 213.

34. R. W. Seton-Watson, A History of
the Roumanians (Cambridge University Press,
1934), p. 394.

35. W. E. D. Allen, The Ukraine: A
History (Cambridge University Press, 1941),
p. 86, quoting Dyboski.

36. S. M. Dubnow, History of the Jews
in Russia and Poland (Philadelphia: The
Jewish Publication Society of America, 1916),
Vol. I, p. 105.

37. Ibid., pp. 104-105.

38. Ibid., p. 113.

39. Quoted by R. W. Seton-Watson, A
History of the Czechs and Slovaks (London:
Hutchinson, 1943), p. 56, at head of Chapter
IV.

40. František Palacký, Dějiny národu
českého, Vol. III, Part II, 3rd ed. (Prague,
1877), p. 43.

41. _Cambridge Medieval History_, Vol. VIII, p. 86.

42. Seton-Watson, _op. cit._, p. 75.

43. See the autobiography _The Memoirs of Prota Matija Nenadović_, ed. and trans. Lovett F. Edwards (Oxford: Clarendon Press, 1969).

43. Slijepčević, _op. cit._, p. 352; Milan Milićević, _Kneževina Srbija_ (Belgrade, 1876), pp. 273-274.

44. _Srpska Pravoslavna Crkva 1219-1969; Spomenica o 750-godišnjici autokefalnosti_ (Belgrade, 1969), illustration opposite p. 296.

45. Milan Milićević, _Knez Miloš u pričama_ (Zagreb, n.d.), illustration opposite p. 208.

46. C. M. Woodhouse, _The Greek War of Independence_ (London: Hutchinson's University Library, 1952), p. 56; Douglas Dakin, _The Unification of Greece 1770-1923_ (New York: St. Martin's Press, 1972), p. 40.

47. An English translation of the epic is given by Woodhouse, _op. cit._, pp. 70-72.

48. Milisav D. Protić, ed., _Knjiga o Djakonu Avakumu_ (Belgrade: Biblioteka Pravoslavlje, 1968). This is a symposium of articles devoted to Deacon Avakum and his cult. The description of his martyrdom and famous last words is taken from Milan Milićević, _Pomenik znamenitih ljudi u srpskog naroda novijeg doba_ (Belgrade, 1888), pp. 5-7. See pp. 9-11 of the Protić edition.

49. Dakin, _op.cit._, p. 111.

508

50. Iurii Samarin in <u>Den'</u>, May 11,
1863, cited in Michael T. Florinsky,
<u>Russia: A History and an Interpretation</u>, II
(New York: Macmillan, 1969), p. 916.

51. Florinsky, <u>ibid.</u>, p. 918.

52. John Paxton, ed., <u>The Statesman's</u>
<u>Year-Book; Statistical and Historical</u>
<u>Annual of the States of the World for the</u>
<u>year 1972-1973</u> (New York: Macmillan, St.
Martin's Press, 1972), p. 791.

53. Albert Rauch, "Kirchen und Reli-
gionsgemeinschaften," in <u>Südosteuropa-</u>
<u>Handbuch</u>, Vol. I, <u>Jugoslawien</u>, ed. by Klaus-
Detlev Grothusen (Göttingen: Vandenhoeck
and Ruprecht, 1875), p. 346.

54. Joint Translation Service, Belgrade, No. 5211, December 29-30, 1968, from
<u>Svet</u>, December 7, 1968, p. 4, column 1.

55. Michael B. Petrovich, "Population
Structure," in <u>Südosteuropa-Handbuch</u>, Vol.
I, <u>Jugoslawien</u>, p. 324.

56. Esad Ćimić, <u>Socijalističko</u>
<u>društvo i religija</u> (Sarajevo: Svjetlost,
1970), p. 93.

57. Paxton, ed., <u>The Statesman's</u>
<u>Year-Book 1972/73,</u> p. 734.

58. Nicholas C. Pano, <u>The People's</u>
<u>Republic of Albania</u> (Baltimore: The Johns
Hopkins Press, 1968), pp. 104-106.

59. Stavro Skendi, ed., <u>Albania</u>
(New York: Published for the Mid-European
Studies Center of the Free Europe Committee,
Inc. by Frederick A. Praeger, 1956), p. 287.

60. <u>Ibid.</u>

61.   Barbara Wolfe Jancar, "Religious Dissent in the Soviet Union," in Dissent in the USSR: Politics, Ideology and People, ed. by Rudolf L. Tokes (Baltimore and London: Johns Hopkins University Press,1975),p. 222.

62.   For an indictment of the Roman Catholic Church of Croatia, see, for example, the work by Viktor Novak, Velika optužba (Magnum crimen), III (Sarajevo: Svjetlost, 1960). The author was a Croat by origin.

63.   "U slavu i čast Cara Dušana Silnog," Pravoslavlje, II, No. 29 (May 23, 1968), p. 1.

64.   "Reči srpskog patrijarha," Pravoslavlie, I, No. 12 (September 28, 1967), p. 7.

65.   For a summary of the history of the Macedonian Orthodox Church written from a Serbian standpoint, зee Djoko Slijepčević, Makedonsko crkveno pitanje (Munich: Iskra, 1969). For a Macedonian description, see "Svetli momenti od najnovata istorija na Makedonskata pravoslavna crkva," Vesnik na Makedonskata Pravoslavna Crkva, XII, No. 5 (October, 1970), 138-142.

66.   Michael B. Petrovich, "Yugoslavia: Religion and the Tensions of a Multi-National State," East European Quarterly, VI, No. 1 (March, 1972), p. 127.

67.   The author himself witnessed this in December, 1975.

68.   "Golemo toržestvo na grobot na svetiot ramnoapostol Sv. Kiril," Vesnik na Makedonskata Pravoslavna Crkva, XII, No. 3

510

(May-June, 1970), p. 84.
    69. Biblija: Stari i Novi Zavjet
(Zagreb: Stvarnost, 1968).
    70. "Novosti Crkve u Hrvatskoj,"
Glas Koncila, VIII, No. 18 (163), September
7, 1969, p. 1.
    71. "Hrvatski 'pohod' na Rim," Glas
Koncila, IX, No. 12 (182), June 21, 1970,
p. 2.
    72. Apostol Mikhailov, "The Bulgarian
Orthodox Church; Past and Present Situa-
tion," in Orthodoxy 1964: a Pan-Orthodox
Symposium (Athens: Zoë, 1964), p. 36.
    73. Ibid.
    74. Paul Miron, "The Orthodox Church
in Roumania," Orthodoxy 1964, p. 239.
    75. Cited by Raoul Bossy, "Religious
Persecutions in Captive Romania," Journal
of Central European Affairs, XV, No. 2
(July, 1955), p. 168.
    76. Ibid., p. 171.
    77. Emil Ciurea, "Religious Life,"
in Captive Rumania: A Decade of Soviet
Rule, edited by Alexandre Cretzianu (New
York: Praeger, 1956), p. 202.

CHAPTER X

1. Seton-Watson, Hugh, <u>Eastern Europe</u>
<u>between the Wars, 1918-1941</u> (London:
Cambridge University Press, 1945 - reprinted
in Hamden, Conn.; Archon Books, 1962), p.
76.

CONTRIBUTORS

CONTRIBUTORS

Paul R. Brass is professor of political
science; chairman of comparative studies
in ethnicity and nationality, School of
International Studies, University of
Washington; author of three books and
several book chapters and articles.
Walker F. Conner is professor of political
science, State University of New York
College at Brockport; Rhodes scholar; NSF
fellow; author of several articles.
Cynthia H. Enloe is professor of political
science, Clark University; NEH fellow in
Malaysia and Fulbright professor in Guayana,
author of two books and several articles.
Joshua A. Fishman is university research
professor, social sciences, Yeshiva University; author of fifteen books and numerous
articles.
Ernest Gellner is professor of philosophy,
London School of Economics; author of seven
books and numerous articles.
Trond Gilberg is associate professor of
political science and assistant director
of Slavic and Soviet Language and Area
Center, Pennsylvania State University;
author of two books and several articles.
Tamás Hofer is section chief of the
Ethnographic Museum in Budapest; editor of
Ethnographia (Budapest); author of four
books in English and German besides numerous
publications in Hungarian; and was visiting
professor at the University of North
Carolina in 1971.

Michael B. Petrovich is professor of
history, University of Wisconsin; author
of five and translator of three books;
author of numerous articles.

Julius Rezler is professor emeritus of
economics, Loyola University of Chicago;
Fulbright professor in India; author of
one book and several articles in English
and several books in Hungarian.

Peter F. Sugar is professor of history,
University of Washington; on the board
of editors, Slavic Review and Austrian
History Yearbook, and on the advisory board,
Historical Abstracts; author of two and
editor of six books.

INDEX

nationalism, 406, 409-10;
recognition, 265; re-
birth, 394; stereotypes,
241; strata, 120; toler-
ance, 7
Culture, 265, 266, 270,
272, 354, 367; common,
186; divisions of, 258-9;
folk, 245, 254, 405;
foreign, 119; German,
272; homogeneous, 253,
255; Italian, 272; Mus-
lim, 403; national, 195,
232; origins of, 117, 118;
peasant, 119, 120, 273;
Polish, 381; and reli-
gion, 403, 404; Romanian,
204; Serb, 400; socialist,
195, 205, 232, 233; Third
World, 275; Yugoslav, 395
Currency reform, 337
Custom, 2, 350, 394
Cvijić, Jovan, 128
Cyprus, 22, 174, 412
Cyril, Bulgarian Patri-
arch, 413
Cyril, Saint, 380, 409,
413
Cyrillic alphabet, 380
Czech: Catholics, 360;
language, 398; middle
class, 23; nation, 398;
nobility, 15; protestants,
360; reformation, 398;
wars of religion, 397
"Czech Brethren", 374, 399
Czech-Slav Ethnographic
Exposition, 115

Czech Socialist Repub-
lic, 329
Czechoslovakia, 44, 45,
52, 55, 159, 162, 165,
167, 184, 186, 189,
192, 193, 195, 196,
202, 281, 304, 305,
306, 307, 310, 316,
317, 318-9, 320, 322,
328-9, 337, 342, 351,
414, 416, 441; con-
stitutions of, 329;
democracy in, 312;
ethnic groups of, 343;
federalism in, 48, 54;
land reform in, 309-
10; Slovaks in, 21
Czechs, 57, 183, 186,
187, 288, 289, 298,
300, 301, 304, 317,
330, 342, 343, 380,
381, 397, 398, 399, 416
Czestochowa, 382

Dacia, 120
Dalmatia, 409
Dance houses, 138, 140
Danilo II, Archbishop
of Montenegro, 408
Danilo II, Prince of
Montenegro, 387
DDR. See East Germany
Decembrists, 270
Decentralization, 202
Democracy, 298; Czecho-
slovak, 312; Polish,
314

Egalitarianism, 255, 262;
and nationalism, 262
Egyptians, 11
Elites, 13, 14, 102, 201,
243, 367; adaptability of,
14, 17; central, 192; co-
operation of, 14, 15;
competition between, 17,
28, 34, 63, 64; communist,
194, 196, 199, 200, 201,
209, 210; culture of, 102;
dominant, 38, 190, 221;
economic, 78, 191; edu-
cated-tribal, 24; and
ethnic symbols, 19; in-
tellectual, 81; native,
197; "new", 33, 35, 38;
"old", 276; Polish, 187;
political, 187, 188, 196,
200, 205; regional, 192,
197; and religion, 18,
19, 20
Emigration, 212, 260; Jewish, 212, 215, 221, 229,
232
Employment: concentration
of, 33; competition for,
34, 35, 64; distribution
of, 52, 224-8, 229, 251,
252, 286, 294, 295-6, 297,
310, 314, 318-9, 340; and
education, 286, 300; mo-
bility of, 268; talent
specific, 243
Endogamy, 3
Entrepreneurship, 428
Equality: of life style,

254; of ownership, 254;
of people, 255
Erdélyi, János, 108,
111, 142
Erkel, Ferenc, 132
Esztergom, Archbishop
of, 374
Eszterházy family, 125
Ethiopia, 160, 175,
179, 276
Ethnarch, 386, 388,
412, 433
Ethnic: awakening, 438;
belonging, 435; bound-
aries, 147, 166-7, 185,
264, 319, 320, 348,
350, 351, 352, 353,
354, 356, 360, 366,
370-1, 421, 426; char-
acteristics, 438; con-
flict, 15, 23-4, 32,
33, 37, 39, 59, 186,
209, 261, 279, 348,
358, 363, 364, 367,
368, 369, 370, 413,
422, 429; conscious-
ness, 106, 116, 121,
123, 199, 202, 203,
209, 233, 235, 367, 381,
423, 435, 444; contact,
351; feeling, 421;
hierarchy, 197; home-
land, 18; identity, 186,
347, 348, 349, 371,
377, 381, 421, 423,
433, 435, 436; ideol-
ogy, 365; intermarriage,

345; mobilization of, 23, 24, 200; in multinational states, 172; and nation, 420; pagan, 379, 380; political organization of, 35, 44, 361; political realignment of, 53-4; political relations of, 38, 191, 210; political significance of, 164; and religion, 352, 353, 359, 366; rights of, 7, 9; in Romania, 203; status of, 279, 280, 284, 285, 289, 290, 300, 306; stratification of, 315-7; territory of, 280; transformation of, 9, 10, 13, 375, 376, 379; under alien rule, 175; in the USA, 355

Ethnic theory: classical Greek, 71, 75, 83, 85, 90; classical Hebrew, 71, 75, 83, 85

Ethnicity, 87, 91, 95, 96, 97, 98, 182, 186, 214, 242, 347, 348, 349, 354, 367, 392, 402, 412, 416, 420, 421, 423, 424, 437, 438, 439, 444; adaptability of, 94; Albanian, 405; and ancestry, 75; authenticity of, 89, 90, 94; basis of, 2; as being, 84-7; benefits of, 72; as cause, 82; claims of, 3; and class, 3; comparative, 101; and

communism, 194, 212; consolidated, 78; Croat, 409; cultural attributes of, 350; definition of, 3; and dialectology, 435; as doing, 87-9; and ethnic categories, 3; and extended family, 71; as feeling, 70; and folklore, 75; "God given", 71, 73, 432, 433; historical scope of, 70; irrationality of, 92; and kinship, 84; as knowing, 90-1; and language, 69, 75, 76, 78, 84, 86, 87, 92, 99, 434; manipulability of, 95-7; and Marxism, 79-80, 81; and minorities, 83; mobilization of, 80, 358; modern European, 77; Muslim, 403; mutable, 92-5; as myth, 79, 80; and national movements, 95, 421, 422, 423; and nationalism, 80, 123; Pakistani, 381; and peasants, 102; politization of, 29, 31; rebirth of, 97, 371; and religion, 72, 73, 349, 353, 354, 355, 357, 358, 359, 362, 370, 371, 375, 376, 377, 393, 403, 404, 406, 411; resurgence of, 10; Romanian, 415; salience of,

Horváth, János, 110
Hubertus, Saint, 434
Hulegu, Mongol Khan, 252
Hungarian: Catholicism,
382-3; ethnography, 112;
electoral laws, 312; folk
poetry, 108; language re-
form, 107; literature,
109; millenary exposition,
114, 125; politburo, 213;
Protestants, 374; revolt
(1956), 326; revolution
(1848), 131; social structure, 132-3, 315-6, 340;
songs, 121
Hungarian Academy of Sci-
ences, 111
Hungarian Ethnographic
Museum, 125, 127
Hungarian Ethnographic
Society, 120, 126
Hungarian National Museum,
114
Hungarians, 190, 192, 234,
288, 291, 297, 301, 302,
305, 320, 332, 344; in
Czechoslovakia, 187, 284,
305, 309, 310, 311, 317,
318-9, 322, 329, 330,
342, 343; deportation of,
283; expropriation of,
330; germanization of, 35;
in Romania, 187, 204, 207,
211, 212, 213, 214, 215,
221, 223, 229, 231, 311,
312, 317, 321, 332-4, 340,

344, 416; in Transyl-
vania,58, 232, 302,
313, 325, 326, 327,
328, 331, 392, 393,
(see also Romania);
in Vojvodina, 328, 331,
332, 333, 342, (see
also Yugoslavia); in
Yugoslavia, 187, 308-9,
313, 314, 317, 341
Hungary, 73, 75, 132,
159, 167, 191, 196, 201,
281, 289, 290, 291, 292,
294, 298, 301, 304, 305,
306, 308, 315, 316, 321,
374, 378, 388, 416, 432,
433; educational sys-
tem of, 300; employ-
ment pattern in, 295;
ethnic groups in, 239;
industrialization of,
299; Jews in, 26, 27;
Turkish occupation of,
297. See also Austria-
Hungary; Habsburg
Empire
Hus, Ian, 397
Hutus, 174

Ibos, 11, 41, 155, 168,
274, 368
Iceland, 153
Identity formation, 5
Ideology, 365, 443;
ethnic, 365; Marxist,
369; nationalist, 439;